THE BOOK OF THE
REVELATION

By LEHMAN STRAUSS

The First Person
The Second Person
The Third Person

Prophetic Mysteries Revealed
The Prophecies of Daniel
Devotional Studies in Galatians
*   and Ephesians*
James Your Brother
The Epistles of John
The Book of the Revelation

Certainties for Today
The Eleven Commandments
We Live Forever

Demons, Yes--but Thank God
*   for Good Angels*

THE BOOK OF THE

REVELATION

Outlined Studies

BY

LEHMAN STRAUSS

LOIZEAUX BROTHERS

Neptune, New Jersey

FIRST EDITION, OCTOBER 1964
ELEVENTH PRINTING, JUNE 1982

ISBN 0-87213-825-9

Library of Congress Catalog Card Number: 64-8641
PRINTED IN THE UNITED STATES OF AMERICA

To

STEPHEN, MICHAEL, MARK,
TIMOTHY AND PETER

the delight of a grandfather's heart

*"Children's children are the crown of old men;
and the glory of children are their fathers."*

Proverbs 17:6

PREFATORY NOTE

The messages in this book were prepared during many weeks and months in a very busy and active pastorate. They are not for scholars and exegetes, but for plain people.

No claim is made for originality, but the writer is deeply grateful for the help he received from many sources including the bibliography to be found in the back of this volume.

Grateful appreciation is extended to Mrs. Lila Giencke who worked faithfully in typing and indexing the manuscript for publication.

LEHMAN STRAUSS

1964

TABLE OF CONTENTS

THE BOOK OF THE

REVELATION

Outlined Studies

AN INTRODUCTION TO
THE REVELATION

The book of the Revelation is one of the most neglected and most controversial books in the Bible. The various viewpoints of different writers make this book confessedly one of the most difficult to interpret. Some seminaries avoid it, barely making mention of it in a New Testament survey course. Man has attempted to do with this book the very thing that God, in the book, told him not to do, namely, "Seal not the sayings of the prophecy of this book: for the time is at hand" (Revelation 22:10). It was written to be read and understood.

This book is a book of consummation, thus it is fitting that it should have been assigned the last place in the Bible. One careful reading of the Bible will convince anyone that this inspired volume forms a complete cycle. Genesis is the book of commencement; Revelation is the book of consummation. Revelation is an excellent finish to the divine library.

Genesis—The commencement of Heaven and earth (1:1);
Revelation—The consummation of Heaven and earth (21:1).

Genesis—The entrance of sin and the curse (3:1-19);
Revelation—The end of sin and the curse (21:27; 22:3).

Genesis—The dawn of Satan and his activities (3:1-7);
Revelation—The doom of Satan and his activities (20:10).

Genesis—The tree of life is relinquished (2:9; 3:24);
Revelation—The tree of life is regained (22:2).

Genesis—Death makes its entrance (2:17; 5:5);
Revelation—Death makes its exit (21:4).

Genesis—Sorrow begins (3:16);
Revelation—Sorrow is banished (21:4).

The first book of the Bible knows no completion apart from the last book of the Bible, and all the rest of the sixty-four books in between are dependent upon each other. No one book in the Bible is an independent contribution to be divorced from the other books.

Before entering upon a study of the book of Revelation we should know at least three schools, or systems, of interpretation inasmuch as one's understanding of the book depends upon the method of approach. I have selected three terms because I believe each term expresses the main point of view in each case.

The Preterist School. A preterist is a person concerned chiefly with the past, the prefix "preter" coming from the Latin *praeter,* meaning past or beyond. In the strict meaning of the term the preterists say that the prophecies in the book of the Revelation have all been fulfilled in the past. They do not see any prophecies in the book having to do with the Second Coming of Jesus Christ. There is reason to doubt that the early Christian fathers ever thought of this theory. Certainly they did not hold that most of Revelation was fulfilled in the days of the Roman Empire under Domitian and that the book has only a literary interest for people of our day. This view we reject.

The Presentist School. A presentist is one who views the events in Revelation, not as actual events *per se,* but rather as an expression of those principles and forces active in any age. Thus their fulfillment may be repeated over and over in history. The presentist is therefore concerned chiefly with the present. He may look back into history and see where they were fulfilled in the past, but he concerns himself mainly with their fulfillment in his own day. For example, the rise of the two beasts in Revelation 13 has no special prophetic anticipation for the presentist. He sees in that chapter the opposition of secular powers to the true Church whenever and wherever that power might arise. This view we reject.

The Prophetic School. This system of interpretation is sometimes called the Futurist School. The futurist holds that the largest part of the book is prophetic, and thus it applies to a period still future. Everything from the fourth chapter to the end of the book is future, and will follow the removal of the Church from the earth at the coming of Christ in the air, according to 1 Thessalonians 4:16-17. Ford C. Ottman states, "Such a view seems also to be in harmony with our Lord's great prophecy in the twenty-fourth chapter of Matthew."

Now it is possible to see a measure of each of these views, for to the student today there is that in the book which is now past, that which applies to the present, and that which is yet in prospect. However, the last of the three above-mentioned views is the one accepted by the present writer.

THE PRELUDE TO THE BOOK

Revelation 1:1-20

I. THE PRESENTATION OF THE BOOK (1:1)

The opening statement presents the book as *"The Revelation of Jesus Christ."* Its title, then, is the first mark of distinction. Notice, it is not "The Revelation of St. John the Divine." There is no authority for this designation. Moreover, John refers to himself as *"your brother, and companion in tribulation"* (1:9). He was a saint in the sense that all true Christians are saints, but he would be the last person to refer to himself as "divine." He was the chosen instrument to be the human penman of the book, but he was not divine.

Please note that the title is singular, not plural—not "Revelations" but "The *Revelation* of Jesus Christ." The word "Revelation" (Gr. *Apokalupsis,* from which we get our English word *apocalypse*), conveys the idea of an appearing, a manifestation, a coming, an unveiling. It is in contrast to an apocryphal (or hidden) book. The word is used once only in the Gospel records (Luke 2:32) where it is translated "lighten," referring to one of the purposes of the Incarnation, namely, to draw away the veil of darkness covering the Gentiles as prophesied in Isaiah 25:7. The same word appears frequently in the Epistles and is translated "manifestation" (Romans 8:19), "coming" (1 Corinthians 1:7), "revealed" (2 Thessalonians 1:7), "appearing" (1 Peter 1:7), "revelation" (1 Peter 1:13). This book is therefore all about the manifestation, the coming, the appearing of Jesus Christ. He shall come in like manner as He was seen going up into Heaven (Luke 24:50-52 cf. Acts 1:10-11). At His next "appearing" on the earth, "every eye shall see Him" (Revelation 1:7). It will be His glorious apocalypse.

II. THE PURPOSE OF THE BOOK (1:1)

The purpose is *"to shew unto His servants things which must shortly come to pass."* Who are His servants? They are Christ's bondmen, His bondslaves. If the Revelation is a closed book to the majority of God's children, it is quite possible that for this very reason it is so. Eight times in the book we find the admonition, "He that hath an ear, let him hear" (2:7,11,17,29; 3:6,13,22; 13:9). It takes the circumcised ear of a willing bondslave of Jesus Christ to hear with the understanding the truths set forth in this book (see Exodus 21:1-6 cf. Jeremiah 5:21; 6:10). It was never God's intention to hold back the meaning of the Revelation, but rather to show, to exhibit, to make known its meaning. All who willingly submit to Christ will have little difficulty with this book.

Christians will do well if they submit to the lordship of Christ, for this book makes known *"things which must shortly come to pass."* These things *must* come to pass. The impersonal verb translated "must" means "it is necessary." The Bible is divinely inspired, and when God says certain things must come to pass, be sure that they will come to pass. But it is a revelation in language which only His *servants* can read and understand.

These "things" will come to pass *"shortly"* (Gr. *en tachei*), an adjective denoting swiftness. Scientists have drawn from this word to give the name "tachometer" to an instrument for measuring velocity. Elsewhere the same word is translated "speedily" (Luke 18:8). When the things in this book come to pass, they will "speedily happen." God has borne along with men patiently, and while some ridicule the prophecies of this book, they fail to see that God is longsuffering (2 Peter 3:9). But the end will come, and when it does it will be marked by suddenness and swiftness. The events will come to pass speedily. Thus the purpose of the Revelation is to show beforehand those things that will speedily happen.

III. THE PENMAN OF THE BOOK (1:1,2,4,9; 22:8)

There is no question that the John mentioned in the Revelation is the son of Zebedee and Salome and the brother of James (Mark 1:19-20; 15:40). His occupation was that of a fisherman (Matthew 4:21). He heard John the Baptist preach and became a follower of Jesus Christ (John 1:35,40). He was one of the three whom Jesus took with Him on several special occasions (Matthew 17:1; 26:37; Mark 5:37). John also was one of the two sent by Christ to prepare the Passover (Luke 22:8). He is referred to as "that disciple whom Jesus loved" (John 13:23; 20:2; 21:7,20), and is mentioned three times in the Acts (Acts 3:1; 4:13; 8:14). He wrote five books of the New Testament, and only he uses Christ's title of "the Word" (*Logos*). (See John 1:1,14; 1 John 1:1; 5:7; Revelation 19:13).

Perhaps no violence would be done this book, or any other book in the Bible, if we did not know definitely the identity of the penmen. But we do know from John's own witness that he saw and heard the things which he wrote (Revelation 22:8). He lived during the reign of Domitian, under whose firm rule the Christians were severely persecuted. He identifies himself with others of the suffering saints as their "brother and companion in tribulation" (Revelation 1:9). He himself was sent in chains as a prisoner to the small and dreary island called Patmos, about twenty-five miles off the coast of Asia Minor, in the Aegean Sea. It was while he was there that God turned his bondage into a blessing. The Patmos of persecution became to John the open door for service. The chains of pagan Rome bound his body but they could not bind his soul. Shut off from the rest of the world, he entered into a communion with his Lord he had never known before.

IV. THE PROMISE IN THE BOOK (1:3)

Blessed is he that readeth, and they that hear the words of this prophecy, and keep those things which are written therein: for the time is at hand (1:3).

No book in the Bible has an introduction and a conclusion quite like this one. It commences with a promised blessing (1:3) and closes with a promised blessing (22:7). Altogether there are seven beatitudes, the word "blessed" appearing seven times. It is the same word used by our Lord in the Sermon on the Mount (Matthew 5:1-11). The beatitudes of the Revelation provide seven texts for an interesting study:

> The Blessed Challenge   (1:3)
> The Blessed Comfort   (14:13)
> The Blessed Cautiousness   (16:15)
> The Blessed Calling   (19:9)
> The Blessed Conquest   (20:6)
> The Blessed Cherishing   (22:7)
> The Blessed Conformity   (22:14)

In the text before us there are three requisites necessary to receiving the promised blessing. First, *"Blessed is he that readeth."* The reader here is no doubt the lector, the one whose duty it was to read publicly in the synagogue or church (Luke 4:16-20; Acts 13:14,27; 15:21; 2 Corinthians 3:15). Paul might have had this in mind when he said to Timothy, "Give attendance to reading" (1 Timothy 4:13). In the early days of the Church before the invention of the printing press, a limited number of handwritten copies necessitated a public reader to go from church to church. There is no doubt in my mind, however, that the promised blessing is to all who take up this book and read it with regularity and reverence.

Secondly, the blessing is promised to those that *"hear the words of this prophecy."* It is, as we have already stated, the open (or circumcised) ear that is required. This admonition is of such tremendous import, it appears at the very commencement, and again at the close of the Book (22:18).

Thirdly, the blessing is promised to all who *"keep those things which are written therein."* F. W. Grant said, "This 'keeping' is observing them in such a way that our practical conduct shall be governed by them." To keep is to give heed to, as of keeping our Lord's commandments (John 14:15); 15:10; 17:6; 1 John 2:3-5; 3:22-24; Revelation 2:26; 3:8,10; 12:17; 14:12; 22:7,9).

"The time is at hand." The word "time" (Gr. *chronos*) denotes a space of time, a season. It can be a short time as in Luke 4:5, or a long time as in Luke 8:27. The statement, "the time is at hand" does not preclude that all the events in the Revelation were to come to pass within a short space of time in John's day. The duration of the "season" is not stated, but we do know from the teaching in the book that those events are related to the Second Coming of Christ.

V. THE PROPHECY IN THE BOOK (1:3)

The Revelation is a book of prophecy. Seven times the noun "prophecy" (Gr. *propheteia*) appears (1:3; 11:6; 19:10; 22:7,10,18,19). It signifies the speaking forth of the mind and counsel of God. Prophecy is not always foretelling in the sense that it is predictive. It is sometimes the forthtelling of the mind of God for the present. But much prophecy is purely predictive. With the completion of the canon of Scripture predictive prophecy ceased, that is, God gave no furthur prediction of things to come.

The "prophecy" spoken of in our text (1:3) doubtless refers to the predictive prophecies in the book (22:7,10,18). That the disclosure of future events is in view here is proved contextually, the largest portion of the book being of a prophetic nature. Every student of the Bible knows that a large part of the Old Testament is prophecy, great and important prophecies concerning Israel and the nations of the world. The book of Revelation is the great prophetic masterpiece of the New Testament, the capstone, the crowning consummation of many unfulfilled prophecies in the Old Testament. There is wonderful harmony in the many prophetic truths found in the Bible, the book of

Revelation being necessary to the whole of divine prophetic revelation. And we must insist that the Revelation is an open book of prophecy (22:10), which dare not be added to (22:18), nor taken from (22:19). This is a solemn warning!

The grand consummation of all predictive prophecy is the coming again of Jesus Christ. Seven times it is stated that He will come (1:7; 2:25; 3:3; 3:11; 22:7,12,20). So then this book is all about His coming. His personal appearing is in view. This was no new truth to the Apostle John. The Holy Spirit led John to write of this blessed event as a challenge to *comfort* (John 14:1-3), *consecration* (John 21:21-23), and *cleanliness* (1 John 2:28; 3:2,3). The Revelation opens with the salutation, *"He cometh"* (1:7), and closes with the supplication, *"Even so, come, Lord Jesus"* (22:20). And between the salutation and the supplication He answers His Church, *"Surely I come quickly. Amen"* (22:20).

VI. THE PARTAKERS IN THE BOOK (1:4,11)

The book is addressed:

> *To the seven churches which are in Asia; unto Ephesus, and unto Smyrna, and unto Pergamos, and unto Thyatira, and unto Sardis, and unto Philadelphia, and unto Laodicea* (1:4,11).

These were distinct assemblies in the several cities and towns named. Asia here is not the whole continent as we know it today, but Asia Minor of which Ephesus was the principal city.

Whether there were more than seven churches in Asia Minor is not intimated by the writer of Revelation. It is this present writer's belief that these churches which partook of the book of Revelation are representative of *the* Church, and therefore present a prophetical unfolding of the history of the Church on earth from the apostolic times to the end of the Church Age, when the Lord shall take her unto Himself.

But why did He choose only seven? The number seven is used more frequently throughout the book than any other. It speaks of completion or perfection. God completes His work in cycles of seven. Seven colors make a perfect spectrum. Seven musical notes make up the scale. Seven days constitute one week. At the fall of Jericho there were seven priests, seven trumpets, and on the seventh day the people marched around the wall seven times. There are seven set feasts of Jehovah (Leviticus 23); seven secrets in the kingdom parables (Matthew 13), and seven sayings of the Saviour from the cross. In Revelation the number seven appears forty-nine times, or seven times seven.

Why did Christ choose these seven in preference to others? The local conditions in each differed, but the seven, when combined, are representative of conditions in Christendom from Pentecost to the end of the Church Age. The universal Church spreads itself out before the omniscient gaze of her Lord and Head. He writes primarily to seven churches, yet speaks to all. But we will have more of this when we study the letters to those churches in chapters two and three.

Immediately following our Lord's naming the seven churches, John turned and *"saw seven golden candlesticks"* (1:12). The word "candlesticks" is a mistranslation of the Greek word *luchnia,* and it should read "lamps" or "lampstands." It is rendered "lampstands" in the Revised Version. We learn that these lampstands symbolize the seven churches (1:20). The churches are to be light bearers (Ephesians 5:8; Philippians 2:15) in the midst of surrounding moral and spiritual darkness. But notice that the Son of Man was seen in the midst of the lampstands. He had said, "I am the light of the world" (John 8:12), thus it is Christ whom the Church is to reflect to the world.

VII. THE PERSON IN THE BOOK (1:5,8,13-18)

We learned that this book is about Jesus Christ, a revelation of Him. The book is both by Him and about Him. He dominates the action of the book. And rightly so, since there is nothing, nor any one, that can quicken the hopes of distressed Christians like a vision of our Lord Jesus Christ. He is portrayed uniquely in several chapters in the Bible. We see Him in His *sufferings* in Isaiah 53; His *splendor* in Matthew 17, Mark 9, and Luke 9; His *submission* in Philippians 2; His *sovereignty* in Colossians 1; and His *superiority* in Hebrews 1. But of all the chapters in the Bible which show forth our blessed Lord, none surpasses Revelation chapter one.

A. *His Dignity*

The faithful witness (1:5).

The book of the Revelation, above all other books, directs our whole being to the one grand Person of history, the preeminent and peerless Christ. He is described first as "the faithful witness" (see also 3:14). Christ was the first to demonstrate perfectly a true and faithful witness. This title was first conferred upon Christ by the prophet Isaiah (Isaiah 55:4). Our Lord said that He came into the world to bear witness to the truth (John 18:37). While on earth He was the Father's faithful witness of the truth. He never lacked courage nor did He ever compromise. The path of our human testimony is strewn with failure and even wreckage. But Christ was faithful unto death.

The first begotten of the dead (1:5).

Having died for that truth to which He faithfully witnessed, He arose from the dead, and He ever remains the first in rank, supremacy, and preeminence in resurrection. This title, already attributed to Christ by the Apostle Paul (Colossians 1:18), has no allusion to chronological order. It simply means that of all those who rise from the dead, He retains supremacy in rank and dignity over all. He was raised never to die again and exalted to a position above all, awaiting the day when every knee shall bow and every tongue confess that Jesus Christ is Lord, to the glory of God the Father (Philippians 2:8-11).

The prince of the kings of the earth (1:5).

Proud earthly monarchs have sought, and still seek, to rule the world, but "the earth is the LORD's, and the fulness thereof" (Psalm 24:1). "The kingdoms of this world are become the kingdoms of our Lord, and of His Christ; and He shall reign for ever and ever" (Revelation 11:15). He is the King of Heaven (Daniel 4:37), the King of the Jews (Matthew 2:2); the King of Israel (John 1:49); the King of the ages (1 Timothy 1:17); the King of glory (Psalm 24:7); the King of saints (Revelation 15:3); and the King of kings (Revelation 19:16). He is the mighty Prince of the kings of the earth (Daniel 8:25).

No sooner is Christ presented in His dignity than John's heart overflows in a doxology of praise:

> *Unto Him that loved us, and washed us from our sins in His own blood* (1:5).

The word "loved" should read "loveth." J. A. Seiss said: "We are apt to think of the great love of God as past; as having spent its greatest force, and reached its highest culmination, when He gave His only begotten Son to humiliation and death in our behalf. But in this we are mistaken. That love is a *present love,* and is as full force at this moment as when it delivered up Jesus to the horrors which overwhelmed Him on the cross." God *continuously* establishes His love in that the death of Christ *remains* as the greatest manifestation of that love. God continues to give proof of His love in that He continues to save any and all who come to Him through Christ. Paul prayed that we might be able to comprehend that love in its four dimensions (Ephesians 3:17-19).

The proof of His continuing love is that He *"washed* [loosed, freed] *us from our sins in His own blood."* The idea here is that He unbound us, released us from our sin. He destroyed its power over us (Romans 6:6) and freed us from it (Romans 6:7), and now "sin shall not have dominion over, you" (Romans 6:14). All the redeemed can sing of His love that is current and changeless. At the tomb of Lazarus we are told that "Jesus wept. Then said the Jews, Behold how He loved him!" (John 11:35-36). The word "wept" (Gr. *dakruo*) is used only of the Lord Jesus, and it appears only this once in the New Testament. The word for "weep" (Gr. *klaio*) in John 11:31,33 is merely a loud expression of grief as one might mourn for the dead. But those Jews saw in the tears of Jesus an expression of divine love. And as Christ felt for that little family in Bethany, even so does He now sympathize with us in all our sorrows (Hebrews 4:14-16; 7:25). His continuing love brings Him to the aid of those who are tempted and tried (Hebrews 2:18). The surroundings of our age may be somewhat different, but His heart of love is the same (Hebrews 13:8).

B. *His Deity*

Twice He says:

I am Alpha and Omega (1:8,11).

The words "Alpha" and "Omega" are the spelled-out anglicized forms of the first and last letters of the Greek alphabet, and they enclose all the rest of the letters necessary to make up words, which in turn are the vehicles of expression. In verse 11 they are translated, "the first and the last" (see also 1:17). Toward the close of the book the two expressions are united: "I am Alpha and Omega, the beginning and the end, the first and the last" (22:13). He is the eternal "I AM," a verb indicating *being* but not *becoming*. He is before all things, the One who *created* all things (Genesis 1:1; John 1:3; Colossians 1:16); who *controls* all things (Hebrews 13), and who will *consummate* all things (Ephesians 1:10). Every thing finds its commencement, course, and consummation in Him. All that letters and language were intended to be, the expression of truth, He is. He only among men and angels could say:

I am . . . the Lord, which is, and which was, and which is to come.
The Almighty (1:8).

This name of God, which appears not less than forty-eight times in the Old Testament, is here applied to our Lord Jesus Christ. It is the Hebrew word *Shaddai,* meaning "the sufficient One." It was to Abraham that God revealed Himself as El-Shaddai (Genesis 17:1-2). The occasion was a confirmation of the promise He had already made to Abraham to make him a great nation (Genesis 12:2), to make his seed as innumerable as the dust of the earth (Genesis 13:16) and as the stars of heaven (Genesis 15:5). Regardless of the age of Abraham and his wife Sarah, God was assuring him that He [El-Shaddai] was equal and sufficient for the carrying out of His promise. Here in the Revelation the all-bountiful and all-sufficient God is none other than our Lord Jesus Christ, "the Alpha and Omega . . . the Lord . . . the Almighty."

C. *His Description*

In these verses John describes *"His head . . . His hairs . . . His eyes . . . His feet . . . His voice . . . His right hand . . . His mouth . . . His countenance"* (1:14-16). *"His head and His hairs were white like wool, as white as snow"* (1:14). This description of our Lord compares with that of Daniel 7:9. The "Ancient of days" is none other than the Jehovah of the Old Testament, "God . . . manifest in the flesh" (1 Timothy 3:16), whose "goings forth have been from of old, from everlasting" (Micah 5:2). The vision here is that of the Judge. In verse 13 He is seen wearing the tribunal garments befitting His royal office. He has arisen from His throne, and He is seen here standing to judge.

His eyes were as a flame of fire (1:14).

Here is a penetrating discernment that searches the inmost depths. John had seen His eyes filled with tears when He wept at the grave of Lazarus (John 11:35), but these are the eyes of the Judge before whom all things are laid bare (Hebrews 4:13). This speaks of His omniscience.

And His feet like unto fine brass, as if they burned in a furnace (1:15).

The brass speaks of righteous judgment for which He firmly stands. It is upon those feet of beauty that He came preaching the gospel of peace, the glad tidings (Isaiah 52:7; Romans 10:15). But when He comes again He shall tread down all abominations and crush those who hate Him.

His voice as the sound of many waters (1:15).

This is the voice of power and authority that shall roar from on high upon His habitation (Jeremiah 25:30). It is the voice that is full of majesty (Psalm 29:4). When He comes again all that are in the graves shall hear His voice (John 5:28). To the unbeliever it will be the voice of final judgment. To His own His voice will give confidence and joy (1 Thessalonians 4:16-18).

And He had in His right hand seven stars (1:16).

The seven stars are the angels [ministers, messengers] of the seven churches (1:20). The world has its stars in the fields of sports and entertainment, but they that turn many to righteousness shall shine as the stars forever and ever (Daniel 12:3). Every minister is under divine authority and receives his orders from Christ. Here the faithful messenger is securely held in the hand of his all-glorious Lord and Head.

Out of His mouth went a sharp two-edged sword (1:16).

It is the Word of God (Hebrews 4:12). Men are trifling with that blessed blade, but they will learn one day that His Word-sword will be all that is needed to judge them (John 12:48).

His countenance was as the sun shineth in His strength (1:16).

John saw that countenance when, with Peter and James, our Lord was transfigured before them (Matthew 17:2). The churches are lamps, but Christ is the sun and we but reflect His glory. Paul saw that countenance the day Christ saved him (Acts 9:1-5), and thereafter he reflected his Lord's glory.

Thus we have seen the dignity, deity, and description of the Person in the book.

VIII. THE PLAN OF THE BOOK (1:19)

Write the things which thou hast seen, and the things which are, and the things which shall be hereafter (1:19).

This verse is the key to the book. It tells us that there is a *past*, a *present*, and a *future* in this book. This is its threefold division, and the divisions are clear.

The things which thou hast seen.

These words doubtless refer to the vision of the glorified Christ which was just shown to John. It constitutes chapter one.

The things which are.

These words refer to the letters to the seven churches, or the history of the Church prewritten from Pentecost to the Rapture. The "things which are" compose chapters two and three, which have to do with the present dispensation.

The things which shall be hereafter.

These are "things" future and they comprise chapters four to twenty-two. Chapter four commences with our Lord's words to John, *"Come up hither, and I will shew thee things which must be hereafter"* (4:1). Everything in the book from chapter four on to the end, will occur after the Church is taken out of the earth.

These three divisions are clear and they do not overlap. Each division is complete in itself and distinct from the other two. This is God's own division of the book. Hold fast to it, and you cannot go astray in your quest to understand its meaning. Do not at any time lift events from one division and attempt to place them in another.

Chapter 1—The Unveiling of His Person (His Glory)
Chapters 2 and 3—The Utterances of His Purpose (His Grace)
Chapters 4-22—The Unfolding of His Power (His Government)

THE LETTER TO EPHESUS

Revelation 2:1-7

To the seven letters themselves we now turn our attention. These are "the things which are." The messages to the churches have a threefold meaning.

First, each letter has a *primary association*, having a local and direct bearing upon the church to which it was written. We must not fail to see this. Certainly the letters were intended to be meaningful and helpful to those Christians in each church who first received the message. Each letter was a measuring rod by which each church could know its standing in the sight of the risen Lord.

Secondly, each letter has a *personal application*. In addition to being historical and local as regards an assembly in each city named, the message to each applies to every individual Christian. To each church Christ says, *"He that hath an ear, let him hear what the Spirit saith unto the churches"* (2:7,11,17,29; 3:6,13,22). It should also be noted that even though Christ addresses each church *as a whole*, the message to overcome is addressed to the individual (2:7,11,17,26; 3:5,12,21).

Thirdly, each church individually, and the seven churches combined, set forth *prophetic anticipation*. I see in them seven ages or stages in the life of *the* Church on earth, commencing with Pentecost and concluding with the Rapture. R. H. Clayton wrote: "It can be no mere coincidence that these Epistles do set out the salient characteristics of the Church through the centuries, and no one can deny that they are presented in historic sequence." When John wrote he probably did not see that each epistle contained an announcement of the future, any more than did David when he wrote Psalm 22. Nevertheless there is a prophetic picture of seven periods of the Church's history on earth. For myself, I do not doubt for one moment that a prophetic foreview of the entire Church dispensation was in the mind of our Lord when He dictated the letters to John. My personal study of church history brings me to this conclusion.

I. THE ASSEMBLY

The Ephesus letter was addressed to the spiritually strong apostolic Church of the first century. Ephesus was a strategic city, the seacoast capital of proconsular Asia, and was one of the great religious, political, and commercial centers. The famous temple of Diana, one of the seven wonders of the ancient world, was situated in Ephesus.

We are not certain as to how or when the Word of God was first preached in Ephesus. We do know however that Paul stayed three years in that city (Acts 20:31). Acts 19 should be read by each student for the necessary background material on the city of Ephesus. The period that is forecast prophetically in this letter runs from the Church's beginning at Pentecost to approximately A.D. 160.

II. THE AUTHOR (2:1)

In each of the seven letters Christ is described differently. Here He is set forth as:

He that holdeth the seven stars in His right hand, who walketh in the midst of the seven golden candlesticks (2:1).

The name "Ephesus" means desirable, and this was indeed the desirable church. The "stars," which are the angels [or messengers], are held in His right hand, the place of power and authority, and the only place where His servants can be sustained and strengthened. In the early days of the Church Christ walked in the midst as the recognized Head, and men took instructions from Him (Ephesians 1:22-23). Christ's true sheep are safe in His hand and are thus led by Him (John 10:27-30). The stars are His light-bearers; He holds them. They derive their light and power from Him. In every assembly of believers where Christ is honored as its Head, He walks among His own and takes a watchful interest in them. Blessed is the assembly whose members are ruled by Jesus Christ! The assembly need not be large in number in order to have the blessings of the Divine Overseer, for He will honor two or three who honor Him (Matthew 18:20). Men may admire the architectural splendors of a building, but Christ is concerned with the "living stones" (1 Peter 2:5).

III. THE APPROVAL (2:2-3)

In each of the seven letters Christ says, *"I know thy works"* (2:2,9,13,19; 3:1,8,15). Having all-seeing and discerning eyes, He knows and is therefore qualified to approve or disapprove.

He approved them for their sacrifical *service,* their *"works and labor"* (2:2-3). The early Church was marked by missionary and evangelistic zeal as seen in the house-to-house witness for Christ, the missionary journeys of Paul, the fervent witness of men and women like Stephen, Philip, Ananias, Barnabas, Priscilla and Acquila, etc. The Greek word for "labor" is translated "toil," and it means diligent labor even unto weariness and exhaustion. The church at Ephesus was a veritable beehive of Holy-Spirit-directed activity.

He approved them for their *steadfastness:*

Hast patience . . . and hast not fainted (2:3).

Amidst Judaism with its legalism and ceremonial law, and paganism with its superstition and immorality, the early Church was fixed, firm, resolute, not fickle. They weathered the storms. Church life did not consist of the folding of the hands and a listless, lethargic sitting through a sermon. This was a working church which pushed forward with anguish of soul for the salvation of lost men and women. In Acts 19 we are told how the Christians in Ephesus were exposed to fierce opposition. They knew what it was to be despised and hated, yet they were neither dispirited nor dissuaded. Trade-unions tried to drive them out of the city, but they stood firm for Christ and His gospel.

He approved them for their *suppression* of evil:

Thou canst not bear them which are evil (2:2).

The early Church was alert to both the mental and moral corruption that prevailed around them, but they saw to it that sinful and corrupt men did not hold office in the assembly. Men were given oversight in the work because of their spiritual power and not because of their social prominence or financial worth. They were intolerant of sin. Today it makes little difference what people are like morally or spiritually, just so we get them into our church and on the membership roll to swell the number. The church at Ephesus was not concerned with the quantity of persons that were added, but rather with the quality.

He approved them for their *spiritual discernment:*

Thou hast tried them which say they are apostles, and are not, and hast found them liars (2:2).

They knew what they believed and why they believed it and they were loyal to the truth. The Apostle Paul had warned them that such men would seek to get in among them (Acts 20:28-31). The Scriptures abound in evidence which should serve as a warning to us (Joshua 9; Ezra 4). Thus we are exhorted to try the spirits (1 John 4:1). At the time the Revelation was written, John was possibly the only living apostle, thus it would be expected that false claimants would arise. Having been rooted and grounded in the truth, they tested every traveling preacher that came their way.

He approved them for their *stand* against the deeds of the Nicolaitanes.

But this thou hast, that thou hatest the deeds of the Nicolaitanes, which I also hate (2:6).

The Nicolaitanes were an early heretical sect. The real origin of this sect, and precisely what it believed and taught, will probably never be known by us. Louis T. Talbot wrote: "The two words *nikao,* meaning 'to conquer,' and *laos,* meaning 'the people' or 'laity,' form the root of the name 'Nicolaitanes.' The term was applied to those who originated the system which divided the Church of Jesus Christ into two divisions—the clergy and the laity. When we come to the study of the situation existing in the churches of Pergamos and Thyatira, we shall find this system in full bloom, with bishops, archbishops, and other religious dignitaries domineering the people." Whatever the deeds of the Nicolaitanes were, Christ said He hated them, and He commended the saints in Ephesus for hating them also.

IV. THE ADMONITION (2:4)

Nevertheless I have something against thee, because thou hast left thy first love (2:4).

They maintained a spirit of sacrifice, steadfastness, separation, and a keenness for detecting heresy, but they were guilty of a sin that no average person could detect. They had left their first love. Our Lord told His disciples, concerning the last days, "The love of many shall wax cold" (Matthew 24:12). Now they could not be charged with having no love at all for Christ, but they had left their *first* love. First love is the love of espousals (Jeremiah 2:2); the tender love of a bridegroom for his virgin bride (2 Corinthians 11:2); honeymoon love. It is the one thing our Lord wants more than anything else and the one thing He asked of Peter before He went away (John 21:15-17).

A wife or husband, for example, may remain faithful and may give evidence of assiduity in matters pertaining to each other, and yet there may be a decline in first love. Similarly, a church member may be very regular in his attendance at the services, but no amount of activity, however intense, can compensate for a lack of love. Sacrifice, even to the point of poverty and martyrdom, if it have not love, shall profit nothing (1 Corinthians 13:3). Like Martha, we can become so occupied with doing *for* Christ as to miss becoming *like* Christ (Luke 10:38-

42). The Lord is jealous of our hearts, and it is no small thing for Him to see our love declining. Love is the first essential in Christian character, and when it commences to decline, the soul begins to drift. It was not in doctrinal errors, but in the loss of first love, that we find the root cause of the falling away in the early Church.

What does Christ's all-searching eyes see in our hearts as He walks among us? Is there a decay of our first love? Are you eager and earnest in your private devotions? Has your heart chilled toward Christ and His Word? Does your Heavenly Bridegroom grieve because you have fallen out of love? Someone has said, "Life holds few things more bitter than the tragedy of unrequited love." It could be said of the church at Ephesus, "The honeymoon is over."

V. THE APPEAL (2:5)

Remember (2:5).

Call to mind those early days when the first-named fruit of the Spirit flooded your soul (Romans 5:5 cf. Galatians 5:22). The first step toward rescuing a church that has left her first love is an acknowledgment of the need. Memory is a precious gift. To look back can be a hindrance, as in the case of Lot's wife, but it can also be a blessing. In this instance the Saviour prescribed retrospection as the first step toward revival in a church whose love was dying. It may wound our pride to compare a victorious and joyous past with a sad and failing present, but there is no other way back.

Repent (2:5).

Do Christians need to repent, confess, and turn back to God? Yes, there must be a change of mind that will lead to a change of direction. Our Lord admonishes His Church to turn from her sins to her first love. "As ye have therefore received Christ Jesus the Lord, so walk ye in Him" (Colossians 2:6). Nothing less than genuine repentance and a return to her "first love" could save Ephesus from complete collapse. Thus remembrance and repentance are stated as two essential factors in recovering the church from its backslidden state. The only proof that the heart is sincere is that the backslider returns to "do the first works" (2:5).

The appeal is to each individual in the Church (2:7). Christ pleads to His Church to give the Holy Spirit His rightful place. Literally and actually Christ is not here in Person. He said that He was going away (John 14:2), and that He would send the Holy Spirit (John 14:16,26). It is the Holy Spirit who testifies of Christ and glorifies Him (John 15:26-27), and it is He who convicts of sin (John 16:7-11). It is the Holy Spirit who regenerates (Titus 3:5) and who chooses the believer's body in which to reside (1 Corinthians 3:16; 6:19). It was to the Ephesian Church that Paul wrote exhorting the saints to "grieve not the Holy Spirit of God" (Ephesians 4:30) and "be filled with the Spirit" (Ephesians 5:18). As we read and meditate and study His Word, He speaks; *"He that hath an ear, let him hear what the Spirit saith unto the churches"* (Revelation 2:7).

But suppose the church refused to repent, then what? Our Lord said, *"Remember . . . and repent . . . or else . . ."* (2:5). Or else what?

Or else I will come unto thee quickly, and will remove thy candlestick out of his place, except thou repent (2:5).

No individual Christian or local assembly can isolate the Holy Spirit and escape disaster. Today nothing is left of the ancient city of Ephesus but a memory, and today nothing is left of some local assemblies but a memory. For the people in the assembly the honeymoon came to an end, and therefore the Lord removed their witness. The light no longer burns and shines as a testimony to Christ and His gospel and the power of the Holy Spirit.

The Apostle Paul never left his first love. He feared being disqualified at the Judgment Seat of Christ (1 Corinthians 9:27; 2 Corinthians 5:10). That first love burned in his soul until his head was removed on the executioner's block. No local assembly or denomination or individual Christian can boast a permanent place in this world as a light-bearer. Let

Christ's admonition and appeal be just as appropriate to us today as it was to Ephesus. Someone has said that ninety-five per cent of the activity in the average local assembly would go on as it is presently even if the Holy Spirit did not exist. Perhaps this is the reason why the average assembly is devoid of spiritual power. There is much activity in many churches, but it is to be feared that most of it is "bootleg" and without any divine purpose and power whatever. Christ's words were literally fulfilled in Ephesus, and history has continuously repeated itself. Remember and repent—or else!

> Where is the blessedness I knew
>   When first I saw the Lord?
> Where is the soul-refreshing view
>   Of Jesus and His Word?
>
> What peaceful hours I once enjoyed—
>   How sweet their memory still!
> But they have left an aching void
>   The world can never fill.

THE LETTER TO SMYRNA

Revelation 2:8-11

I. THE ASSEMBLY

The city of Smyrna received its name from one of its principal commercial products, namely, myrrh. For many centuries it was notably a prosperous seaport city, the port of myrrh. It was situated about forty miles north of Ephesus.

The Greek word *Smurna* is actually a word of Semitic origin, the Hebrew root meaning "bitter." It was a gum resin taken from a shrubby tree and had a bitter taste. It was used as an ingredient in making perfume (Psalm 45:8); as one of the ingredients of the holy anointing oil for the priests (Exodus 30:23); for the purification of women (Esther 2:12); and for embalming (John 19:39). It is most significant that our Lord spoke as He did to the assembly at Smyrna, for this church was in the midst of bitter sorrow and suffering.

Precisely when and under what circumstances the church was planted in Smyrna, history does not state. It is possible that Paul was instrumental in getting it started while on his third missionary journey (Acts 19:10). One thing is certain, Smyrna was a difficult place to maintain a Christian testimony, because the church there was the most afflicted and persecuted of all the churches.

Prophetically, Smyrna sets forth that age or stage in Church history when the Church was persecuted beneath the iron heel of pagan Rome. The persecution had begun in John's day, thus in a primary sense the message applied locally. But the prophetic era extended to about A.D. 312.

II. THE AUTHOR (2:8)

The character in which our Lord presents Himself to the assembly at Smyrna is quite appropriate.

> *These things saith the first and the last, which was dead, and is alive* (2:8).

He thus reveals Himself to them in the way best suited to comfort them in their sorrow and to encourage them in their sufferings. He would console them by reminding them that He had passed through suffering and death and had triumphed over it. In the role of the One "who *became* [the meaning of the aorist tense] dead and lived again," He is able to sympathize with, and succor, them. This persecuted people needed to know that their blessed and glorified Head had defeated death and was now the Master over it (Hebrews 2:18). Having been tempted and tried in all points as they were, He was now their Great High Priest (Hebrews 4:15-16).

Myrrh was associated with Christ in His first coming. After His birth the wise men came and presented unto Him gifts, "gold and frankincense and myrrh" (Matthew 2:11). These items spoke of royalty, deity, and suffering humanity. When He was hanging on the cross they offered Him to drink "wine mingled with myrrh" (Mark 15:23). It was Nicodemus who assisted Joseph of Arimathaea in taking the body of Jesus and preparing it for burial. He brought with him for the embalming "a mixture of myrrh and aloes" (John 19:39-40). When Christ comes again, He shall be presented with gold and frankincense, but not myrrh (Isaiah 60:6). Then He will appear as the mighty Sovereign, not the Sufferer.

III. THE AFFLICTION (2:9)

The Lord approved this suffering church for her works in the face of tribulation and poverty.

> *I know thy works, and tribulation, and poverty, (but thou art rich) and I know the blasphemy of them which say they are Jews, and are not, but are the synagogue of Satan* (2:9).

As Ephesus characterizes the apostolic age of the first century, so Smyrna characterizes the period beginning about A.D. 64 and continuing to the persecution under Diocletian about A.D. 312. Again we might say it is doubtful that John knew the details of the prophetic era that was to continue for some 250 years beyond the time of writing.

The Lord Jesus did say, *"ye shall have tribulation ten days"* (2:10). Many able students of God's Word believe these "ten days" refer to the ten separate attempts to wipe out Christianity prompted by the edicts of ten different Roman rulers. Or it is possible that the "ten days" may allude to the tenth persecution under Diocletian, which lasted exactly ten years. Whatever the precise meaning of the "ten days," it suggests at least that the persecution would be for a limited time.

Dr. Walter L. Wilson sees in the number ten typically that which represents human failure. The ten spies failed to see God's power and provision, so they brought back an evil report (Numbers 13:32). The ten tribes failed to walk with God and do His will, thus they established a separate kingdom given to idolatry (1 Kings 11:31).

But it seems that the number ten might suggest a testing time, not always ending in failure, as seen in the request of Rebekah's mother and brother (Genesis 24:55), or the test of Nehemiah (Nehemiah 5:18), or the Word of the Lord coming to Jeremiah (Jeremiah 42:7), or the request of Daniel (Daniel 1:11-15). Whether the trial results in failure or faithfulness, the number ten is suggestive of a time of testing.

J. J. Van Gorder in *ABC's of the Revelation* lists the ten edicts of ten pagan Roman rulers and their approximate dates:

Nero	A.D. 54	Maximim	A.D. 235
Domitian	A.D. 81	Decius	A.D. 249
Trojan	A.D. 98	Valerian	A.D. 254
Antoninus	A.D. 117	Aurelian	A.D. 270
Severus	A.D. 195	Diocletian	A.D. 284

Christ continued by telling them He was aware of their "poverty." These Christians had literally suffered the loss of all things for Christ's sake. They had lost their possessions, their social prestige and the possibility of working to earn an honest living. But the context suggests that they, like those saints to whom the Epistle to the Hebrews was written, "took joyfully the spoiling of your goods, knowing in yourselves that ye have in heaven a better and an enduring substance" (Hebrews 10:34). The Christian who is laying up treasure in Heaven is rich indeed (Matthew 6:19-21). The poverty of those early saints was a part of their tribulation, but they knew that "a man's life consisteth not in the abundance of the things which he possesseth" (Luke 12:15).

But our Lord knew their poverty as something that He Himself had experienced. "For ye know the grace of our Lord Jesus Christ, that, though He was rich, yet for your sakes He became poor, that ye through His poverty might be rich" (2 Corinthians 8:9). He was born in a borrowed stable, and early in His ministry He said, "The foxes have holes, and the birds of the air have nests; but the Son of man hath not where to lay His head" (Matthew 8:20). Those poor saints in Smyrna were comforted by His words.

However, this church was rich despite her poverty, for Christ added, *"but thou art rich."* Here is one of the many paradoxes in the Bible. Paul expressed it, "as having nothing, and yet possessing all things" (2 Corinthians 6:10). Peter demonstrated the "riches in rags" paradox when he said to the lame man at the gate of the temple, "Silver and gold have I none; but such as I have give I thee: in the name of Jesus Christ of Nazareth rise up and walk" (Acts 3:6). The trusting child of God is never alarmed over the seeming inequality in material things between the righteous and the wicked. The word rich (Gr. *plousios*) is the source of our English word "plutocrat." Christians are the Lord's plutocrats, many of whom have little or no money in the banks of this world, but an abundance of treasure in Heaven. They are rich in their possession of a Saviour, the Scriptures, and the bright and blessed prospect of an eternal home in Heaven.

We cannot leave this parenthesis in Revelation 2:9 without comparing it with the church of Laodicea. To that faithless and self-satisfied church our Lord says:

Because thou sayest, I am rich, and increased with goods, and have need of nothing; and knowest not that thou art wretched, and miserable, and poor, and blind, and naked (3:17).

What a striking contrast between these two churches! Christ designates Smyrna the poor rich church and Laodicea the rich poor church. There is a poverty which is riches and a wealth which is poverty. A man's life may be fed with much goods, but if he spurns the true riches in Christ, God calls him a fool (Luke 12:16-21). The Laodicean letter, being the last of the seven, anticipates prophetically the end of the Church Age, that period immediately preceding the return of Christ for His own. Our materialistic, inflationary times might well mark the end of the present age. Elaborate church edifices with their expensive "educational units" are increasing in number and size with each passing year. A church's wealth determines its stature and importance in these days. But the time is not far off when each of us will have to stand up and be counted either with the poor rich church or the rich poor church.

In addition to the persecution and poverty they suffered, the Lord recognized further how they had to suffer the propagation of false reports. He said:

I know the blasphemy of them which say they are Jews, and are not, but are the synagogue of Satan (2:9).

The word "blasphemy" can be rendered "slander." This church was surrounded by foes. These foes were tearing her reputation to pieces. They were Jews but they were not worthy of the name (Romans 2:28). Rather than representing a true Jewish synagogue, they were a synagogue of Satan (John 8:44). The word "devil" means "slanderer." He is the forger of lies and all manner of false accusations against God's children (Revelation 12:10).

Today the church of Smyrna is behind the iron curtain in Russia; behind the bamboo curtain in China; and behind the purple curtain in Spain, Colombia, Quebec, etc. What it might cost to remain true to Christ none of us can tell. It seems inevitable that America will suffer the same. That there is a present application here, none can deny. Both our Lord and the Apostle Paul wrote of impending tribulation that would arise during the Church Age (John 16:33; 2 Timothy 3:12). Such a time will separate the true believer from the mere professor (Matthew 13:5-6,20-21). Our Lord's seven letters to as many churches supplement and endorse His seven parables in Matthew 13. Both teach the dawn, deterioration, and doom of Christendom.

IV. THE APPEAL (2:10)

Christ tells His church not to fear, and then He adds:

> *Be thou faithful unto death, and I will give thee a crown of life* (2:10).

G. Campbell Morgan points out that the word "faithful" here is from the root which means to be convinced. In chapter 1, verse 5, Christ is said to be "faithful," thus the faithfulness of the saints rests in the faithfulness of the Saviour. Christ was not telling His suffering saints to "keep a stiff upper lip" or to "keep your chin up" or "keep smiling" or "grin and bear it." What He told them was to depend on Him, to be convinced of Him, to let Him be their strength and courage. He knew they would fail if they merely tried to bear up in their own strength. He wanted them to live within the limit of the great assurance that He became dead and is alive.

The "crown of life" is one of five crowns promised to faithful believers when Christ returns. They are: the incorruptible crown (1 Corinthians 9:25); the soul-winner's crown (Philippians 4:1; 1 Thessalonians 2:19); the crown of righteousness (2 Timothy 4:8); the crown of glory (1 Peter 5:4); the crown of life (James 1:12; Revelation 2:10). These are not to be worn on our heads in Heaven, but rather to be presented to our blessed Lord (Revelation 4:10). The Christian philosophy of suffering for Christ is that out of tribulation comes triumph;

out of persecution, the prize; out of death we come to reigning life with Him.

The period in church history, of which conditions in Smyrna were prophetic, dates from about the year A.D. 160 to the beginning of the rule of Constantine in A.D. 313.

THE LETTER TO PERGAMOS

Revelation 2:12-17

I. THE ASSEMBLY

Pergamos was the capital city of Mysia, a Roman province in the northwest of Asia Minor. Paul passed through this province, embarking at the port of Troas, on his first voyage to Europe (Acts 16:7-8). The city of Pergamos was about twenty miles from the sea. It was an illustrious and religious city of wealth and fashion. Unlike Ephesus and Smyrna, it was not a city of commerce.

Pergamos was known chiefly for its religion. There one would find temples erected in honor of many gods. Some of its chief deities were Zeus, Aphrodite, Aesculapius, the latter being the god of medicine who was worshiped under the form of a serpent. Thus our Lord said that this assembly was situated in the city *"where Satan's seat* [throne] *is"* (2:13). Now Satan's throne is not in hell. This whole idea of Satan's headquarters being in hell is preposterous. Satan is "the prince of this world" (John 12:31; 14:30; 16:11). So said Christ Himself on at least three occasions. Paul and John taught likewise that Satan held leadership over this world system (2 Corinthians 4:4; Ephesians 2:2; 1 John 4:3-4; 5:19). His rule extends to both the celestial and the terrestrial spheres.

This religious city was an ideal place for Satan to establish his headquarters inasmuch as his most effective work is accomplished through religious organizations and institutions. While communism and atheism are avowed enemies of Jesus Christ, and therefore under Satan's control, Satan himself operates to his greatest advantage through his demons who pose as ministers of righteousness (2 Corinthians 11:13-15).

It is significant that Christ commences His letter to the assembly at Pergamos with the statement, *"I know . . . where thou dwellest"* (2:13). He knows the environment in which His people live. He is not ignorant of the fact that His Church is in the midst of a religious, non-Christian world. For the present, at least, it is His desire that we remain in the world but not of the world (John 17:14-16; Romans 12:2; James 4:4; 1 John 2:15-17). In no place did the Christians have a more difficult time than in Pergamos, the center of paganism in that day. In Smyrna it is a "synagogue of Satan" (2:9); in Pergamos it is the throne of Satan, his base of operations.

II. THE AUTHOR (2:12)

In order to encourage this assembly our Lord presents Himself as:

He which hath the sharp sword with two edges (2:12).

John had seen this sharp sword issuing from His mouth (1:16). The Holy Spirit prophesied through Isaiah concerning Jehovah's Servant, "He made My mouth like a sharp sword" (Isaiah 49:2). This sword is His Word, used sometimes as an analytical critic of the mind of man (Hebrews 4:12), and at other times as an instrument of war (Ephesians 6:17; Revelation 2:16; 19:15). Every believer knows that the Bible possesses swordlike qualities. It was this weapon that Christ used when He was tempted of Satan in the wilderness (Matthew 4:4,7,10). God's way to overcome satanic error and opposition is by the faithful setting forth of His Word. Nothing but His truth can defeat error, and we have this divinely inspired weapon of victory. Let us use it fearlessly. And when Christ comes to earth again He will use it to smite the nations and to deal with all the false teachers of Christendom.

III. THE APPROVAL (2:13)

Our Lord told them that He knew all about them:

Thou holdest fast My name (2:13).

He praises those, who were dwelling in the shadow of Satan's throne, for their faithfulness to His name. They might have saved themselves from persecution by merely whispering His name among themselves. Or they might have concluded that they must get along with Satan's crowd, and so, in order to maintain peaceful coexistence and satisfy the enemy, they wouldn't make a spectacle of themselves by identifying themselves publicly with Jesus Christ. But no, they maintained a love for, and loyalty to, Christ's name, and He appreciated their stand.

Christ's name stands for Himself. It represents the fullness of His divine Person, His deity, His sinlessness, and His saving work for sinners. Holding fast His name is not the equivalent of carrying a card or wearing a medal to show that one belongs to some "holy name society." Rather, it is holding to the firm conviction that He is the Lord Jesus Christ—"Lord" [Master], "Jesus" [Mediator], "Christ" [Messiah]. His name suggests His honor, His glorious nature, His holy character, and His redeeming power.

In the New Testament we learn that sinners are saved through believing on His name (John 1:12; Acts 4:12). Our Lord gave the assurance that no religious gathering was to be measured by its numerical strength, but by its proper recognition of His name, for He said, "Where two or three are gathered together in My name, there am I in the midst of them" (Matthew 18:20). He taught His disciples to pray to the Father "in My name" (John 14:13-14), and then He assured them that this was one requisite for getting those things for which they prayed (John 15:16; 16:23-24). He warned them that men would hate them for His name's sake (Matthew 10:22), but He promised a rich reward to all who would be willing to forsake all for His name's sake (Matthew 19:29).

He continues His approval of them with these words:

> *And hast not denied My faith, even in those days wherein Antipas was My faithful martyr, who was slain among you, where Satan dwelleth* (2:13).

He praised them for their doctrinal faithfulness. He calls it "My faith." The translators are agreed that, grammatically speaking, *"My faith"* means "your faith in Me" (Berkeley, Guyse, Williams, etc.). They did not merely give intellectual assent to the fact of Jesus Christ; they trusted Him as Saviour and Lord.

One in this church had died for his faith. The secular historians took no note of him, but he is eternally remembered and recorded by the Lord Jesus Christ.

> *Antipas was My faithful martyr, who was slain among you, where Satan dwelleth* (2:13).

All we know about Antipas is that he was Christ's faithful martyr. And the Lord commends this assembly that even in the face of such persecution there were those who remained faithful. We shall meet Antipas, and a host of other martyrs, who, having been faithful unto death, will receive a crown of life. We shall witness their coronation when the Lord Jesus Christ shall say to them, "Well done, thou good and faithful servant."

If your Christian faith and mine were to be exposed to the supreme test, would we stand firm? Would we accept death rather than deny our Lord? Is the name of Jesus Christ more precious to us than life? No trial, however severe, justifies unfaithfulness. "It is required in stewards, that a man be found faithful" (1 Corinthians 4:2).

IV. THE ADMONITION (2:14-15)

After having approved all that He could approve, the Lord proceeds to admonish them.

> *But I have a few things against thee, because thou hast there them that hold the doctrine of Balaam, who taught*

Balac to cast a stumblingblock before the children of Israel, to eat things sacrificed unto idols, and to commit fornication (2:14).

The assembly is not charged with being one with the Balaamites, but apparently had tolerated them in its midst, and that in itself was wrong. It is ever and always sinful to countenance evil among an assembly of believers. It is not enough to be grieved, and even shocked; the guilty one must repent and forsake his evil way. And if there be no repentance, those who have the oversight can take no other course of action except to expel. Though not guilty themselves, they failed to censure those who were guilty. They tolerated them when they should have tried them. The present tendency to minimize sin in the church has reduced her spiritual tone to a subnormal status.

Read 1 Corinthians 5:1-8 for a lesson in church discipline. Paul did not wink at that flagrant example of incest. The member of the church at Corinth who was guilty of immoral relations with his stepmother, and who would not repent, was purged out. Moral dereliction, moral delinquency in the church tends toward the corruption of the whole. "A little leaven leaveneth the whole lump" (1 Corinthians 5:6). Those who have the oversight of the local assembly need to be concerned about the influence that the sins of one person will have upon the whole assembly. When we compromise with evil, we make the word "compromise" a most immoral word in the English language. So said John Morley, and I agree with him.

It is not merely the right of every society to judge evil among its own members; it is a solemn duty. Paul did it, and he did so in the name of our Lord Jesus Christ (1 Corinthians 6:4). We shall not attempt here an explanation of the phrase, "to deliver such an one unto Satan for the destruction of the flesh," whether it means simply excommunication, or the exercise of apostolic authority to inflict on men bodily punishment by the agency of Satan as in Acts 5:1-11; 13:9-11; 2 Corinthians 10:8; 13:10; 1 Timothy 1:20. I am merely making the point that discipline should be exercised in the local assembly whenever and wherever it is needed. There can be no peaceful coexistence between light and darkness, righteousness and unrighteousness, Christ and Belial. Our Lord taught the need for discipline in the Church of God (Matthew 18:15-17), therefore we must not be afraid to exercise it. In this the assembly at Pergamos had failed.

Now precisely what was it for which our Lord admonished them? It was not that any among them professed to be followers of Balaam. Old errors revive under new names or else under no name at all. Neo-orthodoxy is an example of an old error taking on a new name. It is neither new nor orthodox; it is the old modernism in a new dress. Some present-day theologians have changed the label on the bottle but the contents remain the same.

Balaam had introduced a principle of corruption which crept into the early Church. The history of Balaam is recorded in four chapters of the Old Testament (Numbers 22-25). Balaam had the gift of prophecy but, like many of whom our Lord spoke (Matthew 7:22-23), he came to a sorry end. He had God's Word in his mouth while his heart was possessed with a satanic covetousness for the honors and rewards of this world. He made merchandise of the gospel, prostituting it for gain. That Balaam was greedy for gain is supported in 2 Peter 2:15 and Jude 11. He had unusual gifts and was an eloquent preacher, but he was willing to compromise for a price.

Balak, king of Moab, offered Balaam a sizable fee to curse Israel. This Gentile ruler feared the Israelites, who were about to cross over the Jordon River into the promised land. Balaam rejected Balak's first offer (Numbers 22:5-13), but when Balak's messengers returned a second time with the offer of a larger fee and greater fringe benefits, Balaam accepted (Numbers 22:14-21). Three times he attempted to curse Israel, but on every occasion the Lord restrained him (Numbers 23 and 24). At last Balaam conceived an evil scheme that was to produce the downfall of God's people. When he concluded that he could not *curse* them, he proposed to *corrupt* them. He suggested that the Moabite girls should seduce the men of Israel by inviting them to participate in their idolatrous and immoral feasts. In this evil perpetration he succeeded (Numbers 25:1-3 cf. 31:16), and through this unholy alliance, this unequal yoke, this mixed marriage, Israel fell. Balaam had followed Satan's old line. When the devil failed to wipe out the godly line through *murder* (Genesis 4), he resorted to *mixture* (Genesis 6).

This was Balaamism, and it was this evil principle that came into the assembly at Pergamos. The late Donald Grey Barnhouse wrote: "The very word 'Pergamos' has in it the same root from which we get our English words for bigamy and polygamy. It is the word for marriage. The particle which forms the first syllable frequently calls attention to something that is objectionable. 'Pergamos' signifies a mixed marriage in the most objectionable sense of the word, for it is the marriage of the organization of the Church of Jesus Christ with the world." G. Campbell Morgan said: "The doctrine of Balaam broadly stated was undoubtedly that, seeing that they were the covenant people of God, they might with safety indulge themselves in social intercourse with their neighbors."

When and how did the church and the world fall in love? Certainly the mixed marriage ought never to have come to pass. The Lord said to His own, "If the world hate you, ye know that it hated Me before it hated you. If ye were of the world, the world would love his own: but because ye are not of the world, but I have chosen you out of the world, therefore the world hateth you" (John 15:18-19). In His great high priestly prayer He said, "I have given them Thy word; and the world hath hated them, because they are not of the world, even as I am not of the world. I pray not that Thou shouldest take them out of the world, but that Thou shouldest keep them from the evil. They are not of the world, even as I am not of the world" (John 17:14-16). "Marvel not, my brethren, if the world hate you" (1 John 3:13). It follows logically that the world could not bring itself to love the church until the church had first become worldly. The church that is popular with the world today is not the spiritually strong, separated church; rather is it the church that mixes with the world and which welcomes the unconverted worldling into its fold.

Early in the fourth century, after the death of Diocletian

the monarch of the Roman Empire, two men contended for the throne. Constantine in the West and Maxentius in the East were both determined to succeed Diocletian. Old tradition has it that the night before the battle at Milvian Bridge, Constantine saw a vision in the sky in the shape of a cross, bearing the inscription in Latin, *in hoc signo vinces* ("by this sign conquer"). That night he bargained with Satan to join the church and declare himself a Christian if he won the battle. We know from history that Constantine won the battle, declared himself a Christian and Christianity to be the religion of the state. Christian leaders were invited to witness the wholesale baptism of whole regiments of soldiers in Constantine's army. When later almost four hundred bishops met, Constantine was carried on a golden throne and he presided over the council as the recognized head of the church. But with all of the profession and pomp, there is no evidence that he was born again.

After Constantine's declaration, it was popular to be a "Christian." True believers in the Lord Jesus Christ, who were being persecuted, found themselves being lauded by political and civil authorities. Their rags of persecution and their hideouts in the catacombs gave way to softer garments and more comfortable dwellings. Thus the Pergamos stage of history came into being. The church was married to the world.

We have pointed out earlier in these studies the fact that the messages in the seven letters supplement and endorse our Lord's parables in Matthew 13. Pergamos represents the church of the mustard seed (Matthew 13:31-32). Christ speaks of its "greatness" and the fact that the "birds" lodged in its branches. We learn from the first parable that the "fowls" which devoured up the seed represent Satan (13:4,19 cf. Mark 4:15; Luke 8:12). The monstrosity of the "tree" which ought never to have become a tree, according to Genesis 1:11-12, was a freak of abnormal growth. Thus we see Christendom taken over by Satan's emissaries, even as Paul warned in 2 Corinthians 11:13-15. The ecumenical church with its world council is an ugly monstrosity and is a poor facsimile of the true Church of Jesus Christ. The fowls in the topmost branches are Satan's emissaries who attempt to make null and void the sacrificial death of Jesus Christ as man's only hope of salvation. This was typified in Abram's sacrifice when he drove the fowls away (Genesis 15:11).

The story of the church's alliance with the world, and her subsequent failure, is a matter of recorded history. The state church has become Satan's headquarters, where his throne is. Nicolaitanism is fully accepted. It is here to stay. That which was mere "deeds" in Ephesus (2:6), became "doctrine" in Pergamos (2:15), and is today "dogma." The first seeds of the Roman Catholic Church were sown as far back as the fourth century. Today the world is ready to accept the Roman Pope and be subject to him. The Roman Catholic Church claims to be of divine origin, but its "deeds" and "doctrines" are hated by Christ.

V. THE APPEAL (2:16)

Repent; or else I will come unto thee quickly, and will fight against them with the sword of My mouth (2:16).

Here is a sharp command, not to the unsaved holding to the false deeds and doctrines, but to the true Church and its messenger. If we fail to exclude unbelievers from the fellowship of the assembly, we are in error. By allowing them to remain, they imagine they are in a place of safety and security while they are in the place of death and damnation. It is sinful to tolerate Balaamism even though we may not practice it. We are either for Christ or against Him. We cannot serve God and Mammon. No man can serve two masters. It has always been fatal for the church to become identified with the state.

Error will not be suppressed by compromising with it. The false religious ideologies of Christendom can be overthrown only by the sword of the Spirit, the proclamation of the gospel of Christ. And if men will not repent, Christ's saving Word becomes their Judge (John 12:47-48). His holy sword becomes their executioner. Balaam himself was slain with the sword (Numbers 31:8; Joshua 13:22), and so will all those who reject Jesus Christ.

Notice our Lord's discriminating language. He says, "I will come unto *thee* . . . and will fight against *them*." He will gather the wheat and burn the tares. But He calls upon His own to accept His principle of separation, thereby refusing to compromise with either moral evil or religious error.

The period in church history of which conditions in Pergamos were prophetic date from about the year A.D. 313 until the rise of the Papacy, about A.D. 600.

THE LETTER TO THYATIRA

Revelation 2:18-29

I. THE ASSEMBLY

The city of Thyatira, though smaller and less significant than the first three, received the longest letter. It was situated southeast of Pergamos, about half way between that city and Sardis. It was distinguished for its industrial activity and was therefore a prosperous city in trade and commerce. Archaeological discoveries have brought to light the fact that Thyatira was a well-known center for numerous trade guilds. For example, there were organized groups and associations for potters, tanners, bronze workers, and dyers.

It has been said that the water around Thyatira was so adapted to dyeing that in no other place could the scarlet cloth, out of which fezzes were made, be so permanently and perfectly dyed as here. It was Lydia, "a seller of purple, of the city of Thyatira," who had come to Philippi in Macedonia on business, heard Paul preach the gospel there, and received the truth (Acts 16:14). Nowhere is it stated exactly how the assembly got started in the city of Thyatira, but it is not unlikely that Lydia returned to her home there and witnessed to her faith in Jesus Christ. Luke tells us that when she was baptized, other members of her family were baptized with her (Acts 16:15). We do know, however, that when Christ gave these letters to His servant John, the local assembly was in existence and active. It is of interest to note in passing that Lydia was the first recorded convert to Jesus Christ on European soil.

II. THE AUTHOR (2:18)

Our Lord introduced Himself to this church as *"the Son of God"* (2:18). There is a reason for this. Conditions in the church of Thyatira were prophetic of the next period in church history, from the seventh to the sixteenth centuries. During that time from about A.D. 600 to A.D. 1500 the world saw the rapid rise of Romanism. To this church which was prophetic of that long dark period, known as "The Dark Ages," when the Papacy wielded her power malevolently, Christ declares Himself to be *"the Son of God."*

Ford C. Ottman wrote, "As 'the Son of God' He rebukes the church that would degrade Him and keep Him the son of a human mother while exalting *her* above Him as 'the mother of God' and 'the queen of heaven.' " Our Lord knows exactly when and where to insist upon His divine prerogative as the Son of God. He would have all usurpers, with their queenly assumptions, know that He is the very Son of God who alone speaks with supreme and final authority. He would have all men know that they are not dealing with prophets like Moses and Elijah, nor with apostles like Paul and Peter. They are dealing with Deity, with the divine Son of God Himself. The rise of Romanism made Jesus popular as "the son of Mary," a position that robs Him of His essential deity and thereby degrades Him. But God had a Son, coeternal and coequal with the Father. While it was truly prophesied that " a virgin shall conceive and bear a son" (Isaiah 7:14), it is equally true that the Son was given before ever He was born of Mary (Isaiah 9:6).

Romanism teaches those under its power that they must pray to Mary in order to get through to God. This fallacy is nowhere hinted at in the Holy Scriptures. On the contrary, our Lord taught that the Father was to be approached in the Son's name (John 14:13-14; 16:23-24). In anticipation of the claims of Rome, our Lord plainly refers to Himself as "the Son of God." He knew the day would come when His true followers would be hated for His name's sake (Matthew 19:29).

In Pergamos they were holding fast His name (Revelation 2:13). In Thyatira conditions were foreshadowing Rome's efforts to lower the dignity of His name.

He is further described as the One:

Who hath His eyes like unto a flame of fire (2:18).

Joseph A. Seiss said: "There is nothing more piercing than flaming fire. Everything yields and melts before it. It penetrates all things, consumes every opposition, sweeps down all obstructions, and presses its way with invincible power. And of this sort are the eyes of Jesus. They look through everything; they pierce through all masks and coverings; they search the remotest recesses; they behold the most hidden things of the soul; and there is no escape from them. As the Son of God He is omniscient as well as almighty." This is a most solemn truth!

Hagar knew that His burning eyes pierced the night of her sorrow and loneliness, for she cried, "Thou God seest me" (Genesis 16:13). Jeremiah testified of Him who tries the mind and heart of all men (Jeremiah 11:20; 17:9-10; 20:12). The apostles recognized that His eyes like unto a flame of fire pierced human hearts and minds when they prayed, "Thou, Lord, which knowest the hearts of all men" (Acts 1:24 cf. 15:8). The words in the Authorized Version, "which knowest the hearts of all men," are the translation of one Greek word (*kardiognostes*) and means "heartknower."

The Divine Heartknower pierced the Pharisees with His omniscient gaze "When He had looked round about on them with anger, being grieved for the hardness of their hearts" (Mark 3:5). "He knew all men. . . . He knew what was in man" (John 2:24,25). "Jesus knew from the beginning who they were that believed not, and who should betray Him" (John 6:64). He read the hearts of Nathanael (John 1:48) and the woman of Samaria (John 4:28-29). Simon Peter never could erase from his memory the vision of Christ's gaze when "the Lord turned, and looked upon Peter . . . and Peter went out, and wept bitterly" (Luke 22:61,62), for after the resurrection he said to Jesus, "Lord, Thou knowest all things" (John 21:17).

No human has ever yet escaped His all-knowing gaze (Hebrews 4:13). Let us then learn to walk in His presence as the One who knows all.

John describes the Lord further:

His feet are like fine brass (2:18).

Here Christ takes on the symbol of judgment. As the One whose feet are as polished brass, "He treadeth the winepress of the fierceness and wrath of Almighty God" (Revelation 19:15). Brass is a metal used in Scripture as a symbol of judgment. The serpent of brass in Numbers 21:9 represented our Lord Jesus Christ who, under the divine judgment of Heaven, bore the penalty for our sins on the cross (John 3:14-15). Sin must be judged. God can never remain silent and inactive where sin is present. If the guilty in Thyatira, or America, or Asia, or Africa, or Europe, or in any other place, will not repent and come to Christ as their Saviour and Lord, then they must face Him when He comes again to judge the living and the dead. The description of the Judge with feet like burnished brass tells us His judgment will be strong and righteous. All judgment is committed to Jesus Christ, and He will execute it infallibly. But this is the day of grace when His feet are a thing of beauty as He brings good tidings of salvation (Isaiah 52:7 cf. Romans 10:15). Oh, that sinful men and women would see this truth!

III. THE APPROVAL (2:19)

Here are blessed qualities indeed!

I know thy works, and charity (2:19).

The Christ of the lampstands credits this church with "charity" (love). With all the faultiness in this church, as we shall see, there was much good. Love led the list of virtues. Where love was waning in Ephesus (2:4), it was gaining in Thyatira.

Love in its very essence is the divine nature (1 John 4:8,16). It is that eternal and essential attribute of God, that principle of God's nature, whereby He is moved in compassion toward the worst of sinners, regardless of any sacrifice on His part (Romans 5:8; 2 Corinthians 5:19; 1 John 3:16). Now all Christians are "partakers of the divine nature" (2 Peter 1:4), thus "the love of God is shed abroad in our hearts by the Holy Ghost which is given unto us" (Romans 5:5). It is called by the Apostle Paul the greatest of the Christian characteristics (1 Corinthians 13:13) and the first manifestation of the ninefold fruit of the Spirit (Galatians 5:22). It is God's love in us experientially that begets love to men (1 Thessalonians 4:9; Romans 13:10). There were saints in Thyatira who were dwelling together in love because God was dwelling in them (1 John 4:16), and apparently their love for each other was increasing (2 Thessalonians 1:3).

I know thy . . . service.

By their service Christ meant their ministry, which was their love in action toward those in need, the lack of which would have raised reasonable doubt that God's love dwelt in them (1 John 3:17). The Greek work for "service" is *diakonian* meaning "ministry." It is used of the collective ministering of a local assembly (as in Acts 11:29; Romans 15:26; 1 Corinthians 16:1; and 2 Corinthians 9:1). It was not merely the mechanical function of the job for which they were responsible, but rather that tender and loving unofficial kindness. A man may be zealous to perform with detailed accuracy his official work, and yet sadly lack the tender touch of loving-kindness. G. Campbell Morgan said, "So many men are ready to spread a banquet, and slow to give a cup of cold water." It is possible to labor without love, but the saints at Thyatira, like those at Thessalonica, possessed the desirable combination, namely the "labor of love" (1 Thessalonians 1:3). Many of their names were not perpetuated, nor did they find a place in church history, but the blessed Lord remembered them. And when He comes again He will remember and reward all such (Matthew 25:31-40).

He then approves them for their faith.

I know thy . . . faith.

The word used here for "faith" is *pistos,* suggesting the idea of faithfulness, fidelity, loyalty. These saints were dependable, reliable. Fickle and faltering saints are not faithful, but occasional and spasmodic. Some Christians run well at the outset of the race but, like the Galatians, they tire quickly and fall by the way or else are led astray (Galatians 5:7 cf. 6:9). But the tender, loving care of the Christians in Thyatira for others was carried on faithfully.

The Lord commends them further for their patient endurance.

I know thy . . . patience.

As service grows out of love, so patience is the sequence of faith, and these saints had patience. They maintained an equal mental and emotional balance under pressure. Our Lord commended them for their patience because He sets great value upon this virtue. This fragrant flower of faithfulness was present at Ephesus (2:2), and in His letter to Philadelphia Christ speaks of "My patience" (3:10).

Do we have this capacity to be still when all around us is storm-tossed? Think of Christ's patience with sinners; with His blundering disciples; with those who tormented and tried Him unjustly and then crucified Him; with you and me! There was always that readiness to endure and suffer. The word for patient is *hupomone* (from *hupo,* "under," and *meno,* "to abide"). We are to abide in Christ under tribulation (Romans 12:12) for it is through trial that patience grows (James 1:3), and this is acceptable with God (1 Peter 2:20). Moreover, patience perfects Christian character (James 1:4), so let us run the race with patience (Hebrews 12:1).

In our Lord's final word of approval, He said:

I know . . . thy works; and the last to be more than the first (2:19).

Twice He mentioned their "works" in the course of His commendation. He did this in order to point out the highly commendable quality of continued growth and development. Their last works were more than the first. As a pastor I have observed quite often that type of person who commences a task with cheerfulness and enthusiasm, and then comes to a standstill, offering weak excuses for his failure. It is a worldly principle of the unsaved cheerfully to do their best when taking on a new job, and then lessen their efforts. But there were believers in Thyatira who were known for their continued progress and increased usefulness. They were neither slipping backward nor standing still, but they were advancing steadily in their Christian course.

How is it with *you?* Is your last state worse than your first (Matthew 12:45)? Is your latter end worse than the beginning (2 Peter 2:20)? Or is your faith growing and your love increasing (2 Thessalonians 1:3)?

IV. THE ADMONITION (2:20-24)

What was wrong in the church at Thyatira? Our Lord is specific.

> *Notwithstanding I have a few things against thee, because thou sufferest that woman Jezebel, which calleth herself a prophetess, to teach and to seduce My servants to commit fornication, and to eat things sacrificed unto idols* (2:20).

At once we notice a contrast between the church at Thyatira and the church at Ephesus. Ephesus would not tolerate evil but was waning in love (2:2,4); Thyatira was gaining in love but tolerating evil. These two extremes are with us today. They have never departed from the churches. In some assemblies we find the moral and doctrinal perfectionists, Pharisees, who are loveless and sometimes ruthless in their dealings with brethren whom they believe to have departed from the faith. In other places there are those who preach love and toleration, even to the extent of seeking peaceful coexistence between good and evil. No one will argue against the fact that the Bible tells us to love everybody, but it tells us also that righteousness has no fellowship with unrighteousness (2 Corinthians 6:14).

Now who was Jezebel? Her very name has come to be associated with evil. The Old Testament Jezebel was the notorious daughter of Ethball, the pagan king of the Zidonians. His subjects in Tyre and Sidon were Baal-worshipers. Jezebel married Israel's wicked King Ahab, after which she set up the worship of Baal in Israel (1 Kings 16:29-33). When God raised up His prophet Elijah and sent him to rebuke Ahab, Jezebel threatened Elijah and frightened him so badly that he fled for his life and was ready to resign from the ministry (1 Kings 19:1-4). Read the revival under King Josiah in 2 Kings 23, particularly verse 7, and you will have some idea of the depths of degradation to which Jezebel led the children of Israel. Our Lord refers to it as "the depths of Satan" (Revelation 2:24). Jezebel is associated with sodomy. Dr. Barnhouse pointed out that "every sanctuary in a sacred wood was at the same time an asylum of debauchery and adultery, institutions of male and female sexual practices. The priests of Baal were wicked sex perverts."

In Thyatira a woman had influenced God's servants. Christ called her "Jezebel." I believe she was a real woman, but that our Lord used the Old Testament Jezebel to express what this woman was, a seductive and wicked influence among God's people. As Balaam contaminated Israel before her, so Jezebel polluted Israel by her moral and doctrinal impurities (2 Kings 9:22). The Jezebel of the Old Testament had been dead for almost a millennium, but the demon that had possessed her was now controlling another woman of the same name in order to corrupt the church at Thyatira with ethical and doctrinal errors.

Our Lord said she *"calleth herself a prophetess"* (2:20). Just as Jezebel in Elijah's day took the lead in changing the religious doctrines and deeds of the people, so the self-styled prophetess in Thyatira boldly taught her nefarious philosophy with little or no opposition. They were so sweet and pleasant in that church that they tolerated even Jezebel. And why not? Her philosophy did have some truth in it. But then all heresy has enough truth in it to hold the errors together. Vance Havner said, "We used to have an old clock that wouldn't run and it was right two times every day. But the Word of God is right any time of the day!" Beware of tolerating the Jezebel type of person. They may claim to be inspired and to have received some new revelation from God, and yet touch the deep things of Satan. Mrs.

Mary Baker Eddy, Mrs. Ellen G. White, Joseph Smith, Charles Russell, and a host of others claimed divine inspiration and revelation for their views and philosophies, and the results have been disastrous. Many servants of God have been seduced. Jezebel may have been a member of the local congregation but she did not belong to *the* Church of Christ. I am wary of anyone who claims to have fathomed the deep and unrevealed mysteries of life, and then seduces God's servants in the name of Christ and His Church.

It was stated in the beginning of this chapter that the Thyatiran period in church history extended for about nine centuries and was known as "the Dark Ages" when the Papacy ruled ruthlessly. A man is enthroned and addressed as "holy father." A woman is put in the man's place and is substituted for Christ. But the Holy Scriptures know nothing of this. In the New Testament the Church is set forth in the simile of a woman, never a man (2 Corinthians 11:2; Ephesians 5:22-33). Even though the Bible is clear that a woman is in subjection to the man and that a woman is never to usurp authority over the man (1 Timothy 2:11-12), Romanism has reversed this order and millions of Roman Catholic men worship an image of Mary and offer prayers to her.

We have suggested before that these seven letters endorse and supplement our Lord's parables in Matthew 13. In the parable of the leaven it was a woman who hid the leaven in the three measures of meal, till the whole was leavened (Matthew 13:33). The parable of the leaven is the fourth in the series of seven, as the letter to Thyatira is the fourth in that series of seven. In each instance a woman introduces an evil influence. In each the evil influence works from within, not from without. Jezebel is being tolerated in the congregation. Christendom is gradually being influenced by the evil of Romanism. One day the whole will be leavened.

Dr. Barnhouse wrote: "The conflicting claims of Jezebel and the Scripture present an interesting comparison. Both pretend infallibility. The Roman prophets claim infallibility which must not be tested, but which must be received, without any question of testing. The Scriptures which everywhere claim for themselves finality and infallibility, submit themselves to every possible test." He then goes on to make clear his view, that the Jezebel form of religion was projected prophetically in the mind of Christ to the end of the age. He continues: "Judgment is prophesied upon ecclesiasticism. It is definitely stated here that the Jezebel form of Christianity shall pass through the Great Tribulation (2:22). We shall see, however, when we come to the message to the church at Philadelphia, that the real believers will be kept from the hour of tribulation that is to come upon the earth. The details of God's judgment upon ecclesiasticism occupy a large section of this prophecy."

Christ said that the method of Jezebel, the self-styled prophetess, was *"to teach and seduce My servants"* (2:20). Rome professes to teach with authority. She claims to be the only church that cannot err in matters pertaining to faith and morals. The average Roman Catholic knows next to nothing about the meaning of Scripture. Taught to "hear mother church," Roman Catholics know only what "the church teaches." Walter Scott said in his book, *Exposition of the Revelation of Jesus Christ:* "Her teachings and seductions, however contrary to Scripture and repellent to human understanding, must be accepted as authoritative and infallible. This is a dogma with Rome. She cannot err, therefore she cannot progress. It is thus that Rome and ignorance, Rome and superstition, as history abundantly testifies, go together. Rome dreads the light and fears the Bible." And then he adds: "Teaching and preaching are not gifts conferred upon the church, nor is it responsible to do either. The church is taught, but does not teach. Both teaching and preaching are the exercise and gift by individual servants of the Lord" (Ephesians 4:8-12).

> *And I gave her space to repent of her fornication; and she repented not* (2:21).

Jezebel refuses to repent and is therefore judged. The Jezebel of the last 1,500 years has not changed. Rome never does change. But this Babylon of prophecy will meet with divine judgment when the sovereign Head of the Church comes back to earth again. Read Revelation 17 and 18 for a detailed account of her doom. One of the last acts of the Old Testament Jezebel was to paint her face in an attempt to conceal her identity, but she died a horrible death nevertheless (2 Kings 9:30-37). Rome has been pretending for centuries to be something other than what she is, but the Lord knows her and will finally judge her.

V. THE APPEAL (2:25-29)

Christ has one final word of appeal to His faithful followers.

Hold fast till I come (2:25).

This might seem to be a small thing, but in the midst of infidelity it means much to Him. He reminds the true children of His Kingdom that He is coming. Here is a strong incentive to carry on with courage until the end. Our Lord is coming back for His own, and nothing will please Him more than to find us loving His appearing and looking for Him (1 John 2:28).

THE LETTER TO SARDIS

Revelation 3:1-6

I. THE ASSEMBLY

The town of Sardis, situated in the fertile valley at the foot of Mount Timolus, lay about thirty miles southeast of Thyatira. It was a city affected gravely by the horrible results of war and the great earthquake of the first century. Very little that was worth while in that ancient city has survived till modern times. As the ancient capital of Lydia it was one of the richest cities in the world. Its excellent climate and gorgeous palace were the center of attraction.

When or by whose ministry the local assembly was founded in Sardis we are not told. Joseph A. Seiss says: "The ruins of a Christian edifice have been identified as the church of St. John, and he perhaps was the man who first planted Christianity there. The only name historically associated with the church of Sardis is that of Melito, who was its bishop about the middle of the second century. But there is everything to beget the belief that it was a church of distinguished prominence."

The word Sardis means "escaping ones," or "those who come out." The period in the history of Christendom suggested here is the Reformation period from about A.D. 1517 to A.D. 1750. In the midst of spiritual darkness there were those who escaped its contamination. Among those who "escaped" or "came out" were Luther, Knox, Wycliffe, Zwingli, and others. These were the great reformers who broke with Rome. The intolerable condition under papal rule reached its climax on October 31, 1517, when Martin Luther nailed his "Ninety-Five Theses" to the door of the church in Wittenburg, Germany. When Luther's voice resounded throughout the German Empire, it found response in many a heart that was completely weary of the Roman system.

II. THE AUTHOR (3:1)

Our Lord addressed Himself to this church as:

He that hath the seven Spirits of God (3:1).

This takes us back to the vision of Christ recorded in the first chapter where we see "the seven Spirits . . . before His throne" (vs. 4). This symbol speaks of the Holy Spirit in the plenitude of His power and perfect work. "Seven" is the divine number for expressing completeness, fullness. For obvious reasons, which we shall see later in our study, Christ would have the church in Sardis know that He desires to control His Church by the effective work of the Holy Spirit. In each of the seven epistles, the descriptive term He uses of Himself suits perfectly the condition of the particular church addressed.

The present Church Age is the dispensation of the Holy Spirit, the third Person of the blessed Holy Trinity. Now all three Persons in the Godhead—Father, Son, and Holy Spirit—are coequal and coeternal. In 1:4-5 the "seven Spirits" are linked with the Eternal Father and with Jesus Christ as the one and only source of grace and peace. Thus all needed grace and peace are assured the local assembly whose members are filled with the Spirit. Scott points out that "the closeness of these 'seven Spirits' to the throne (4:5), and their intimate relation to Jesus Christ (5:6), suggest the same conclusion that they are the Holy Spirit." Wherever sin and failure mark a local assembly, one can be certain the Holy Spirit has not been in command in the hearts of the people. The Word of the Lord to Zerubbabel needed to be re-emphasized in Sardis, "Not by might, nor by power, but by My spirit, saith the LORD of hosts" (Zechariah 4:6).

Our Lord's further description of Himself in the words, *"He that hath . . . the seven stars,"* was given to remind all who were in the church at Sardis that the oversight brethren are in His right hand (1:16,20). They must take their orders from Him. He is the sovereign Head of His Church, and through the Holy Spirit He carries out His program (Acts 1:8). Could it be that in Sardis some individual, or group, had usurped authority? Many a local assembly can attribute its lack of life and love to the fact that Christ is no longer owned as the Head and Lord over the people.

III. THE ADMONITION (3:1)

Thou hast a name that thou livest, and art dead (3:1).

Before examining our Lord's complaint, it should be observed that the church in Sardis was not lacking in works. He said, *"I know thy works."* In all probability it was a beehive of organized activity. When Christ said, *"Thou hast a name that thou livest,"* I conclude that there was little lacking in the outward appearance of that church. It had a reputation for being a progressive church. No doubt others in the surrounding communities were saying, "Now that church in Sardis is a live church for you." Had you inquired of any pagan on the streets of Sardis for the location of this church, I venture to say he could have told you at once. It was well attended, and well advertised. But more than this, it had a reputation for being alive. It was known as "the live church." Christ said, *"Thou hast a name that thou livest."* It was engaged in all those activities which characterize a live church. Most people had a high estimate of this church. Had you been moving from any one of the cities of Ephesus, Smyrna, Pergamos, or Thyatira to Sardis, your pastor would no doubt have suggested that you attend this church.

But the startling and terrible truth about the church in Sardis was that it was dead. It would be difficult to convince its members that this was so, but we know the church was dead because our Lord said it was. It was functioning largely on its reputation of a once glorious past. They were still reciting their beliefs and saying their prayers and paying their bills, but the fire had gone out. You have seen lovely looking flowers that thrilled you, until you examined them closely, only to discover that they were artificial. Actually those artificial results of the craftmanship of man's hands had no right to the name of flower. Outward appearances can be notoriously deceptive.

The eyes of Christ pierced beyond the flesh to the skeleton. It was as dead as was Lazarus, of whom Jesus said, "Lazarus is dead," and Martha added, "By this time he stinketh" (John 11:14,39). It all depends upon the eyes through which the church is being diagnosed; we are prone to forget that "the LORD seeth not as man seeth; for man looketh on the outward appearance, but the LORD looketh on the heart" (1 Samuel 16:7). He knows the difference between life and a corpse wrapped in graveclothes.

He said:

I have not found thy works perfect before God (3:2).

The word "perfect" literally means "finished" or "complete" or "fulfilled." They were not carrying out God's purpose for their existence. The *"name"* (verse 1) was a name among men, but not *"before God."* This church was living a lie. Its members were physically alive and at the same time spiritually dead. The Apostle Paul describes it thus, "But she that liveth in pleasure is dead while she liveth" (1 Timothy 5:6), "alienated from the life of God" (Ephesians 4:18). When the Great Physician felt their pulse He pronounced them dead. Do we know the difference between appearance and reality? God does! In every generation He has had to pronounce against certain ones, "This people draw near Me with their mouth, and with their lips do honour Me, but have removed their heart far from Me" (Isaiah 29:13).

Our Lord fiercely condemned every outward appearance of religious activity not directed by the Holy Spirit. He warned those hypocrites who made their contributions "that they may have glory of men"; who said their prayers "that they may be seen of men"; and who "disfigure their faces, that they may appear unto men to fast" (Matthew 6:2,5,16-18). Toward the end of His ministry He said, "But all their works they do for to be seen of men" (Matthew 23:5). "Woe unto you, scribes and Pharisees, hypocrites! for ye are like unto whited sepulchres, which indeed appear beautiful outward, but are within full of dead men's bones, and of all uncleanness. Even so ye also outwardly appear righteous unto men, but within ye are full of hypocrisy and iniquity" (Matthew 23:27-28). These are stinging remarks aimed at all hypocritical make-believe. The Lord is never deceived by the outward attractiveness of a well-kept mausoleum, knowing that on the inside there are the bones of a dead man. The sight of death is bad enough, but a corpse that is made to look alive is a ghastly, frightening spectacle.

The Reformation raised up a group of men who came out from Romanism and who rescued much from the mortuary of Rome. But they did not go far enough. State churches were organized, many of which are in operation today in Germany, Holland, and other countries. Denominationalism with its sacraments, forms, and ceremonies became a cold, lifeless formalism. Ministers became ministers of the church, not of Christ. Dr. Barnhouse wrote: "There is nothing wrong with the Augsburg Confession, with the Thirty-Nine Articles, with the Heidelberg Confession, with the Westminster Confession. Go throughout Christendom, however, and you will find the gospel in a coffin. There are, indeed, believers but dead, formal orthodoxy too frequently characterizes the scene."

IV. THE APPROVAL (3:4)

> *Thou hast a few names even in Sardis which have not defiled their garments; and they shall walk with Me in white: for they are worthy* (3:4).

In the midst of death and degradation in Sardis, there were a few who had kept themselves free from the encumbrances of the world. The word "few" (Gr. *oligos*) is an adjective denoting "small, slight, little." Those who had not defiled their garments were in a minority, not many in number. But then, those who choose to identify themselves with Jesus Christ never are in the majority. Our Lord said, "Enter ye in at the strait gate: for wide is the gate, and broad is the way, that leadeth to destruction, and many there be which go in thereat: because strait is the gate, and narrow is the way, which leadeth unto life, and few there be that find it" ((Matthew 7:13-14). There are but two ways. The way of the "many" is the broad way and leads to destruction, that is, to the eternal loss of well-being, the loss of all that makes one's existence worth while. The way of the "few" is the narrow way, but it leads at last to life in its highest form. The sad contrast between the "many" and the "few" marks the twofold division of the human race. All men travel on one or the other of these two roads. Those who travel with the crowd and stand for nothing might find a certain feeling of security in doing what the majority do. But it is a false security. The fact that so many persons are doing the same thing does not make it right. Thank God for the "few" who maintain a good witness for Christ, and who have not become bogged down in the quagmire of this world's doubts and defilements.

In every generation God has His "fews"—a Noah, a Daniel, or a Job, of whom He testified to His servant Ezekiel: "The word of the LORD came again to me, saying, Son of man, when the land sinneth against Me by trespassing grievously, then will I stretch out Mine hand upon it, and will break the staff of the bread thereof, and will send famine upon it, and will cut off man and beast from it: though these three men, Noah, Daniel, and Job, were in it, they should deliver but their own souls by their righteousness, saith the Lord GOD" (Ezekiel 14:12-14). These in Sardis were those who kept themselves "unspotted from the world" (James 1:27). Now it is much easier to live for Christ when you are surrounded by noble and godly Christian people. But the "few" in Sardis were the spiritual among the unspiritual, the sincere among the hypocrites, the humble among the proud, the separated among the worldly. They were the saints who were leading pure, wholesome Christian lives in the midst of corruption. There were only a few, but the Lord took account of them by name. He saved Noah and his family from the flood, He rescued righteous

Lot from the brimstone and fire He sent upon Sodom and Gomorrah, and in Elijah's day He had seven thousand in Israel who had not bowed the knee to Baal (1 Kings 19:18). When Christ was here on the earth He called His followers a "little flock" (Luke 12:32). He has always known His faithful ones by name, and our generation is no exception. In most local assemblies one can find God's remnant, His faithful few, the Master's minority.

Our Lord's testimony about the "few" was that they *"have not defiled their garments."* This word "garments" is used in a figurative sense. What garments are to the body, so habits are to the real self. How we dress is important. It makes a difference whether our clothes are clean or dirty, whether they fit or do not fit, whether they become us or do not. A soldier must dress the part of a soldier, a marine the part of a marine, and a naval man the part of a sailor. Each knows that his uniform must fit well and be kept clean at all times. So, too, the Christian must exercise care about the wardrobe of his soul. The old moth-eaten garments of the unregenerated life must be discarded. "But now ye also put off all these; anger, wrath, malice, blasphemy, filthy communication out of your mouth. Lie not one to another, seeing that ye have put off the old man with his deeds" (Colossians 3:8,9). Then the new garments are to be worn. "Put on therefore, as the elect of God, holy and beloved, bowels of mercies, kindness, humbleness of mind, meekness, longsuffering; forbearing one another, and forgiving one another, if any man have a quarrel against any: even as Christ forgave you, so also do ye. And above all these things put on charity, which is the bond of perfectness" (Colossians 3:12-14). Read our Lord's parable of the wedding supper. When the king examined the guests and discovered there a man who did not have on a wedding garment, he ordered that man to be banished to outer darkness, and then He concluded the parable with the words, "For *many* are called, but *few* are chosen" (Matthew 22:11-14). It was the few in Sardis who were properly clothed.

Concerning the few, Christ promised:

They shall walk with Me in white: for they are worthy (3:4).

"White" is always the color of Heaven. The redeemed of the Great Tribulation are seen wearing robes washed white in the blood of the Lamb (7:14). Then there follows the white cloud (14:14); the white horse (19:11); the white horses (19:14), and finally the great white throne (20:11).

V. THE APPEAL (3:2-3)

Be watchful, and strengthen the things which remain, that are ready to die (3:2).

This word "watchful" (Gr. *agrupneo*) expresses the idea of being wakeful, sleepless, as the watchfulness of one who is intent upon a thing. It comes from two Greek words meaning "to chase sleep." Our Lord calls upon the few to be vigilant and strive to strengthen and revive what remains but is at the point of death. Apparently the "few" were not watchful, and the result of not having been so was that more were failing and ready to die. There were those who had been vibrant with life and energy, but now were languishing from lack of it. He appeals to the "few" to salvage those gifts and talents before it is too late. The church is admonished to get busy and by prompt action rescue all that were on the verge of death. This appeal was needed then, and it is needed even more now. A situation such as this demands a vigilance that will take hold of every opportunity for improvement. A competent and compassionate physician will stand guard over the least remaining evidence of life and nourish it with the greatest of care. *"Hold fast,"* Christ tells them—and us.

If therefore thou shalt not watch, I will come on thee as a thief, and thou shalt not know what hour I will come upon thee (3:3).

Here our Lord used His coming again as an incentive to action motivated by the Holy Spirit. What did He mean when He said, *"I will come on thee as a thief"?* If we suspect that a burglar might break into our house, there would be fear and suspense on our part. No one welcomes the coming of a thief for fear of what he might take from us or the harm he might inflict upon us. The residents in Sardis were acquainted with all of this, for robbers lurked in the hills and caves, and frequently swooped down upon the unsuspecting. They were not ready for the coming of those hoodlums, thus they knew well the loss, and sometimes sorrow, that resulted. The city was built on a hill, surrounded on three sides by cliffs. Twice enemies came in and besieged it, once when Croesus and his soldiers slept, thinking they were safe. At another time, when Achneius was ruler, Antiochus the Great attacked the city and it fell. Those Christians in Sardis understood full well the meaning of Christ's words.

The coming of the Lord means different things to different people. The attitude one has toward this doctrine is a sure test of his spiritual condition. If I am like the "many" in Sardis, the announcement of His coming is one of terror. If I am of the "few," the very thought of His appearing is as a lovely refrain to the soul. The "many" in Sardis desired to see His coming postponed, the "few" were living in the spirit of joyful expectation. This is a very real test of our spiritual condition. Every time the "few" in Sardis heard that Christ was coming again, they responded with the words, "Even so, come, Lord Jesus."

Christ does not come upon His waiting Bride as a thief, but in such manner He will come upon all apostates and the unregenerated. Paul wrote, "For yourselves know perfectly that the day of the Lord so cometh as a thief in the night. . . . But ye, brethren, are not in darkness, that that day should overtake you as a thief" (1 Thessalonians 5:2,4). The Thessalonian believers were witnessing, working, and waiting for God's Son from Heaven (1 Thessalonians 1:9-10). Is the coming of the Lord your daily expectation? Remember, when He comes, it will be too late to repent of your deeds.

THE LETTER TO PHILADELPHIA

Revelation 3:7-13

I. THE ASSEMBLY

Clovis G. Chappell said: "Were it my privilege to go back across the years and attend a service at one of these seven churches, I think I should choose the church at Philadelphia. Then, should I have the further privilege of choosing at just what particular service I should be present, I should select the one at which the pastor read this letter that we have for our present study." I like Dr. Chappell's choice.

The city of Philadelphia was located about thirty miles southeast of Sardis leading to Laodicea. Bounded by Mount Timolus, it shared the rich, fertile soil which characterized Sardis. However, it was in a precariously dangerous position because that entire section of Asia was subject to frequent earth tremors and occasional earthquakes. Philadelphia suffered severely from the earthquake of the first century that completely demolished Sardis. But toward the end of the century the city had been completely rebuilt and a testimony for Jesus Christ established.

The name *Philadelphia* means "brotherly love." The city was built by Attalus Philadelphus, whose name it bore. Its elevation was about nine hundred feet. Owing to the volcanic nature of the soil, the city became famous for the cultivation of fine grapes. Its name now is Ala-Sheher, which means "City of God."

II. THE AUTHOR (3:7)

We have mentioned in these studies that the risen Lord presents Himself to each of these churches in a different character and always in keeping with the need in each church. The titles and descriptive phrases by which He presents Himself are all taken from the description of Him found in chapter one. Dr. Barnhouse points out that "all of them are more or less indicative of judgment. He has spoken as the One holding the churches in the right hand of authority, as the One who is risen to take that authority, the One who has the two-edged sword, eyes as a flame of fire, feet like fine brass to march in judgment against the iniquiters."

These things saith He that is holy (3:7).

He commences with an attribute by which He declares Himself to be God. Holiness is an essential attribute of deity. In the Old Testament Jehovah refers to Himself as "the Holy One" (Isaiah 40:25). On a number of occasions He said, "I am holy" (Leviticus 11:44). Jesus quite naturally assumes it, and rightly so, for He is "holy, harmless, undefiled, separate from sinners, and made higher than the heavens" (Hebrews 7:26). Peter testified of Him as the One "Who did no sin, neither was guile found in His mouth" (1 Peter 2:22). Holiness is what Christ is in Himself, in His essential character. Because He is holy, every word He ever spoke and everything He ever did was perfect. It could not be otherwise. He is the embodiment of holiness. John testified that "in Him is no sin" (1 John 3:5). Paul adds that He "knew no sin" (2 Corinthians 5:21). Both Pilate's wife and Pilate himself called Him a "just" [or righteous] Man (Matthew 27:19,24). As a matter of fact, because Christ was essentially holy in His nature, it was impossible for Him to commit sin.

Our Lord then speaks of Himself as *"He that is true"* (3:7). Persons are sometimes spoken of as being true, but no created being possesses the moral glory of being, in his essential nature, "the True One." G. Campbell Morgan distinguishes between being "holy" and "true." He says that as the "holy" One, Christ is right in character; as the "true" One, He is right in conduct. He could not be different in His actions from what He is in His attributes. When character is right, conduct will be right. Because holiness inherently resides in Him, truth does likewise. Since He is perfect in what He is, He is also perfect in what He does. He only could say, "I am . . . the truth" (John 14:6). In this He claimed oneness with the Father when He prayed, "And this is life eternal, that they might know Thee the only *true* God, and Jesus Christ, whom Thou hast sent" (John 17:3). The Apostle John closed his first Epistle with the words, "And we know that the Son of God is come, and hath given us an understanding, that we may know Him that is *true,* and we are in Him that is true, even in His Son Jesus Christ. This is the *true* God, and eternal life" (1 John 5:20). It is this vision of Christ as the "holy" and "true" One that keeps the Christian when lawlessness and dishonesty prevail all about him.

Our Lord's description of Himself concludes with the words:

He that hath the key of David, He that openeth, and no man shutteth; and shutteth, and no man openeth (3:7).

I know of only one passage in the Bible which contains a reference to this symbol, and from which our Lord may have drawn His words. It is in Isaiah 22, the chapter entitled "The burden of the valley of vision" (22:1), by which phrase the prophet designates Jerusalem as a place shut in and protected by God, and a place where He will give His prophets visions of His plans and purposes for the future. The time was during the reign of Hezekiah. The Assyrian armies of Sennacherib were already on the march against Israel. The people should have been in a spirit of mourning and repentance, but instead there was a spirit of frivolity and careless living. The people said, "Let us eat and drink; for tomorrow we shall die" (22:13). Their leader was Shebna, who was also the treasurer of the palace, or the chamberlain over the king's household. He was a frivolous, reckless, and selfish man. It was to him, because of his hard and rebellious heart, that the Lord said, "I will drive thee from thy station" (22:19). Isaiah predicts that the Lord will toss him about like a ball into a foreign, wicked land, and there he shall die (22:18).

Shebna's position will be taken by Eliakim the son of Hilkiah (Isaiah 22:20). Of Eliakim God said, "And the key of the house of David will I lay upon his shoulder; so he shall open, and none shall shut; and he shall shut, and none shall open" (22:22). The significance of the key of David is clear. It is the rule over David's house. What is said of Eliakim marks him as a type of Christ. Like many prophecies in the Old Testament, this one in Isaiah 22 has a double fulfillment. To Eliakim was committed the key of David, which was the key to the royal treasury, over which he was given authority to open and shut as he deemed it wise. The great and final fulfillment of this prophecy is plain. Of Christ the prophet wrote: "The government shall be upon His shoulder. . . . Of the increase of His government and peace there shall be no end, upon the throne of David, and upon His kingdom, to order it, and to establish it with judgment and with justice from henceforth even for ever" (Isaiah 9:6,7). The angel said to Mary, "He shall be great, and shall be called the Son of the Highest: and the Lord God shall give unto Him the throne of His father David: and He shall reign over the house of Jacob for ever; and of His kingdom there shall be no end" (Luke 1:32-33). Christ is the absolute Ruler in His kingdom. The key to the house of David is His by legal right and by lineage. He is sole Heir to the throne of David, and until He comes again to reign, the Jews can have no true sovereign. The key is the symbol of His authority, and this authority was given to Him over Heaven and earth (Matthew 28:18).

First, Christ holds the key to the door of *salvation*. If you wish to enter the gate that leads to life everlasting, you must come to Christ. No individual or church can assure you of entrance into Heaven nor keep you from entering. The key is in the hand of Christ. It is true that Christ said to Peter, "I will give unto thee the keys of the kingdom of heaven" (Matthew 16:19), and it is also true that Peter used those keys. Through his preaching of the gospel he opened the door to the

Jews on the day of Pentecost (Acts 2:14-47). Through his ministry the first Samaritan believers received the Holy Spirit (Acts 8:14-17). As the result of his witness the first Gentile, Cornelius the Roman centurion, was saved (Acts 10:44-48). But Peter has long since been dead. Now the keys are back in the hands of Christ. He said, "I am He that liveth, and was dead; and, behold, I am alive for evermore, Amen; and have the keys of hell and of death" (Revelation 1:18).

I have set before thee an open door. . . . (3:8).

The tense is perfect. The door He opened remains open today. That door is Christ Himself. He says, "I am the door; by Me if any man enter in, He shall be saved, and shall go in and out, and find pasture" (John 10:9). You had better enter while the door is still open. When Noah and his family were safely in the ark, "the LORD shut him in" (Genesis 7:16). The door which shut Noah safely on the inside sealed the doom of all unbelievers on the outside. God had shut the door and the day of salvation for that generation came to an end. Read again our Lord's parable of the ten wedding attendants. Five were wise in that they filled their lamps with oil and were ready. Five were foolish in that they made no preparation, thus their lamps were empty. When the bridegroom came, the five wise attendants that were ready went in with him to the marriage, "and the door was shut." The five foolish attendants returned too late. They frantically pounded against the door, and cried, "Lord, Lord, open to us. But he answered and said, Verily I say unto you, I know you not" (Matthew 25:1-13). Rise up, and come through the door at once before it is too late.

Secondly, Christ holds the key to the door of *service.* He said to the saints at Philadelphia:

I have set before thee an open door, and no man can shut it (3:8).

While it is true that Christ opens doors for us, He will not enter them for us. It is His part to open that door. It is ours to enter. The great Apostle Paul was alert to the many doors Christ had opened for him. He said, "For a great door and effectual is opened unto me, and there are many adversaries" (1 Corinthians 16:9). "Furthermore, when I came to Troas to preach Christ's gospel, a door was opened unto me of the Lord" (2 Corinthians 2:12). It was Paul's prayer that he would never force his way unceremoniously through doors which the Lord never opened (Colossians 4:3). Any man of God in the will of God will find an open door for Christian service, and there is no power on earth or in hell that can shut the door which God has opened. Rome had padlocked the prison doors and set a guard over Peter, but the iron gate was opened by an unseen hand of the supernatural Christ (Acts 12:5-11). At Lystra Paul was beaten and stoned (Acts 14:19), but God raised him up, and when he returned to his brethren at Antioch, he testified to the church there "all that God had done with them, and how He had opened the door of faith unto the Gentiles" (Acts 14:27).

Christ has opened many doors of service, but too many of us have been so blinded by greed, selfishness, and the lust for pleasure that we fail to see the open door. Many doors that were open at one time our Lord has now shut. He has shut the door to China, parts of Europe and Latin America. Other doors are being shut. I wonder how many doors, that are now shut, we have failed to enter while they were open.

Our study of church history leads me to believe that this period described by the letter to Philadelphia followed that of the Reformation. The period of the open door extended from about 1750 A.D. to approximately 1950 A.D. During the past two hundred years God raised up men like William Carey, John and Charles Wesley, George Whitefield, Adoniram Judson, Charles Finney, Dwight Moody, "Billy" Sunday, and many more. The great missionary movements were in full swing. No one could ever stop the forward movement of the gospel when the Church took advantage of the open door to service.

But a great tragedy has struck the Church of Christ. Many Christians have gone soft and indifferent. After World War II Japan was a wide open door to Christian workers. General Douglas MacArthur called upon Christians of America to send five thousand missionaries through that open door. We failed to answer that call. In 1960 the President of the United States, Dwight D. Eisenhower, was prevented from visiting Japan by several hundred thousand demonstrating communists.

Many church pulpits that at one time were occupied by men of God who loved and preached the Bible as God's Word, are now taken over by modernists who ridicule any literal belief in the Bible. We are now in the Laodicean period. True, Christ has kept a few doors open. But prophesied apostasy is increasing, and the icy fingers of Romanism, modernism, and communism are putting the death grip on opportunities for service in the name of our Lord Jesus Christ. We seem to be approaching the end of the Age of Grace. I believe the world is getting its last chance to believe on the Lord Jesus Christ and be saved. Many countries have already had their last opportunity, and Christ has closed the door. Oh, Christian, arise and step through the door of service that is still open for you.

Thirdly, Christ holds the key to the door of *safety*. He said:

> *I also will keep thee from the hour of temptation, which shall come upon all the world, to try them that dwell upon the earth* (3:10).

The open door is not merely that of salvation and service. It is a door of safe deliverance from the Great Tribulation. Dr. Morgan wrote: "While that promise may have had its partial fulfillment in the escape of the church at Philadelphia from some wave of persecution that swept over the district, its final fulfillment will undoubtedly be realized by those who, loyal to His word, and not denying His name, shall be gathered out of the world at His Second Coming before the judgment that must usher in the setting up of His Kingdom upon the earth." I believe that the tribulation is the time of God's wrath upon the earth (Revelation 6:17), but that the Church will be saved, not merely from the tribulation, but from the very "hour" of it (1 Thessalonians 1:10; 5:9). Those who will be in this time of testing are referred to as *"them that dwell upon the earth,"* that is, earth dwellers, those who have had no interest in Heaven but who have settled down in the earth. But

Christ promises to deliver His own in safety out of the tribulation. He holds the key to the door of deliverance.

III. THE APPROVAL (3:8)

Only good is spoken about this church. There is no admonition. The Lord said:

> *I know thy works . . . for thou hast a little strength*
> (3:8).

The Christians in Philadelphia were apparently few in number. They had little numerical strength. This does not mean
they were marked by feebleness. Contrariwise, they made full
use of the strength they possessed. They were faithful.

I do not read that our Lord's followers were ever in the numerical majority. Abraham had but three hundred and eighteen
men when he defeated the armies of four kings (Genesis 14:14-
16). Gideon and his band of three hundred put to rout a whole
army of Midianites (Judges 7:19-23). Elijah on God's side
was more than a match for the four hundred and fifty prophets
of Baal (1 Kings 18:21-40). Jesus referred to His disciples
as a "little flock" (Luke 12:32). After more than three years
of public ministry, there were a mere one-hundred-and-twenty.
They were the Master's minority. They had little power as
man reckons power, but it pleased God to make the fullness
of His power available to the faithful, even though they were
small in number and lacking in social prominence. Christ assured the faithful few in Philadelphia that He can use them
and that He keeps a door wide open to them. They might not
have exerted any great influence on the city politically or
economically, but they could be Christ's flaming evangelists.
"Power belongeth unto God" the Father (Psalm 62:11), God
the Son (Matthew 28:18), God the Holy Spirit, and to all who
are indwelt by the Spirit (Acts 1:8).

Christ testified further of them, *"Thou hast kept My Word"*
(3:8). These people were true to the gospel. They were loyal
to the Word of Christ. They did not yield to the majority who

raised doubts and speculations about His Word. We live in a time when to doubt the Bible is looked upon as a mark of intellectual cleverness. Recently (February 13, 1961) a leader in the Episcopal Church spoke of "the myth of the Garden of Eden." He said, "I do not know a single member of the Anglican Communion—bishop, presbyter, deacon, or layman—who believes this story literally." The newspaper reported that, "He [speaking of the bishop] described the virgin birth as a myth which churchmen should be free to accept or reject." Then the bishop concluded his tirade by saying, "Our church has long left room for differing degrees of acceptance as to the details of the narrative late inserted by humans into the gospel accounts."

I suppose that the church in Philadelphia possessed but little numerical and pecuniary strength compared with the Episcopal Church mentioned above. But it was dear to Christ, who thinks more of quality than of quantity. The Lord does not blame us for having little strength, but for having little faith and little regard for His Word. Those Christians to whom Christ addressed Himself had kept His Word. This means they received the Word, they believed the Word, they loved the Word, and they obeyed the Word. To them God's Word was a treasure, a holy thing, thus they kept and guarded it, even under great disadvantages. I have come to the place in my life where I could find it easier to die than deny the Word of my Lord.

Christ's word of approval continues. He says:

Thou . . . hast not denied My name (3:8).

Being loyal to the Scriptures, they were loyal also to the Christ of the Scriptures. It is no small matter to love and honor the name of Jesus Christ in times when so many speak His name lightly and even blasphemously. The "Name" of Christ in Scripture stands for all that He is. His full name is "Lord Jesus Christ." He is Lord [Master], Jesus [Mediator], Christ [Messiah]. In the New Testament the name of the Lord Jesus Christ is invested with all that the name "Jehovah" implied in the Old Testament. That name suggests His deity, honor, glory, majesty, holiness, eternality, omnipotence, omniscience, and omnipresence.

Sinners are saved through faith in His name (Matthew 1:21; John 1:12; 20:31; Romans 10:13), and in His name only (Acts 4:12). Conversely, all who have not believed in the name of the only begotten Son of God are "condemned already" (John 3:18). Our Lord taught His followers to pray in His name as an essential requisite to receiving answers to their prayers (John 14:13-14; 15:16; 16:23-24). He gave promise that "where two or three are gathered together *in My name,* there am I in the midst of them" (Matthew 18:20). He promised further an abundant reward for any sacrifice one would make for His name's sake (Matthew 19:29).

Not surprisingly, however, we learn that the name of our Lord Jesus Christ provokes the hatred of those who do not love Him. He said, "And ye shall be hated of all men *for My name's sake*" (Matthew 10:22; Acts 9:16). But some of His followers were faithful and did not deny His name. Peter got off to a right start at Pentecost when he said, "Repent, and be baptized every one of you *in the name of Jesus Christ* for the remission of sins, and ye shall receive the gift of the Holy Ghost" (Acts 2:38). At the gate of the temple he said to the lame man, "*In the name of Jesus Christ of Nazareth* rise up and walk" (Acts 3:6). When the crowds gathered to see the man who had been lame now walking and leaping, Peter said to them, "And *His name* through faith *in His name* hath made this man strong" (Acts 3:16). Then the religious hierarchy asked Peter, "By what *name* have ye done this?" (Acts 4:7) Then Peter, filled with the Holy Ghost, said, "Be it known unto you all, and to all the people of Israel, that *by the name of Jesus Christ of Nazareth,* whom ye crucified, whom God raised from the dead, even by Him doth this man stand here before you whole" (Acts 4:10). "For there is none other *name*" (Acts 4:12). Then they commanded Peter and John "not to speak at all nor teach *in the name of Jesus*" (4:18), and let them go. Those who had not denied the name of Christ joined with others of our Lord's followers to pray. Together they praised God that He had performed signs and wonders *"by the name of Thy holy child Jesus"* (4:30). Later they were arrested again and brought before the authorities who asked them, "Did not we straitly command you that ye should not teach *in this name?"* (5:28) The apostles answered their question by saying, "We ought to obey God rather than men" (5:29). Then they beat the apostles and "commanded them that they should not speak *in the name of Jesus,* and let them go. And they departed from the presence of the council, rejoicing that they were counted worthy to suffer shame *for His name"* (5:40-41). These had not denied His name.

Shortly after Saul of Tarsus was converted, the Lord sent His servant Ananias to assist the new convert. Ananias expressed his reluctance to go, on the grounds that Saul had authority from the chief priests to imprison all persons who called *on Christ's name* (Acts 9:14). The Lord urged Ananias to go, assuring him that Saul was truly saved, "A chosen vessel unto Me, to bear *My name* before the Gentiles, and kings, and the children of Israel:" and then He added, "For I will shew him how great things he must suffer for *My name's sake"* (9:15-16). From that moment on, the great apostle was known as one who "spake boldly *in the name of the Lord Jesus"* (9:27,29). When Agabus besought Paul not to go to Jerusalem so that his life might be spared, God's servant replied, "I am ready not to be bound only, but also to die at Jerusalem *for the name of the Lord Jesus"* (21:13). Paul never denied Christ's name.

Holding to the name of Christ will result in unswerving loyalty to Him and to His cause. Wherever there has been a tendency to treat lightly His holy name, there has been an absence of His power and blessing. Remember, "Thou shalt not take the name of the Lord thy God in vain; for the Lord will not hold him guiltless that taketh His name in vain" (Exodus 20:7). The cost of acknowledging the name of Christ was high in the days of the apostles, and the day is upon us again when we will pay a price for declaring His name, but, blessed be God, we hallow "a name which is above every name" (Philippians 2:9).

IV. THE ACCOUNTING (3:9)

Behold, I will make them of the synagogue of Satan, which say they are Jews, and are not, but do lie; behold, I will make them to come and worship before thy feet, and to know that I have loved thee (3:9).

In Philadelphia there were those who were in opposition to the truth. They were Jews who brazenly claimed to be Christians, but their actual character is revealed in no uncertain terms. Our Lord said they are *"of the synagogue of Satan."* This makes four of the seven churches in which Satan is found (2:9,13,24; 3:9). As in the case of Sardis, these enemies of the gospel are identified with the synagogue of Satan, the great opponent of the assembly of Christ's own. The Lord says that they lie, a severe description He earlier attributed to Satan (John 8:44). They boasted that they were the people of God but they are written off as impostors and liars.

At the time the Lord spoke these words He probably made reference to the Judaizing teachers who were prevalent in the early days of the Church. It was doubtless this very problem the Apostle Paul faced when he wrote the Epistle to the Galatians (Galatians 2). Prophetically they might well refer to modern-day cults which deny Christ's deity and claim to be the 144,000 saved Jews referred to in Revelation 7. But whoever they are, one thing is certain: the day of accounting will come for them. In that day they will admit that Philadelphian Christians, who have kept Christ's Word and have not denied His name, are loved by Him.

We learn from this that those who are true to Christ and His Word need not attempt to vindicate themselves nor seek vengeance against Satan's emissaries who are in their midst. Such false apostles and deceitful workers will present themselves as ministers of righteousness, but their "end shall be according to their works" (2 Corinthians 11:13-15). These are the tares of whom our Lord spoke in His parable (Matthew 13:24-30; 36-43). Paul declared, "The mystery of iniquity doth already work" (2 Thessalonians 2:7). John added, "Ye have heard that antichrist shall come, even now are there many antichrists" (1 John 2:18). Jude said, "For there are certain men crept in unawares, who were before of old ordained to this condemnation, ungodly men, turning the grace of our God into lasciviousness, and denying the only Lord God, and our Lord Jesus Christ" (Jude 4). These are spurious Christians who come among us with another gospel (Galatians 1:6-9). They are not wicked and immoral men who peddle lawlessness. To the contrary, they advocate a form of righteousness, but "they being ignorant of God's righteousness, and going about to establish their own righteousness, have not submitted themselves unto the righteousness of God" (Romans 10:3). But God will vindicate both Himself and His children. The day of God's vengeance is not yet (Isaiah 61:2 cf. Luke 4:18-20). "Vengeance is Mine; I will repay, saith the Lord" (Romans 12:19 cf. Deuteronomy 32:35), "When the Lord Jesus shall be revealed from heaven with His mighty angels, in flaming fire taking vengeance on them that know not God, and that obey not the gospel of our Lord Jesus Christ" (2 Thessalonians 1:7-8). The Philadelphian believers can afford to await the vindication of God's time (2 Timothy 4:14). Some of us may not live long enough to see the enemy sit at our feet, but God will see to it in His time. When our Lord comes again, His ancient people will know how He "loved the church, and gave Himself for it" (Ephesians 5:25).

V. THE APPEAL (3:11)

Behold, I come quickly: hold that fast which thou hast, that no man take thy crown (3:11).

This is the third time in as many chapters we find it clearly stated that Christ is coming again (1:7; 2:25; 3:11). Frequently in Scripture His Second Coming is associated with the rewards He will give to His faithful servants. "And, behold, I come quickly; and My reward is with Me, to give every man according as his work shall be" (Revelation 22:12 cf. Matthew 16:27; 1 Corinthians 3:13). Indeed He is "a rewarder of them that diligently seek Him" (Hebrews 11:6).

Satan would use those of his synagogue to steal our rewards from us. Thus we have Christ's appeal, *"hold that fast which thou hast."* And why? *"That no man take thy crown."* The crown is not our salvation. Neither man nor demon nor angel, in time present nor in time to come, can separate us from the love of God which is in Christ Jesus our Lord (Romans 8:38-39). (See also John 10:28-30.) We are saved by faith and not by works, but we are saved to work, and for our works we shall be rewarded (Ephesians 2:8-10).

In every assembly there are various forms of evil to steal our crowns. A cold heart overcame the saints in Ephesus. In Smyrna the believers were tempted by discouragement through tribulation and poverty. In Pergamos there were the opposing doctrines of Balaam and the Nicolaitanes. In Thyatira Jezebel held undisputed sway. Sardis had a name to live by and was dead. In Philadelphia there were tares among the wheat. We may lose our crowns through discouragement, worldliness, social life, success, friends, and even our families. In our Lord's parable some seed fell among thorns, and the thorns choked the good seed (Matthew 13:7). The thorns He calls "the care of this world, and the deceitfulness of riches" (Matthew 13:22). These choke the Word so that the believer becomes unfruitful. Oh, Christian, guard well the sacred deposit Christ has entrusted to you. Be certain that no one takes your crown. Hear the blessed Lord say, "Be thou faithful unto death, and I will give thee a crown of life" (Revelation 2:10). And when He comes again to take us to the home He has prepared for us in Heaven, we shall cast our crowns before His throne, and say, "Thou art worthy, O Lord, to receive glory and honour and power: for Thou hast created all things, and for Thy pleasure they are and were created" (Revelation 4:10-11).

Hold that fast which thou hast (3:11).

What did they have? A little power, His Word, His name, and the promise of His coming again. If we give up these things, we may expect to lose our reward. "Let us not be weary in well doing: for in due season we shall reap, if we faint not" (Galatians 6:9). If the battle grows wearisome and the burdens weightier, take courage. Ere long, faith will give way to sight, and we shall see Him. Hold fast! "Let no man beguile you of your reward" (Colossians 2:18). "Look to yourselves, that we lose not those things which we have wrought, but that we receive a full reward" (2 John 8).

THE LETTER TO LAODICEA

Revelation 3:14-22

I. THE ASSEMBLY

Laodicea, the chief city of Phrygia, was strategically situated in the Lycus Valley about forty-five miles southeast of Philadelphia. Located at the confluence of three much traveled highways, the city grew into a highly successful commercial and financial center. It was a city of wealthy bankers and financiers. The many millionaires combined to build theaters, a huge stadium, lavish public baths, and fabulous shopping centers.

We have no record of the founding of the Christian church at Laodicea, nor are we told in the inspired text that Paul ever visited the city. It is possible that Epaphras played an important role in gathering the believers together. We do know, from Paul's letter to the Colossians, that the great apostle wrote a letter to the Laodicean assembly (Colossians 2:1; 4:12-16). Some scholars believe that the epistle to the Laodiceans is none other than the Epistle to the Ephesians, it being a circular letter requested by Paul to be read in several assemblies in different cities. We do know from the references in Colossians to the assembly at Laodicea that Paul was acquainted with the work there and very much interested in it. He prayed for the saints at Laodicea as he did for those at Colosse (Colossians 2:1-2).

Perhaps we should mention here one other reference, in the Authorized Version, to the assembly at Laodicea. It appears in an appended note at the close of Paul's first Epistle to Timothy. It reads, "The first to Timothy was written from Laodicea, which is the chiefest city of Phrygia Pacatiana." The revisers claimed they could find no authority for this statement and therefore omitted it.

In our comments on chapter 1, verse 11, we pointed out the fact that God completes His work in cycles of seven. The Laodicean letter, which is the last in our Lord's series of seven, brings to a close His prophetic foreview of the Church's earthly history. From chapter four on to the end of the book, the Church is nowhere mentioned as being viewed on earth. The true believers have been caught up to be with the Lord (4:1).

The Laodicean age commenced about the turn of the century, a time within the memory of some living today. Laodicea represents twentieth-century Christendom with its blatant denials of great truths of historic Christianity. Christ is seen outside the church, standing at the door and knocking (3:20). His virgin birth, vicarious atonement, and bodily resurrection have been denied by men who claim to be the spiritual leaders in Christendom. The tares among the wheat are becoming more and more obvious. And it should be remembered that the root cause of this sad condition goes back to the first of the seven assemblies addressed by Christ, "Thou hast left thy first love" (2:4).

II. THE AUTHOR (3:14)

Our Lord appropriately presents Himself to this assembly.

These things saith the Amen (3:14).

This is now the fourth time we have met this word "amen" in the Revelation (1:6,7,18). It is translated from Hebrew into both Greek and English, meaning *truth*. In Deuteronomy 7:9, God is called "the faithful [amen] God." In Isaiah 65:16 He is called "the God of truth." Here the word "truth" is from the Hebrew "amen," and is, to the best of my knowledge, so translated here only in the Old Testament. Literally Jehovah is the God of the *amen*. He is the faithful and true One, the Amen God. He only can add "amen" to every word He utters. It would be difficult to find a more fitting word to describe the God of the Bible. Man may search the greatest libraries in existence, and when he has ransacked the records of literature the world over, he will never find another bearing this name. To every one of His utterances we are compelled to say, "so be it (amen)."

Once in the New Testament, here in Revelation 3:14, "Amen" is used as one of Christ's official titles. He only among man is the affirmation and confirmation of the mind of God. Because He is God's last Word, there is no improving upon Him. *Amen* is stamped upon the very image of Christ, "For in Him dwelleth all the fulness of the Godhead bodily" (Colossians 2:9). He is the Amen. This title is equivalent to His words, "I am the truth" (John 14:6). His ministry of words and works fulfills every promise of God, "For all the promises of God in Him are yea, and in Him *Amen*" (2 Corinthians 1:20). What the church at Laodicea should have been and failed to be, Christ is.

The equivalent of the word *amen* in Greek is our Lord's oft repeated "verily." In the Gospel according to John the double "verily" appears twenty-five times and is rendered in the King James Version by "verily, verily":

1:51	5:24	6:53	10:7	13:38
3:3	5:25	8:34	12:24	14:12
3:5	6:26	8:51	13:16	16:20
3:11	6:32	8:58	13:20	16:23
5:19	6:47	10:1	13:21	21:18

These verses show the frequency with which Christ used the word when introducing some great revelation of the mind of God. He was really saying, "Amen, amen," or "It is true, it is true." He only could say, "To this end was I born, and for this cause came I into the world, that I should bear witness unto the truth" (John 18:37). It is not uncommon to hear someone say, "Amen," to the truth of Christ's words. What is meant is, "It is true," for everything He says is faithful and true. He is neither two-faced nor double-tongued. He is *"the faithful and true witness"* (3:14). Every promise He has made and every warning He pronounced shall most certainly come to pass.

Our Lord describes Himself further as *"the beginning of the creation of God"* (3:14). This statement does not mean that Christ was the first of God's created beings, but rather the One in whom creation had its beginning. To say that Christ is the first creature created by God is contrary to all Scripture, for He Himself is "the beginning and the ending" (1:8), the original Agent in God's creative work. "All things were made by Him" (John 1:3). "For by Him were all things created" (Colossians 1:16). The church that was wealthy and worldly needed to know this truth. Their wealth was as nothing compared with Christ and His wealth. One may be in Christ and yet be poor, "as having nothing, and yet possessing all things" (2 Corinthians 6:10), for, "if any man be in Christ, he is a new creature: old things are passed away; behold, all things are become new" (2 Corinthians 5:17). Thus Christ is the Agent of both the material and spiritual creation of God. This is a solemn reminder that one must be born again, be a new creation in Christ, in order to be saved (John 3:3).

I once heard it said (I do not remember where or by whom) that there were three significant creations: A *natural* creation over which God placed Adam as its head. A *national* creation over which God placed Abraham as its head. But man's history from Adam on has been marked by sin and failure, so that God introduced—A *new* creation with Christ as its Head.

God allowed man to go only so far. When the first man, who was of the earth, had failed, God sent the Second Man, the Lord from Heaven (1 Corinthians 15:47). He introduced the new creation. In this sense also He is "the beginning of the creation of God."

III. THE ADMONITION (3:15-17)

Seeing nothing in this church He can approve, the Lord proceeds to admonish them. He says:

I know thy works, that thou art neither cold nor hot: I would thou wert cold or hot. So then because thou art luke-warm, and neither cold nor hot, I will spue thee out of My mouth (3:15-16).

The condition of the Laodicean church was nauseating to the

Saviour. They were straddlers, fence-sitters, middle-of-the-roaders. Any attitude is better than that of being tepid. A church that is neither enthusiastic nor antagonistic is most difficult to deal with. Halfheartedness will paralyze any effort. Jesus looks upon lukewarmness on the part of Christians as disgusting. It is no compliment to a church when it cannot be called either cold or hot.

But why should the Lord desire that they be cold rather than lukewarm? When you have read again our Lord's statement to the Pharisees, then His desire as He expressed it to the Laodicean church can be understood. "And Jesus said, For judgment I am come into this world, that they which see not might see; and they which see might be made blind. And some of the Pharisees which were with Him heard these words, and said unto Him, Are we blind also? Jesus said unto them, If ye were blind, ye should have no sin: but now ye say, We see; therefore your sin remaineth" (John 9:39-41). This is a deeply solemn and significant statement! The Pharisees were not sensitive to their blindness. Like many others they would say, "We are not blind; we can see. We are not ignorant; we know." And yet, for all their boasted light and knowledge, they rejected Christ. It is far better for the poor sinner who admits he has no light or knowledge. Had the Pharisees recognized their own blindness, they would have received Him who is the Light of the world and He would have cleansed them from their sins. But in their refusal to confess their blindness, their sin remained. Thus the Lord is saying to those at Laodicea that, if instead of being lukewarm, they were so cold as to feel the bitterness and severity of that coldness, they would flee to the true warmth for refuge. If we are really cold, and admit to the fact, our confession will lead to the removal of our sin.

There follows our Lord's awful indictment given in strange but sobering imagery. He said:

> *So then because thou art lukewarm, and neither cold nor hot, I will spue thee out of My mouth* (3:16).

Notice Christ did not say, "So then because thou art no longer orthodox and have denied the great truths of the faith."

The truth of the matter is that they had not denied the gospel. Their major problem lay in the fact that they were not "hot." The Greek word for "hot" is *zestos,* from which the English word *zest* is derived. It appears only here in the New Testament and means "boiling hot" (from *zeo,* to boil). The members in the church at Laodicea were not boiling hot; they were not ardent Christians. They had no enthusiasm, no emotion, no zeal, no urgency. It is possible to have a large measure of doctrinal correctness without the fire of spiritual fervor and affection. To such a church in the last days our Lord says, *"I will spue thee out of My mouth."* Of course the language is metaphorical, but this use of words does not empty them of their meaning. Lukewarm liquid is used as an emetic. It creates nausea. It is not merely tasteless, but positively distasteful. John Stott has said, "Christ's forceful expression is one of disgust. He will utterly repudiate those whose attachment to Him is purely nominal and superficial." It is possible, then, for one to be religious and at the same time to be repulsive to Christ. All such He must eject (Matthew 7:21-23; 25:11-12).

Like the Pharisees who were blind and did not know it, so the Laodicean church did not know their real condition.

> *Because thou sayest, I am rich, and increased with goods, and have need of nothing; and knowest not that thou art wretched, and miserable, and poor, and blind, and naked* (3:17).

Their condition can be summed up in two phrases, *"thou sayest . . . and knowest not."* They said they were rich and had need of nothing, and all the while they were wretched, miserable, poor, blind, and naked. It was their estimate of themselves compared with Christ's declaration of their true condition. A true indication of this church's spiritual decay is witnessed by the fact that she speaks of herself and not of Christ. She boasts of her material riches and resources but never utters one word of praise for her Lord. Imagine the Apostle Paul being the pastor of that church and preaching to its Sunday morning crowd on one of his favorite texts, "But God forbid that I should glory, save in the cross of our Lord Jesus Christ, by whom the world is crucified unto me, and I unto the world" (Galatians 6:14). It is pitiable when a church cannot stand together and say from their hearts, with a loud voice, "Worthy is the Lamb that was slain to receive power, and riches, and wisdom, and strength, and honour, and glory, and blessing" (Revelation 5:12). We need the gift to see ourselves as our Lord sees us, and not until then will we offer praise to Him.

He said, *"Thou art wretched."* The word "wretched" means "distressed." The only other appearance of this word in the New Testament is where Paul used it of himself when he cried, "O wretched man that I am!" (Romans 7:24). When Paul saw himself through the eyes of the Lord, he could only groan under the burden of indwelling sin and long for deliverance by a power greater than himself. Once when I led a woman to Christ, a woman possessed of wealth, health, and beauty, I watched a face grow pale and saw a soul in distress as, in verse after verse from the Bible, God showed her how wretched she was. But that day she found true and abiding riches in Jesus Christ.

He described that church further as being *"miserable."* The Greek word means *pitiable,* a word appearing here, and in 1 Corinthians 15:19 where we read, "If in this life only we have hope in Christ, we are of all men most miserable." Actually the poor rich people in Laodicea needed to be pitied, certainly not envied. They possessed much for this life but had nothing for the life to come. The Lord looked upon them with pity. He actually felt sorry for them.

Then Christ told them they were *"poor."* They said, "We are rich, and have need of nothing." They were quite right in one sense of the word. They were rich in material things. This prosperous city was known for its wealth. The local inhabitants were proud of their accumulated riches. But the Lord knew their true state. Who is more to be pitied than an individual who, in his delusion, imagines that he is rich, whereas in reality he is a beggar? He revels in his fancied possessions while the Lord stands by in pity, and says, *"Thou art poor."* I once read of a man who visited a wealthy church. A deacon showed him around the property. He pointed out the expensive architecture, the costly chandeliers, tapestries, carpets, and pews. And then he said to his guest, "You name it and we have it." The visitor then asked, "When did you have a revival in your church?" The deacon replied, "Oh, some churches have revivals, but we don't need that sort of thing here." They thought they were rich; Christ says they are poor. They were miserably deceived. Little wonder He pitied them.

IV. THE APPEAL (3:18-20)

How, then, did Christ appeal to this church?

I counsel thee to buy of Me gold tried in the fire, that thou mayest be rich; and white raiment, that thou mayest be clothed, and that the shame of thy nakedness do not appear; and anoint thine eyes with eyesalve, that thou mayest see (3:18).

These people were merchants. They were used to buying and selling. In this way they had accumulated large fortunes. But theirs was the gold of this world. They had gained it by trading with the merchants who came from the East to Laodicea with their camels laden with goods. This, however, is not the coin of the realm in the Kingdom of God. The Laodiceans were traders in garments made of the world's finest wool, but these were no covering for the nakedness of a man's soul. They were dealers in expensive ointments, but such ointments could never heal their poor spiritual vision. There are no doubt many people in the world who are like the man in our Lord's parable, of whom Christ said, "Thou fool, this night thy soul shall be required of thee. . . . So is he that layeth up treasure for himself, and is not rich toward God" (Luke 12:20-21). On the other hand, there are those who are sanctified in Christ Jesus to whom Paul wrote, "Ye are enriched by Him. . . . Now ye are full, now ye are rich" (1 Corinthians 1:5; 4:8). The Laodiceans had been trading in the world's mart only. Now the ascended Lord recommends that they turn to Him. He does not command them; He counsels them. He respects their right to choose for themselves, but He offers them the best advice.

He says, *"I counsel thee to buy of Me."* Why does He appeal to them to *buy* of Him? How can wretched, miserable, poor, blind, and naked people *buy* anything? Is salvation to be purchased? Our Lord was using language apropos to these merchandising-minded men. He would have them turn from the salesmen who peddled the wares of this world to the One who said, "Ho, every one that thirsteth, come ye to the waters, and he that hath no money; come ye, buy, and eat; yea, come, buy wine and milk without money and without price" (Isaiah 55:1). Buying "without money and without price" is indeed a figure of grace. Dealing with Christ is within the reach of the poorest. As a matter of fact, the deeper the need the better the chance of consummating the purchase. Is there anything in all the world more wonderful than this? Your right to come and buy without money is your recognition of your own deep need and poverty. Christ is appealing to the church as He sees her, not as she thinks she is. In effect, He says, "If you are but conscious of your poverty, I have riches for you." How graciously He offers to provide their need!

He advises them *"Buy of Me gold tried in the fire, that thou mayest be rich."* The "gold" here is not literal, but figurative. They said they were rich; He said they were poor and needed His gold. The gold here is that divine righteousness that will stand every test and never decrease in value even in the worst depression. Job expected that the trials and sufferings through which he was passing would remove the dross from his life, and that he would emerge from this experience more righteous than he had ever been before, even as gold (Job 23:10). There is a proverb which teaches us that the unrighteous acts of a beautiful woman are as inconsistent as a gold ornament worn by a pig (Proverbs 11:22). From another proverb we learn that righteous [or right] words well spoken are like a beautiful picture of gold framed in silver (Proverbs 25:11). Right words have a beautiful effect upon those who hear them. The Prophet Isaiah quotes the Lord as saying He can adorn a man with His righteousness much greater than man can adorn himself with the gold of this world (Isaiah 13:12). In the New Testament the righteous deeds of the Christian, that shall have God's approval in the day of judgment, are compared to gold (1 Corinthians

3:12-13). Thus we can see that our Lord was but offering the Laodiceans His righteousness that would enrich their lives on earth and for eternity. Gold purified in the fire is what God is to the believer in Christ. Actually Christ's appeal was a call to hear and heed His word (Psalm 19:7-11).

He urged them further:

> *Buy of Me . . . white raiment, that thou mayest be clothed, and that the shame of thy nakedness do not appear* (3:18).

The language here in the third chapter of the last book in the Bible resembles that which we read in the third chapter of the first book in the Bible. The sin of Adam and Eve disclosed to them the shame of their nakedness. They immediately made aprons of fig leaves, a false covering which proved to be nothing more than an excuse or an alibi (Genesis 3:7). God Himself had to provide coats of skins for them, a covering which was the result of a substitutionary sacrifice (Genesis 3:21). The finery of the Laodiceans could never cover their moral nakedness. All of man's righteous deeds are as filthy rags in God's sight (Isaiah 64:6). It is a case of being ignorant of God's righteousness and going about to establish his own righteousness (Romans 10:3). Thus Christ says, "Buy of *Me* . . . white raiment." This is divine righteousness which God imputes to every believing sinner in Christ (1 Corinthians 1:30). He only can clothe their nakedness with the clean white linen of His righteousness (Revelation 19:8), without which no man can see the Lord.

For their blindness Christ says:

> *Anoint thine eyes with eyesalve, that thou mayest see* (3:18).

They could well afford to travel the known world of their day, but Christ could open their eyes to perceive a spiritual world they had never known. Our Lord opened many blind eyes during His earthly ministry, and He still makes men to see. The patent-medicine eye ointment of liberalism and neo-orthodoxy leaves men blind. Only the Great Physician can show men the true light (John 8:12). Spiritual perception is greatly needed in our day, and be certain the natural man does not have it (1 Corinthians 2:14-16). If you are conscious of your blindness, He has "eyesalve" for you. Let Him anoint you with the Holy Spirit and you will see a world of which you never dreamed (1 John 2:20-21). He possesses all that the church so sorely lacks, and until men turn to Him they can never be cured of their distorted vision.

> *As many as I love, I rebuke and chasten: be zealous therefore, and repent* (3:19).

He asserts His love for all in the congregation, the unfaithful as well as the faithful. But they must know that divine love will never overlook wrong. He will not force His recommendations upon them, but their disobedience will bring chastening. He will not tolerate their condition indefinitely. In every dispensation the Lord has rebuked and chastened those whom He loves (Proverbs 3:11-12; Hebrews 12:5-6). His love is never so complacent that it condones sin in our lives. We see Him yearning over Jerusalem just prior to the time when the ax was laid to the root of the tree (Matthew 23:37-38). If He had not loved the church at Laodicea He would not have bothered to appeal to her and counsel her. But her members must repent at once and completely, without mental reservations. They must turn from all that displeases Him. He will not tolerate lukewarmness. They must get hot and stay hot or else He will spue them out. *"Be zealous therefore, and repent."*

Though He was excluded from the church at Laodicea, Christ appeals to the individual. Observe His use of the singular pronoun in the appeal:

> *Behold, I stand at the door, and knock: if any man hear My voice, and open the door, I will come in to him, and will sup with him, and he with Me* (3:20).

Someone has said, "History affords little ground for optimism that an organization that has departed from Christ will return." But our Lord does appeal to the individual, whether that individual is in this group or that, or in no group at all. We should rejoice that the gospel is addressed to "whosoever will," to "any man." There is little likelihood that Christendom as a body will surrender to Jesus Christ and allow Him to take over the reins of sovereignty. When He comes, "shall He find faith on the earth?" (Luke 18:8) Hardly! His true followers never were in the majority. He called them His "little flock" (Luke 12:32). But, thank God, many individuals will open to Him. Even in Laodicea, where we find the worst of the seven churches, our Lord stands at the door and appeals to "any man."

He is the risen, exalted Christ, standing at the closed door of the human heart, desiring entrance. We speak of sinners finding Christ, as though men go about knocking on doors seeking Him. This is not true. The fundamental fact of Christianity is that this loving Saviour is ever seeking men and appealing to them one by one. I see in this text a touch of divine, infinite long-suffering and patience. Christ both knocks and speaks, as He has been doing for nineteen centuries, and His voice is clear to all who will hear. Do not confuse that voice of Christ with the jargon of men. Knowing it is He, let Him in, for He brings with Him a rich feast of personal fellowship, the like of which you have never known. Though He is not wanted by denominations and church systems, He will continue to deal with individuals until this Age of Grace has run its course.

While Christ appears in the midst of the seven lampstands (or churches) (1:12-13), we dare not conclude that Christendom is God's habitation through His Spirit. He indwells any assembly only as He indwells individuals in that assembly (1 Corinthians 3:16; 6:19-20). "Now if *any man* have not the Spirit of Christ, he is none of His" (Romans 8:9). He never enters into a system en masse; He comes into the hearts of individuals. For the most part the Laodicean church of the last days does not claim Christ. Its leaders are taken up with their own importance and self-sufficiency. History has repeated itself. Before Christ came, conditions were so bad as to cause the departure of the glory of the LORD from the temple (Ezekiel 10:18). So also in Christ's day. At one time in His ministry He referred to the temple as "My house" (Matthew 21:13 cf.

Isaiah 56:7) and "My Father's house" (John 2:16), but not long afterward He said, "Behold, your house is left unto you desolate. . . . And Jesus went out, and departed from the temple" (Matthew 23:38; 24:1). It is the same with Laodicea. Christendom has become man's house; it is no longer God's house. Our Lord described a true assembly when He said, "For where two or three are gathered together in My name, there am I in the midst of them" (Matthew 18:20). You see Him in the midst of His little flock after His resurrection (John 20:19). But this is not so in Laodicea. Instead of being "in the midst," He is seen on the outside, appealing for admittance.

"If any man hear My voice, and open the door, I will come in to him"—not into the whole assembly at Laodicea. Christendom's doom is sealed. Man's church of the last days is a spewed-out church. But, thank God, in the last days and last phase of the professing church, individuals may enjoy fellowship with the Lord Jesus Christ.

Many of you have doubtless seen Holman Hunt's famous painting of Christ standing outside a closed door, knocking, and seeking admittance. One day an artist friend looked at Hunt's picture and said to him, "Haven't you made a mistake by painting the door without a latch?" To this Hunt replied, "No, I have not made a mistake. The latch is on the inside. You and I control the latch." If Christ comes in we must open the door. And when we admit Him into the dwelling of our hearts, He brings an end to all poverty. To the hearing ear Revelation 3:20 is one of the great texts of the Bible. As a matter of fact, it is one of the greatest since it appears at the close of the Church Age just prior to Christ's return. The world's Saviour is still the waiting Guest, seeking earnestly and knocking appealingly. This is all He can do. He will not force Himself in.

Never say that Christ has not knocked at the door of your heart. Reflect seriously on your past life, and you will recall, I am sure, a variety of ways in which the Saviour has knocked at your door. He has knocked through suffering, poverty, the death of a loved one, a marital rift, the clear gospel witness through a sermon, the personal testimony of someone concerned for your soul, or the quiet godly life of some child of God. But He has been there knocking, and He is there again, right now. While you are alive and able, let Him in at once to take over your whole personality.

THE OVERCOMERS

In each of the seven letters our Lord issues a promise *"to him that overcometh"* (Revelation 2:7,11,17,26; 3:5,12,21). The history of the Church, as previewed prophetically by Christ in the seven letters, seems to be the history of conflict. The foes are many and varied, from traitors and temptations within, to taunts, tribulations, and tyranny from without. The true Christian in any local assembly, where mere professors are often found also, learns quickly that conversion is not the end of Christian experience; it is not the beginning of an easygoing life without trials and opposition. The children of Israel faced their foes in their dispensation, and the Christian faces his today.

Now it is not my intention here to go into detail as to the nature of the conflict. I will merely say concerning it that the Lord has not left us without warning nor without weapons. The objective in this study is an attempt to clarify misunderstanding as to the identification of the overcomers. Most commentaries I have read view them as an inner circle of victorious Christians, known among themselves for the terms and phrases they use, and for a life of holiness above fellow believers. Now none of us will deny that there are different levels of spiritual experience, and that some Christians are far out in front of other Christians in matters of Christian growth. There are the "spiritual" and the "carnal" (1 Corinthians 3:1), the "fathers," "young men," and "little children" (1 John 2:13), the "babe" that uses milk and "them that are of full age" and partake of "strong meat" (Hebrews 5:12-14). But are the overcomers the more spiritual among believers? Are they the more mature who have grown in grace above their fellows? Are they those in preferential circles who are designated by one descriptive term or another? If you answer "yes" to these questions, I am quite strongly convinced that your answer lacks scriptural authority.

The Scriptures do teach that there will be rewards for Christians, and that some of God's children will reap more than others. This is borne out in many passages such as Matthew 10:42; 16:27; 25:19; Luke 19:10-26; 1 Corinthians 3:11-15; 9:24-25; 1 Thessalonians 2:19; 2 Timothy 4:8; 1 Peter 5:4; Revelation 22:12; and others. But the promises made to the overcomers in the seven letters are, in some instances, of such a nature that the casual reader might conclude that those who are not overcomers could lose their salvation. This of course can never be.

Now I must strongly oppose the man who was heard to say, "A Christian can do anything but be lost." A man who knows the grace of God in truth will never speak as loosely as this. On the other hand, Jesus did say, "My sheep hear My voice, and I know them, and they follow Me; And I give unto them eternal life; and they shall never perish, neither shall any man pluck them out of My hand. My Father, which gave them Me, is greater than all; and no man is able to pluck them out of My Father's hand. I and my Father are one" (John 10:27-30). Here Jesus is speaking of salvation, not rewards. Christians might lose rewards, but salvation—never!

The promises made to the overcomers are a part of the great salvation provided by God in grace for all those who have been redeemed through faith in Christ's blood. What I am saying is that all *true* believers in the Lord Jesus Christ are the overcomers in Revelation 2 and 3. If some of my brethren find it difficult to accept this view, I only beg your patience and prayers. But I must remind you that if only one of these promises could be proved to be the common property of all truly born-again people, I have proved my point. And if the failure to appropriate or win for one's self that reward, which one of these promises offers, results in a soul's being lost, my thesis is doubly strengthened, at least among those brethren who believe in the eternal security of the Saviour.

Keep in mind the setting in which the promises appear. The seven letters trace the dawn, development, and decline of Christendom, showing clearly that the religious trends of the last days preceding Christ's return are away from the truth of the Biblical historical Christian faith. The successive periods in the history of the Church are marked by a growing apostasy and defection from the doctrine of the apostles. The course has been in the line of deterioration. This is exactly as the Scriptures predict and it is in harmony with the increased evil in the world. Our Lord predicted the rise of "false prophets" (Matthew 24:11,24). Paul warned the Ephesian elders, "For I know this, that after my departing shall grievous wolves enter in among you, not sparing the flock" (Acts 20:29). In our Lord's parables the tares and the wheat grow up together (Matthew 13:24-30, 38-40), the good fish are mingled with the bad (Matthew 13:47-48). All of this is stating simply that Christendom is a mixture of true believers and false professors.

In the church at Smyrna there were those of the synagogue of Satan (Revelation 2:9). In Pergamos there were those who held the doctrine of Balaam and of the Nicolaitanes (Revelation 2:14-15). In Thyatira there was Jezebel and those who followed her (Revelation 2:20). In Sardis there were those who professed to have been born again but who were spiritually dead (Revelation 3:1). In Laodicea a state of spiritual poverty existed in which state the members are described by Christ as being wretched, miserable, poor, blind, and naked (Revelation 3:17). This is Christendom, a mixture of the saved and unsaved. It is exactly the situation we find today in the World Council of Churches.

The overcomer is the truly born-again-one, not the one who claims never to have been overcome, but the one who overcomes at last.

Presently there is only one perfect Overcomer. He could say, "I also overcame, and am set down with My Father in His throne" (Revelation 3:21). All other overcomers are such by virtue of their position in Him. Jesus said, "Be of good cheer; I have overcome the world" (John 16:33). I am so glad that our Lord Jesus Christ has overcome the world because I know that I never could.

The Apostle John wrote, "For whatsoever is born of God

overcometh the world: and this is the victory that overcometh the world, even our faith. Who is he that overcometh the world, but he that believeth that Jesus is the Son of God?" (1 John 5:4-5) The overcomer here is he who has been born again. The verb rendered "overcometh" is in the aorist tense, and this takes us back in point of time to when we first received Christ by faith and were born again, when we passed spiritually out of death into union with Christ. Faith in Christ did not merely make us God's children, but overcomers as well. The day we trusted Christ was a day of victory, the day we overcame the world. "Who is he that overcometh the world, but he that *believeth* that Jesus is the Son of God?" Not merely certain ones among the believers, but all of them. From the very moment of our conversion we were overcomers. "This is the victory that overcometh the world"—even our fighting? No! "Even our faith." Since our blessed Lord overcame the world, must we fight the battle all over again? How foolish! Rather do we trust Him who by His death and resurrection has won the battle for us.

John comments further on the subject of overcoming. "Ye are of God, little children, and have overcome them: because greater is He that is in you, than he that is in the world" (1 John 4:4). The antichristian spirits are in the world, but the children of God are said to have overcome them. How? Certainly not by any strength in the Christian himself, but by the victorious Lord who indwells him. There is not the slightest hint in this verse that only some of God's born ones are overcomers. Contrariwise, they are all God's "little children" who are indwelt by Him, the mighty Victor. Twice John says to the "young men," "Ye have overcome the wicked one" (1 John 2:13-14). Again, let me point out that the overcomer is not one who claims never to be overcome, but one who must overcome at last because he is Christ's. God sees His children as having overcome the wicked one; they are already "sanctified in Christ Jesus" (1 Corinthians 1:2); in His plans they are already "glorified" (Romans 8:30). "We are more than conquerors through Him that loved us" (Romans 8:37).

I. THE PROMISE TO EPHESUS (2:7)

To him that overcometh will I give to eat of the tree of life, which is in the midst of the paradise of God (2:7).

Only those who have eternal life may eat of the tree of life. Now the tree of life is not reserved for a preferential few chosen from among God's children; it is for all who possess eternal life. In Eden, which was man's paradise, there was the tree of life (Genesis 2:9; 3:22). To eat of that tree was to become immortal, that is, incapable of dying. This right was forfeited by man when he sinned. The promise to the overcomer is that he shall be given perpetuity of life, complete conquest over further liability to die. Now is this promise made only to certain of the redeemed in Heaven? Certainly not! Jesus said, "Whosoever liveth and believeth in Me shall never die" (John 11:26). Here He is not referring to a select number from among those who believe. Is Paul's inspired word to some —or to all—believers when he says, "This mortal must put on immortality" (1 Corinthians 15:53)? I do not know of one evangelical teacher of the Bible who would limit Paul's words to a mere part of Christ's true Church. Paradise lost in the Garden of Eden brought death. Paradise restored means the abolishment of death. The immortality of the Christian is not dependent upon his own faithfulness, but upon Him "Who hath abolished death, and hath brought life and immortality to light through the gospel" (2 Timothy 1:10). The paradise of God and the tree of life will be shared by all who are in Christ. It is the lot and portion of all the redeemed.

Our Lord knew well that the entire local assembly as such would not inherit the promise, inasmuch as there were unbelievers among the believers. So the promise was made to each individual believer in the assembly, "to *him* that overcometh." Salvation is a personal and an individual matter. The gate into the Paradise of God is still open with its access to the tree of life. Each must decide for himself whether or not he will enter. Every soul who trusts Christ now may be assured that one day our blessed Lord will escort him to the tree of life where he shall eat and never die again. And remember, the right to the tree of life and immortality is not to those who struggle but to those who are saved.

Dear Robert McCheyne must have been a great soul, judging from all that I have read about him, but I feel he missed our Lord's meaning in His promise to the overcomers at Ephesus. McCheyne wrote in his pamphlet, *The Seven Churches of Asia*, concerning Christ's promise in Revelation 2:7: "I know there are some of you who are struggling, struggling hard, and you *are* overcoming. Well, then, you shall eat of the tree of life." In this I cannot concur. Our right to the tree of life is not through our struggling but through Christ's suffering. That for which man was created will be reached at last, not because we struggled here on the battleground of human life, but because we have been redeemed through the sacrifice of God's dear Son. If you want to be an overcomer, then come to Christ. Unbelief and immortality cannot coexist in Heaven where God dwells. You need the salvation that God offers to you through faith in the Lord Jesus Christ. Come to Him at once and you shall overcome at last.

II. THE PROMISE TO SMYRNA (2:11)

He that overcometh shall not be hurt of the second death (2:11).

We have no difficulty in identifying the "second death." It is clearly marked out for us twice in this same book.

And death and hell were cast into the lake of fire. This is the second death (Revelation 20:14).

But the fearful, and unbelieving, and the abominable, and murderers, and whoremongers, and sorcerers, and idolaters, and all liars, shall have their part in the lake which burneth with fire and brimstone: which is the second death (Revelation 21:8).

The language here is plain. The "second death" is the judgment of hell, that everlasting banishment from the presence of the Lord which awaits the wicked.

Now dare we assume that deliverance from the "second death" is here promised to a certain class of Christians only? Perish the thought! Who among us would have any assurance that we would be delivered if such were the case? No Christian can expect to escape physical death, which is the separation of his spiritual part from his body, except that the rapture of the Church occur before he dies. But of a truth every Christian is assured that he will escape the lake of fire and torment. The unbeliever dies and finds a "second death" awaiting him; the believer dies and finds eternal life. The point our Lord made in His letter to Smyrna is that they might have to pass through physical death, but they will not be hurt of the "second death." This promise describes a blessed future for all the redeemed. But if it is allocated to a preferential circle, what remains for the circle of ordinary Christians, of which some of us are a part?

I believe that this promise draws a cleavage between the true believers and the mere professors in the local assembly. It is too much for me, as a pastor, to say that all in our local assembly are overcomers. I am obliged to face the fact that possibly there are those who have not been born again. The promise of our Lord is not extended to those persons who merely give assent to a creed or a doctrine or a set of church by-laws. It is for those who have heard and believed the gospel of Christ and thereby have "passed from death unto life" (John 5:24).

"Blessed and holy is he that hath part in the first resurrection: on such the second death hath no power" (Revelation 20:6). Now there is a resurrection to life and a resurrection to judgment. Those who are called out from the dead at the first resurrection are the ones whom God has justified, thus it will be "the resurrection of the just" (Luke 14:13-14). They are those who are "in Christ," thus "the dead in Christ shall rise first" (1 Thessalonians 4:16). They are those who have passed out of death into life (John 5:24; Ephesians 2:1), thus they will have part in "the resurrection of life" and not in "the resurrection of damnation" (John 5:28-29). The Bible does not teach one general resurrection for all mankind. The resurrection of the redeemed, over whom the second death has no power, are those raised at the Rapture when Christ comes for His own before the millennium. There are some failing Christians, of whom I have been one, but I know that not one Christian will be in the lake of fire. The overcomers clearly include all true children of God.

III. THE PROMISE TO PERGAMOS (2:17)

> *To him that overcometh will I give to eat of the hidden manna, and will give him a white stone, and in the stone a new name written, which no man knoweth saving he that receiveth it* (2:17).

Three things are here promised to the overcomer. First, he is *"to eat of the hidden manna."* Some able teachers feel that the words "to eat" should be omitted from the text. Whether or not this is so is not important to our understanding of the promise. What is the "manna"? Let us apply the law of first mention. We meet this word for the first time in connection with Israel's experiences in the wilderness. When the people complained to Moses about their shortage of food, God said, "I will rain bread from heaven for you" (Exodus 16:4). And when the children of Israel saw it, they said one to another, "It is manna" (Exodus 16:15). Manna then was the portion of God's people, His provision for them as they journeyed through the wilderness. It was not ordinary food, but miracle bread from Heaven.

Now manna has always stood as a type of our Lord Jesus Christ. When the people asked Him for a sign that they might believe in Him (John 6:30-31), He replied, "Verily, verily, I say unto you, Moses gave you not that bread from heaven; but My father giveth you the true bread from heaven. For the bread of God is He which cometh down from heaven, and giveth life unto the world. . . . I am the bread of life: he that cometh to Me shall never hunger; and he that believeth on Me shall never thirst" (John 6:32-35). Christ is the portion of His people. He is the true Bread. He said further, "I am that bread of life. Your fathers did eat manna in the wilderness, and are dead.

This is the bread which cometh down from heaven, that a man may eat thereof, and not die. I am the living bread which came down from heaven: if any man eat of this bread, he shall live for ever: and the bread that I will give is My flesh, which I will give for the life of the world. . . . Verily, verily, I say unto you, Except ye eat the flesh of the Son of man, and drink His blood, ye have no life in you. Whoso eateth My flesh, and drinketh My blood, hath eternal life; and I will raise him up at the last day. For My flesh is meat indeed, and My blood is drink indeed. He that eateth My flesh, and drinketh My blood, dwelleth in Me, and I in him" (John 6:48-56). A large segment of Christendom, both Roman and Protestant, have distorted Christ's words by making the eating of His flesh and the drinking of His blood apply to the Lord's Table. J. J. Van Gorder said, "If sinners receive eternal life by partaking of the Lord's Table, then instead of hedging it about with numerous restrictions, it should be assembled on the most prominent intersections where sinners may be invited to partake." But how inconsistent can men be? The same chapter adds, "It is the spirit that quickeneth; the flesh profiteth nothing: the words that I speak unto you, they are spirit, and they are life" (John 6:63). The fact that Christ is the satisfying portion of His people cannot be stressed too much. Believers have their souls' hunger satisfied by the blessed Lord, the Bread of Life. It would be difficult for me to conceive how Christ, the Bread of Life, could be given to a mere portion of Christians and not to all. Not to partake of the Bread of Life is to be without Christ, hence without eternal life.

But why does our Lord refer to it as *"hidden* manna"? The trials which had beset the Christians at Pergamos were unusually difficult for them. They were called upon to bear witness for Christ in the very headquarters of Satan's operations. Balaamism and Nicolaitanism prevailed right in the local church in Pergamos. How did the Christians survive and maintain their testimony in the midst of such satanic evil? They partook daily of Christ. He was hidden from the view of those who rejected Him. The believer has meat to eat that the world knows not of. He feeds upon Him who alone can satisfy. In the midst of this world's corruption the child of God draws from that eternal source of sustenance and supply which is hidden in the secret of God's presence. The Christian need never compromise with the world for satisfaction, as did Balaam, for he finds satisfaction in Christ.

Some commentators see in the "hidden manna" a reference to the golden pot of manna which was kept in the most holy place in the Tabernacle as a memorial to God's faithfulness and a token of His supply for subsequent generations (Exodus 16:32-34; Hebrews 9:4). Hid in the ark, it was kept from the gaze of the people. Only the eye of Jehovah rested upon it, the symbol of His beloved Son.

But the promise to the overcomer is in the future tense. Exactly! He who is our life in this world will still be so in Heaven, but in a greater degree. "Now I know in part; but then shall I know even as also I am known" (1 Corinthians 13:12). Christ is wonderful to us now, but then, "We shall see Him as He is" (1 John 3:2). When we see Him it will be in all of His eternal glory and splendor. We think we know Him now, but wait, beloved child of God. The best is yet to be.

The overcomer is promised *"a white stone."* A wide variety of interpretations of the white stone have issued from the commentators. I have found nothing in Scripture which tells me precisely what this white stone might be. But whatever allusions one might have, and whatever conclusions to which he might arrive, we do know that a name is to be engraved upon it. If you ask me whether the name is that of the believer or of Christ, it would seem to me that it is the Lord's own name here in view. This is inferred from the later promise in 3:12. The name of the Lord is the important and significant name among men and angels (see 14:1). The one receiving the name is the only person who knows what that name is, suggesting to us that in Heaven each redeemed person will have his own personal and intimate knowledge of his Lord. Each will enjoy an intimacy with His Lord which no other can share. Only the redeemed who receive His name can reign with Christ. Jehovah said, "I will set him on high, because he hath known My Name" (Psalm 91:14).

IV. THE PROMISE TO THYATIRA (2:26-27)

And he that overcometh, and keepeth My works unto the end, to him will I give power over the nations: and He shall rule them with a rod of iron; as the vessels of a potter shall they be broken to shivers: even as I received of My Father (2:26-27).

The scene here is an earthly one. The emphasis is upon a demonstrated authority over the nations on the earth. There is a problem here for those who deny that there is to be a literal kingdom of Christ on earth in which His saints will rule with Him. I see in this promise strong support in favor of the millennium.

The promise here has a direct connection with the second Psalm. In this Messianic Psalm the Father says to the Son, "Ask of Me, and I shall give Thee the heathen for Thine inheritance, and the uttermost parts of the earth for Thy possession. Thou shalt break them with a rod of iron; Thou shalt dash them in pieces like a potter's vessel" (Psalm 2:8-9). The promise to the overcomer assures him that he is to share with Christ in His judgment administrations over the nations. Jude wrote, "The Lord cometh with ten thousands of His saints, To execute judgment upon all, and to convince all that are ungodly among them of all their ungodly deeds which they have ungodly committed, and of all their hard speeches which ungodly sinners have spoken against Him" (Jude 14-15). Here, as well as in the promise to Thyatira, the Holy Spirit speaks about things associated with Christ and His Church at His Second Coming.

This idea of the saints reigning with Christ is in keeping with the original purpose of God for man. In the Genesis account of the creation of man, the first of the divine injunctions was regal in character. God said, "Let them have dominion . . . over all the earth" (Genesis 1:26). The failure of the first Adam with reference to his rule over the earth did not mean that man had lost forever his divinely-bestowed dominion. It is to be restored. Christ assured the disciples, "It is your Father's good pleasure to give you the kingdom" (Luke 12:32); "Ye also shall sit upon twelve thrones, judging the twelve tribes of Israel" (Matthew 19:28). Paul wrote, "And if children, then heirs; heirs of God, and joint-heirs with Christ; if so be that we suffer with Him, that we may be also glorified together" (Romans 8:17). This is the wonderful outlook for the child of God. "Do ye not know that the saints shall judge the world?" (1 Corinthians 6:2) "Know ye not that we shall judge angels?" (1 Corinthians 6:3). "But the saints of the most High shall take the kingdom, and possess the kingdom for ever, even for ever and ever" (Daniel 7:18). This fact is asserted three times within the space of that single chapter (Daniel 7:18,22,27). I am sure that this promise of coming authority is not confined to a select few from among the saints, but for all saints. It seems fitting that it should be so.

The promise to Thyatira continues with the words:

And I will give him the morning star (2:28).

The meaning of this statement is not difficult to trace. In the closing words of the book Jesus said, "I am . . . the bright and morning star" (Revelation 22:16). Saints and angels are elsewhere in Scripture called stars, but this Star is peculiarly and preeminently different. This Star is Christ Himself. Balaam in his prophecy said, "There shall come a Star out of Jacob, and a Sceptre shall rise out of Israel" (Numbers 24:17). Balaam saw Him afar off, but the world is much closer now to seeing Him in His new earthly role. True, there is still the world's darkness because of Satan and sin. We Christians sometimes wonder how brightly the gospel light shines through the present blackness. But then we press on to let our light shine, for one day Christ will present Himself to us again, not as our Redeemer to die for us, but as the world's Ruler to reign with us. Then will be fulfilled the prophecy of Zacharias, "The dayspring from on high hath visited us, to give light to them that sit in darkness and in the shadow of death" (Luke 1:78-79).

In promising this Star to the overcomer, then, Christ is but pledging Himself, not to a select few from among His own, but to all who are truly His. The Morning Star will usher in the majestic glory and splendor of the preeminent Christ. "We have also a more sure word of prophecy; whereunto ye do well that ye take heed, as unto a light that shineth in a dark place, until the day dawn, and the day star arise in your hearts" (2 Peter 1:19).

V. THE PROMISE TO SARDIS (3:5)

> *He that overcometh, the same shall be clothed in white raiment; and I will not blot out his name out of the book of life, but I will confess his name before My Father, and before His angels* (3:5).

The promise here is threefold. First, the overcomer is to receive *"white raiment."* It is his new garment whereby he shall be known for his purity and righteousness. This is the final robing of all saints, not a special garment for a preferential few. There were those in Sardis who had defiled their garments. They might have professed to be Christians but they had not been clothed in Christ's righteousness. These shall in no wise enter Heaven. The man without a wedding garment cannot be present at the marriage supper of the Lamb (see Matthew 22:11-14).

The overcomer is not the one who earns the white garment by struggling and succeeding, but he receives it because he was made white through faith in the blood of the Lamb. Whether a man is a pretribulation saint or a tribulation saint, his robe can be made white only "in the blood of the Lamb" (cf. Revelation 7:14). The promise here is that all believers shall enjoy the full realization of what they have been made in Christ. Man's garment is as "filthy rags" in God's sight (Isaiah 64:6), but in Christ we are "made the righteousness of God in Him" (2 Corinthians 5:21). Of the true believers Jesus says, "They shall walk with Me in white: for they are worthy" (Revelation 3:4). Their worthiness is the worthiness of Christ, the garment given by the Bridegroom to His Bride. As Christ appeared in dazzling white at His transfiguration (Luke 9:29), so *all* believers shall appear with Him in glory (Colossians 3:4).

Secondly, Jesus promises, *"I will not blot out his name out of the book of life"* (3:5). The book of life is the register of all who ever lived. It is God's record of the names of men, the name whereby He knows each. Let there be no problem in our minds about this book and those whose names are erased from it. Let me say clearly that every person has his name in this book. Those whose names are erased are those who never were saved. This book was well known to Moses as containing the names of both the forgiven and unforgiven. Moses was willing to forfeit his eternal life for those who as yet were not forgiven. He prayed, "Yet now, if Thou wilt forgive their sin—; and if not, blot me, I pray Thee, out of Thy book which Thou hast written" (Exodus 32:32). Of course we know that God could never honor such a request any more than He could honor a similar desire in the heart of the Apostle Paul (Romans 9:3). The blotting out of any name involves eternal death (Revelation 20:15), while the preservation of that name in the book of life is said by our Lord to be of the highest importance (Luke 10:20). Now since the blotting out of a name involves eternal death, dare we assume that all Christians, except those on a preferred list who supposedly overcome in this life, lose their salvation and suffer eternal death? I am certain that this could not be so.

There are names in that book now which will not be there at the final opening of it. Those whose names will be missing never were saved. Each individual must determine for himself whether or not his name remains in the book of life. This is just as true of the Jew as it is of the Gentile (Daniel 12:1). Christ alone, to whom all judgment is committed, will determine whose names are to be blotted out. In a Messianic Psalm we hear Him saying, "Let them be blotted out of the book of the living, and not be written with the righteous" (Psalm 69:28). What each of us does with Christ now will be the determining factor in the day of judgment. Your name is written in the book of life. Will you receive Christ at once and thereby see to it that your name shall never be blotted out? And if you reject Him now, the day is coming when you must worship Him even though your name has been erased from the book of life (Revelation 13:8). But eternal blessedness with Him is reserved for those whose names remain written in His book of life (Revelation 21:27).

Finally, our Lord promises the overcomer, *"I will confess his name before My Father, and before His angels"* (Revelation 3:5). In addition to not removing the names of all the redeemed, Christ promises to confess their names before His Father. This very promise our Lord stated clearly when He was here on the earth (Matthew 10:32; Luke 12:8). Great will be the difference between the names Jesus will confess and some of the names made famous in this world. But we may be certain that He will be forever true to the man who confesses Him.

VI. THE PROMISE TO PHILADELPHIA (3:12)

Him that overcometh will I make a pillar in the temple of My God, and he shall go no more out: and I will write upon him the name of My God, and the name of the city of My God, which is new Jerusalem, which cometh down out of heaven from My God: and I will write upon him My new name (Revelation 3:12).

The promises to Philadelphia are more numerous than those to the other churches. To the people in this church there is only commendation; there is no accusation, hence there is nothing in particular mentioned that they must overcome. Ephesus had left its first love. Smyrna was being persecuted. Pergamos was worldly. Thyatira was unequally yoked with Jezebel. Sardis had a name to live by but was dead. What then do they overcome in Philadelphia? The promise might serve as a warning to any mere professors in that assembly since it is offered only to the overcomers who are the genuine believers.

The overcomers, Jesus says, *"Will I make a pillar in the temple of My God."* In Solomon's temple there were two pillars. The right pillar was called Jachin, which means "He shall establish." The left pillar was called Boaz, which means "He is my strength" (1 Kings 7:15-22). This was a fitting promise to the Philadelphia overcomer. In Philadelphia he had but a "little strength." In Heaven he shall be established and made a pillar of strength. Some of God's children have only a little strength and are not too well established here on earth. But, thank God, in Heaven all of God's children will be made pillars—stable, strong, established. Nothing will shake us there, not even a Samson. Here we often fail to abide in God's presence, but in Heaven we *"shall go no more out."* Some so-called pillars in our churches today are not very steady or permanent. Peter, James, and John seemed to be pillars in the early church (Galatians 2:9). I suppose they were more firm and fixed than are some pillars in the twentieth-century church. Be that as it may, in Heaven we all will be firmly rooted forever in Him, our blessed Lord and Saviour.

Some will say that this promise could be only for some specially distinguished ones. W. Hoste says that this might have weight if pillars in the Scriptures usually meant the support of a fabric, instead of a trophy or witness, like Jacob's four pillars, or the brazen pillars, Boaz and Jachin, which supported nothing, but bore perpetual witness to the power and faithfulness of Jehovah. All the people of God will be pillars in His temple, perpetual witnesses to what grace can do.

Christ continues:

> *And I will write upon him the name of My God, and the name of the city of My God.*

In Heaven all the redeemed will be openly associated with God and with the heavenly Jerusalem. In order that all would know that the Israelites were God's people, God said to Moses, "And they shall put My name upon the children of Israel" (Numbers 6:27). It is the same idea here. When the redeemed come back to earth to reign with Christ, all who are in the earth will know them, for each shall bear both the name of God and the fact that he is a citizen of Heaven. I do not question that too often we fail to bear His name here on earth, and by our failure the unsaved do not know we are citizens of Heaven. We have at times been ashamed to speak His name, afraid to identify ourselves with Him, embarrassed into silence when we should have witnessed of Him.

And then Christ concludes:

And I will write upon him My new name.

We will be identified with the Saviour who bought us. Why this would be true of only some of the saints is not clear. Our Lord did not write a book during His earthly sojourn, but in Heaven He will write upon each of the redeemed His new name. This name will not be "Jesus" (Matthew 1:21), nor the scores of other names and titles by which He is identified in the Scriptures, but a new name. Thus every one in Heaven will be a table of testimony. Then when we return to earth for the millennial reign, we will be known and read of all men. This is the prospect for all who are in Christ. We shall all share with Him in His kingdom and glory, for His new name will be "KING OF KINGS AND LORD OF LORDS" (Revelation 19:16).

VII. THE PROMISE TO LAODICEA (3:21)

To him that overcometh will I grant to sit with Me in My throne, even as I also overcame, and am set down with My Father in His throne (3:21).

In one respect this promise exceeds all the rest. A throne is the symbol of authority and conquest. The promise Christ gave to the twelve in Matthew 19:28 now becomes a blessed reality to all the redeemed. As Christ shared the Father's throne, both before His incarnation in eternity past (John 17:5), and after His ascension (Revelation 3:21), so the Christian will share Christ's throne in the coming manifestation of His kingdom. Dare we assume that association with Christ in His kingdom is for some of the redeemed only and not for all? We dare not assume any such thing because there is no scriptural authority for it. This promise is not given to those who successfully struggle to the end; it is assured every one who has been born again into that kingdom. In that day Christ's prayer will be answered, namely, that all believers may be one (John 17:21). The throne of Christ will be shared with all His followers.

How did Christ overcome? In many ways and at various times, but more specifically when He was tempted of the devil in the wilderness. "Again, the devil taketh Him up into an exceeding high mountain, and sheweth Him all the kingdoms of the world, and the glory of them; and saith unto Him, All these things will I give Thee, if Thou wilt fall down and worship me. Then saith Jesus unto him, Get thee hence, Satan: for it is written, Thou shalt worship the Lord thy God, and Him only shalt thou serve" (Matthew 4:8-10). Satan was showing our Lord an easy way to get the kingdom of this world without the Cross, without the suffering and crucifixion. But He overcame Satan and death and the grave, and sat down with His Father in His throne. Now all believers are made kings unto God (Revelation 1:6; 5:10), and will therefore reign with Christ when He establishes His throne (Revelation 20:6). These are royal prerogatives reserved for all saints. The end of our salvation is not to sit on clouds and play harps. When Christ sits on the throne of His glory (Matthew 25:31), then shall we sit on thrones and rule with Him (Luke 22:29-30). Our rights to that throne are blood rights (Revelation 1:5-6).

These promises to the overcomers form the fullest description to be found in all the Word of God of those things which God has prepared for His redeemed ones. They open to us the bright prospects of the life to come for all the saved. "He that overcometh shall inherit all things" (Revelation 21:7), a statement set in contrast, not with failing Christians, but with the "unbelieving" who "shall have their part in the lake which burneth with fire and brimstone: which is the second death" (Revelation 21:8). Let all who read these words and who have not yet yielded to Jesus Christ, receive Him at once. The dispensation of grace is coming to a close. Do not delay your decision to believe on the Lord Jesus Christ and be saved.

THE THRONE IN HEAVEN

Revelation 4:1-11

The third section of this book commences with chapter four. The seven letters in chapters two and three sketched the prophetic history of the Church on earth. We have seen that the local assemblies had in them many who were mere professors, and that as the Church Age ran its course, there was a growing apostasy and defection from the faith. With the passing of time Christendom has become increasingly corrupt doctrinally. The world has not gotten better, but worse. And all the while God has kept busy with His program of calling out "a people for His name" (Acts 15:14). One by one He has been adding to His true Church as many as would believe on Christ and receive Him.

At this point we should be reminded of the threefold division of the book as it appears in 1:19:

"The things which thou hast seen"—the vision of the glorified Christ in chapter 1.

"The things which are"—the history of the Church on earth prewritten from Pentecost to the Rapture as seen in the letters to the seven churches in chapters 2 and 3.

"The things which shall be hereafter"—the future events to take place after the true Church has been taken out of the earth as set forth in chapters 4 through 22.

From 4:1 to the end of the book all the events follow the rapture of the Church. By this time God will have completed His Church and the Church will have completed her mission on earth. In fact, the word "church" does not appear again in the book until the end, where the glorified Lord speaks to the churches (22:16). We are now living somewhere toward the close of the second period designated by the phrase, *"the things which are,"* awaiting our Lord's coming to rapture the Church to Himself. Thus we are about to view the thrilling panorama of wonders which are to take place after the Church's mission on earth has ended and she is caught up to be with Christ, *"things which must be hereafter."* If we miss this divine division of the book we have lost the key to its understanding.

The key word in chapter 4 is "throne." It appears twelve times in these eleven verses and not less than thirty-seven times in the entire book. The book commences with a "throne" (1:4) and concludes with a "throne" (22:3). Revelation is the "throne book" of the Bible. Thrones often speak of judgment, and in the chapters we are about to study, there are divinely inspired prophecies of coming judgments upon the wicked living and the wicked dead. At no time has God vacated His throne. He has never relinquished His sovereignty and majesty, thus we are reminded of God's power and authority of which the throne is a symbol. "The LORD hath prepared His throne in the heavens; and His kingdom ruleth over all" (Psalm 103:19). Presently, during this Age of Grace, God's throne is one of grace and mercy where sinners and saints may come boldly to "obtain mercy, and find grace to help in time of need" (Hebrews 4:16). But the throne in Revelation 4 appears after the rapture of the saints, when the present dispensation has ended and a new dispensation of judgment has begun.

> *After this I looked, and, behold, a door was opened in heaven: and the first voice which I heard was as it were of a trumpet talking with me; which said, Come up hither, and I will shew thee things which must be hereafter* (4:1).

What is the significance of the door opened in Heaven? A door is an opening through which one may pass from one place to another. The Bible tells us that there is only one door into Heaven. Our Lord Jesus said, "I am the door: by Me if any man enter in, he shall be saved, and shall go in and out, and find pasture" (John 10:9). He only is the way of access to

God. As sinners alienated from God we have no access except through Christ. Remember, there are not two or more doors, but one. The open door in Heaven that John saw was Christ's final call to all the redeemed, both dead and alive, to enter Heaven.

This is the fourth time the word "door" is used in Revelation. It first appears in the letter to the church at Philadelphia where our Lord said, "I have set before thee an open door, and no man can shut it" (3:8). This is the open door for a gospel witness. The second door occurs in the letter to the church at Laodicea where Christ says, "Behold, I stand at the door, and knock" (3:20). The third appearance of the word "door" is in this same verse where He says, "If any man hear My voice, and open the door, I will come in to him, and will sup with him, and he with Me" (3:20). Here we see the closed door of the human heart. While the door remains open for gospel preaching and Bible teaching, Christ stands at the door of the individual's heart, knocking and asking to be admitted. Many continue refusing to let Him enter, while a few, who recognize their lost and sinful state, receive Him. But at the close of this present age, when the last soul has received Him, He will open the door into Heaven and call His own to their heavenly home which He has been preparing for them that love Him (John 14:1-3). It is this great event to which we give attention now.

But I must remind the unsaved reader of these lines that you are in grave danger. The present Age of Grace could come to an end at any moment. If you have not received Christ, you have chosen to be lost forever. Open the door of your heart to Him, and He will open the door of Heaven to you.

The apostle writes what he heard through the open door.

> *The first voice which I heard was as it were of a trumpet talking with me; which said, Come up hither, and I will shew thee things which must be hereafter* (4:1).

I see in these words one of the briefest yet one of the clearest statements on the rapture of the Church. It is symbolic of the fulfillment of the believer's "blessed hope." Our Lord promised that He would keep His own from the hour of trial that is to come upon the whole world (3:10). Thus we see in the Apostle John a representative figure of those who will be "caught up" to meet the Lord in the air and be with Him forever.

John said the voice of the Lord *"was as it were of a trumpet."* This is the same trumpet voice which Paul described in his divinely inspired prediction of the Rapture. "Behold, I shew you a mystery; We shall not all sleep, but we shall all be changed, In a moment, in the twinkling of an eye, at the last trump: for the trumpet shall sound, and the dead shall be raised incorruptible, and we shall be changed" (1 Corinthians 15:51-52). This will be the last trumpet sound of the present dispensation of grace calling up both those who have died in Christ and those in Him who are alive at that time. This will not be the last trumpet in point of time. Seven trumpets more are to be sounded after the Church is caught up to Heaven, but these are trumpets of judgment sounded by angels (Revelation 8:7,8,10,12; 9:1,13; 11:15). This is a trumpet of blessing sounded by God before judgment is poured out on the earth (1 Thessalonians 4:16-17). As the trumpet voice summoned John to Heaven, so we await its sound calling us to that meeting in the air. Symbolically, then, this open door in Heaven is to permit the saints to enter.

I will shew thee things which must be hereafter (4:1).

Heaven is the vantage point of all true and accurate prophecy, the only safe place of vision. Men may make predictions of events which are to take place on the earth, but if those predictions are not from God's point of view, they are not to be trusted. Man tells us the world is getting better; God says it will become increasingly worse. Man says that peace among nations is close at hand; God says there will be wars and rumors of wars, nation fighting against nation. Man predicts that in years to come he will have won the battle against disease, famine, and hardship; God says there is to be a fearful looking forward to judgments of disease, famine, and hardship.

We do not wonder that modern ministers shun the book of the Revelation. They will not face the fact of coming judgment upon the world. They lull people to sleep with false utopian theories and remain silent about the real issues. If we are to see future things we must know the plans and counsels of God, and these are laid in Heaven. The things that are to transpire on earth have their hidden source in the secret chambers of Heaven. From John's viewpoint on Patmos the picture is dark for the Church and bright for the world which hates her and her Lord. But when John is able to see things from God's point of view, the picture is changed radically. He sees the true Church caught up to Heaven, God is on His eternal throne, and manifestations of divine wrath are in store for the earth dwellers who have rejected His Son. The words *"after this"* and *"hereafter"* make it clear that what follows is to take place on the earth after the Church Age has run its course. Let us not be occupied with prophecy from an earthly viewpoint but from Heaven's vantage point.

The apostle writes, *"And immediately I was in the spirit"* (4:2). The translation of John from earth to Heaven was *"immediately"* (at once). Even so will the rapture of the Church take place at once, "in a moment, in the twinkling of an eye" (1 Corinthians 15:52). Other men before John had gone into Heaven. There were Enoch (Genesis 5:24), Elijah (2 Kings 2:11), and Paul (2 Corinthians 12:1-5), but they tell us nothing of what they saw. There is no throne and Him that sat upon it flashing back through the open door. There is no vision of the occupants there. But with John all is different. What he heard and saw he is told to write for the blessing of the whole Church.

He adds, *"I was in the spirit."* Some men say that to be consistent we must interpret this expression with the identical expression in 1:10. I would not say as much. There is much more to be considered here in chapter 4. John is summoned by the Lord to *"come up hither."* Actually what happened was that his spirit was projected from his body and caught up to Heaven. In some mysterious and miraculous way, John was instantaneously translated from Patmos to the third Heaven, the abode of Almighty God.

I. THE PERSON "ON THE THRONE" (4:2-3)

> *And immediately I was in the spirit: and, behold, a throne was set in heaven, and one sat on the throne. And He that sat was to look upon like a jasper and a sardine stone: and there was a rainbow round about the throne, in sight like unto an emerald* (4:2-3).

Among His last words to the church at Laodicea, Christ refers to His throne and His Father's throne (3:21). Which, if either, did John see in chapter four? I am not certain that he saw either of these. Seiss points out that the throne was being set as John was looking. He says, "The expression is in a tense which denotes unfinished action, reaching its completion at the time of the seeing. This is exactly what the original expresses. The passage is an exact parallel, both as to subject and phraseology, to Daniel 7:9, where the prophet says: 'I beheld till the thrones were set (not *cast down,* as our version has it), and the Ancient of days did sit. . . . His throne was like the fiery flame.'" That which is eternal cannot be placed in position or be set at any given time. The throne in John's vision is temporal and moveable. The vision included the placing of the throne as well as the throne itself.

The Sitter upon the throne is not named. And it will be difficult for me to attempt an identification of just which Person in the Godhead is the occupant on this throne. Seiss says that here is "the unnameable, indescribable Godhead, in which Father, Son, and Holy Ghost are consubstantial, and the same." We do know that His appearance was *"like a jasper and a sardine stone,"* not as to shape, for Deity does not take on any particular shape, but in the brilliance and glory of the splendor of God. The language is symbolic, *"like* a jasper and sardine stone." Both stones are found in the breastplate of the Jewish high priest (Exodus 28:17-20), and in the New Jerusalm which descends from God out of Heaven (Revelation 21:10,11,19-20). I cannot say more than that these stones are divinely chosen as being emblematic of God's glory as displayed in His righteous government. They are precious stones which speak of what the triune God is.

II. THE PLEDGE "ROUND ABOUT THE THRONE" (4:3)

And there was a rainbow round about the throne, in sight like unto an emerald (4:3).

When we view a rainbow from earth, we see only a semi-circle, a reminder of the pledge God made to Noah that He would never again destroy the earth by water (Genesis 9:11-17). The rainbow from Heaven's viewpoint is a complete circle, not broken by the line of the horizon as it is when seen from the earth. The gorgeous green, the blend of the colors of the spectrum, is suggestive of promise and hope. However, the hope is not for the earth, because the day of judgment has come. God has another covenant with His Son, and He is about to fulfill it. He promised that one day the earth would be Christ's "footstool," a word denoting that which is under one's feet, or that which is in subjection to someone (Psalm 110:1 cf. Acts 2:34-35; Hebrews 1:13; 10:13). For God's children, the storm is over, since Christ bore the judgment for all their sins. The sun hid in darkness when Christ, the mighty Maker, died for man the creature's sin. But the throne in Heaven is encircled as the pledge of God's faithfulness. He is about to begin judgment against all who have rejected His Son, thereby preparing the earth for Christ's reign.

III. THE PERSONS "ROUND ABOUT THE THRONE" (4:4)

And round about the throne were four and twenty seats: and upon the seats I saw four and twenty elders sitting, clothed in white raiment; and they had on their heads crowns of gold (4:4).

The word "seats" is the same word in the Greek translated "throne," so that actually there were twenty-four thrones. In the center there was the majestic throne of Deity, and in a circle around it were twenty-four other thrones, or royal seats.

Who are these favored ones occupying the regal seats in Heaven? They are a royal and priestly company. We know they are not angels, but human beings, for the song they sing shows them to be redeemed ones. "And they sung a new song, saying, Thou art worthy to take the book, and to open the seals thereof: for Thou wast slain, and hast *redeemed* us to God by Thy blood out of every kindred, and tongue, and people, and nation" (Revelation 5:9). The fact that they give honor to Christ for redeeming them shows that they are redeemed sinners gathered from every part of the earth. Their association with Deity is a royal one. Actually they are reigning with Christ even as Paul wrote to Timothy (2 Timothy 2:12).

But why are there twenty-four? H. A. Ironside writes: "I do not think we need be in any doubt as to their identity if we compare Scripture with Scripture. . . . In 1 Chronicles 24, we read of something very similar. . . . Twenty-four elders were appointed by King David to represent the entire Levitical priesthood. He divided the priests into twenty-four courses, each course to serve for two weeks at a time in the temple which Solomon was to build. The same arrangement was in force when our Lord's forerunner was announced. Zacharias was 'of the course of Abia,' the eighth in order (Luke 1:5). The priests were many thousands in number. They could not all come together at one time, but *when the twenty-four elders met* in the temple precincts in Jerusalem, the *whole priestly house* was represented. And this is the explanation, I submit, of the symbol here. The elders in Heaven represent the whole heavenly priesthood—that is, all the redeemed who have died in the past, or who shall be living at the Lord's return. . . . The Church of the present age and Old Testament saints are alike included. All are priests. All worship. There were twelve patriarchs in Israel, and twelve apostles introducing the new dispensation. The two together would give the complete four and twenty."

They are described as being *"clothed in white raiment; and they had on their heads crowns of gold"* (4:4). These dazzling white garments speak of perfect righteousness, "the righteousness of saints" (Revelation 19:8). The redeemed and the raptured are now with Jesus and like Jesus (1 John 3:2), fashioned like unto Him (Philippians 3:20-21), saved from the presence and possibility of sin. They are in Heaven, forever free from that constant struggle against evil which characterized their earthly sojourn.

The golden crowns on their heads disclose their royal dignity. Having been washed from their sins in Christ's blood, they have been made both "kings and priests" (Revelation 1:5-6). They are the overcomers, thus all are crowned with the royal authority common to all saints in Heaven. There have been no rewards given out as yet. John's vision here is of that which takes place after the Church is caught up into Heaven. No saints will be crowned until "that day." The Apostle Paul wrote: "I have fought a good fight, I have finished my course, I have kept the faith: Henceforth there is laid up for me a crown of righteousness, which the Lord, the righteous judge, shall give me at that day: and not to me only, but unto all them also that love His appearing" (2 Timothy 4:7-8). The expression "at that day" refers to the day of Christ's coming for His own. He says, "And, behold, I come quickly; and My reward is with Me, to give every man according as his work shall be" (Revelation 22:12).

IV. THE PROCEEDINGS FROM "OUT OF THE THRONE" (4:5)

And out of the throne proceeded lightnings and thunderings and voices: and there were seven lamps of fire burning before the throne, which are the seven Spirits of God (4:5).

Bear in mind that the throne of Deity here is the throne of judgment. There is no throne of grace because the day of grace is already past. The reason why God does not judge the world today, in spite of the prevailing wickedness, is because He is seated upon a throne of grace. But here John is given to see the day when judgment will issue forth from the throne of Deity. *"Out of the throne proceeded lightnings and thunderings and voices."* A dreadful storm is about to burst on the earth beneath. Let us say that this is Justice Day for the earth, for justice means judgment. Lightnings, thunderings, and voices are symbols of judgment. These signs appeared at the giving of the law at Sinai when God was not then dealing in grace (Exodus 19:16). They will appear again when the present day of grace is past (Revelation 8:5; 10:3; 11:19; 16:18).

V. THE PORTRAYAL "BEFORE THE THRONE" (4:5)

And there were seven lamps of fire burning before the throne, which are the seven Spirits of God (4:5).

The number seven has been used characteristically of the Holy Spirit (Revelation 1:4; 3:1; 5:6). These are not seven different spirits, but rather the sevenfold fullness and completeness of the Holy Spirit's omniscience and omnipotence. Here the Holy Spirit takes on His judicial character, fire being a symbol of divine judgment at the second coming of Christ to the earth with His saints (2 Thessalonians 1:7-8). This is far different from the divine fire in the present power and activity of the Holy Spirit in the Church (Acts 2:3). The Holy Spirit descended upon Jesus as a dove, but here He is "the spirit of judgment, and the spirit of burning" (Isaiah 4:4). Each member of the Holy Trinity is viewed in connection with the righteous character of the throne. Each is prepared to execute judgment.

And before the throne there was a sea of glass like unto crystal (4:6).

The laver in the tabernacle (Exodus 30:18-21), and the sea in Solomon's temple (1 Kings 7:23-27) were for priestly purification. But in Heaven the sea is solidified. In Heaven, where there is a fixed state of holiness and purity, there is no need for cleansing. Heaven is the place of perfection. There the saints will have entered into perfect sanctification. The backslidings of the heart and the failures of the flesh are forever past.

VI. THE PRAISE "IN THE MIDST OF THE THRONE" (4:6-11)

John saw *"four beasts full of eyes before and behind"* (4:6). The Greek word for "beast" is *zōon,* and is translated "living creature," as in the Revised Version. It appears at least twenty times in the book of Revelation. These living creatures are created beings. They are full of eyes before and behind, able to see all things with accuracy.

They must be regarded as mere symbols as the language indicates. "The first . . . was *like* a lion, and the second . . . *like* a calf, and the third . . . had a face *as* a man, and the fourth . . . *like* a flying eagle" (4:7). Like the twenty-four elders, they were redeemed by Christ's blood, so then they must have been at one time a part of the fallen race of man. Their representations of the animal creation might indicate the dominion given to man over the animal world. Judging from what is said of them in later passages, they seem to be administrators of divine government and authority. They stand ready to render service to God in any part of the universe. They possess strength like the lion, they render service like the ox, they possess intelligence as does man, and they are swift like the eagle. Now I am not going to add to the confusion which already exists as to precisely who these living creatures are and what they represent. It is not wise to go beyond that which the Bible teaches. I have examined thirty-nine different commentaries on this passage, and they leave me convinced that many of the brethren have engaged in mere speculation and fanciful interpretation.

We come now to the most important aspect of the six verses under consideration, namely, the praise ascribed to God by these living creatures.

> *They rest not day and night, saying, Holy, holy, holy, Lord God Almighty, which was, and is, and is to come* (4:8).

The praise is increasing. It reveals the nature of the thrice-holy God: Father, Son, and Holy Spirit. This same expression of praise was offered by the seraphims in the Temple (Isaiah 6:3). These glorified beings are intimately connected with the holiness and justice of God. In the prophecy of Isaiah they sound God's praise and execute His judgment by taking the coals of fire to purge the lips of the prophet. Here they are doing the same. Before the fury of God's wrath is poured out, His holiness is magnified. It is because of His holiness that He must judge sin. We are reminded of His holiness, deity, and eternalness. The names "Lord God Almighty" [Jehovah Elohim Shaddai] suggest that God is getting ready to resume His relationship with Israel. These names were first given in connection with His chosen people.

> *And when those beasts give glory and honour and thanks to Him that sat on the throne, who liveth for ever and ever, The four and twenty elders fall down before Him that sat on the throne, and worship Him that liveth for ever and ever, and cast their crowns before the throne, saying, Thou art worthy, O Lord, to receive glory and honour and power: for Thou hast created all things, and for Thy pleasure they are and were created* (4:9-11).

At the sound of "Holy, holy, holy" coming from the four living creatures, the twenty-four elders rise from their thrones and fall before the triune God to join the ascription of praise. First, they *"worship Him."* Worship in the Scriptures has several connotations, such as obeisance, reverence, homage, honor, service. I have never found in Scripture any definition of worship. Worship is not confined to praise. W. E. Vine wrote, "Broadly it may be regarded as the direct acknowledgement to God, of His nature, attributes, ways, and claims, whether by the outgoing of the heart in praise and thanksgiving or by deed done in such acknowledgement." The first and fundamental claims of God upon His redeemed ones is that they worship Him. The devil would claim the worship of men, but God only must be worshiped (Matthew 4:9-11). How it must grieve Him when we become weak in our worship! Here on earth we rob Him of the honor, homage, and service that is due Him. But in Heaven we shall worship Him as we ought.

As part of their worship they *"cast their crowns before the throne."* They lay aside their given glory to add to His glory, thereby ascribing all glory to Him. They realize that they owe their victory to Him who sits upon the central throne, thus He alone is worthy to receive their crowns. Here on earth we want to get credit for what we do, and while it is true that crowns of reward will be given for faithfulness in service, in Heaven we will recognize that we are not worthy of them. We will lay them at the feet of Him who saved us by His matchless grace. At that day we shall admit that we were unprofitable servants, not even worthy to serve Him.

Their paean of praise concludes with the words:

> *Thou art worthy, O Lord, to receive glory and honour and power: for Thou hast created all things, and for Thy pleasure they are and were created* (4:11).

We praise God for saving us, but seldom have I heard a believer praise God for creating him. In Heaven we will know the joy of having been created. There are no songs of evolution in Heaven, only of creation. Our Saviour is the Origin and Source of all creation (John 1:3; Colossians 1:16). He caused all things and all creatures to exist. This is the reason why the elders worship Him. They acknowledge God as the Source and Sustainer of the universe and of all life.

Such were the scenes which John saw in Heaven. Our blessed Lord is worshiped as the Creator of the earth upon which He is about to pour out divine judgment. His enemies have raged against Him, but He is unmoved.

THE SEVEN-SEALED BOOK

Revelation 5:1-14

The importance of this chapter in the book of Revelation cannot be overemphasized. It contains the key to the right understanding of the rest of the book. If we err here we will be wrong the rest of the way. The scroll in the right hand of Him that sat upon the throne is the official document which determines the great crisis and climax of human history. The nations of the world hold no document in their possession as significant and accurate as this scroll. World leaders have made their plans and predictions, but they all must come to nought. We are about to see unfolded before our very eyes a detailed description of the earth's future.

The closing part of Daniel's prophecy has reference, I believe, to this seven-sealed scroll. There were details concerning the time of the end which Daniel did not understand. The prophet said, "I heard, but understood not: then said I, O my Lord, what shall be the end of these things? And He said, Go thy way, Daniel: for the words are closed up and sealed till the time of the end" (Daniel 12:8-9). The book, "closed up and sealed" by Daniel, has since been in the possession of Him who gave the message contained in it. A similar scroll is mentioned in Ezekiel 2:9-10. What is contained in the book will come before us now as the seals are broken in succession and its message disclosed. The literal unveiling of God's purposes for the world, as divinely written in the scroll, will not take place until after the Church has been taken up to be with her Lord.

Chapter 5 continues progressively in thought and detail

after chapter 4, so that there is no need for a chapter break at this point. I mention this so that we do not miss the continuity of divine revelation connected with this scene in Heaven. The outline which follows is given to assist us in correctly interpreting the message in the scroll.

I. THE SUBJECT

The *subject* of the sealed scroll is *redemption*. He who opens the scroll is the "Lamb," still bearing the scars of crucifixion. His death was the "one sacrifice for sins for ever" (Hebrews 10:12), the wounds of which still bear witness to the substitutionary feature of that death (Zechariah 13:1,6). Then, too, the *song* that is sung is one of *redemption* (5:9). The scroll, while containing a message of divine revelation pertaining to prophecy, speaks of redemption. True, redemption has its roots in the past, but its final fulfillment lies in the future. Redemption is not confined solely to our Lord's first coming to earth; it is very definitely linked with His Second Coming. When Jesus spoke to His disciples concerning those things which are to precede His Second Coming, He said, "And when these things begin to come to pass, then look up, and lift up your heads; for your *redemption* draweth nigh" (Luke 21:28). The Holy Spirit gave the Apostle Paul to see that redemption is still largely a subject pertaining to the future. He says to believers, "Ye were sealed with that Holy Spirit of promise, Which is the earnest of our inheritance until the redemption of the purchased possession" (Ephesians 1:13-14). The possession has been purchased but not yet fully redeemed. All creation groans waiting to be redeemed, "Even we ourselves groan within ourselves, waiting for the adoption, to wit, the redemption of our body" (Romans 8:22-23).

The subject of the seven-sealed scroll, then, has to do with redemption. In order to interpret the scroll we must examine the Biblical laws and customs in Israel's history as they are recorded in the Old Testament. Included in the numerous laws which God gave to His people, there was a law which dealt specifically with redemption. Three things could be redeemed:

(1) A man could sell himself into servitude, that is, if he had no money he could sell himself as a servant. However, a near kin could redeem him from his servitude (Leviticus 25:47-55). The one who redeemed him, then, was called the kinsman-redeemer.

(2) If a woman's husband died, and he left no unmarried brother to marry her, or if a living brother of the deceased man chose not to marry his brother's widow, as provided for in Deuteronomy 25:5-10, then the nearest of kin could marry her. This man was likewise a kinsman-redeemer. Boaz marrying Ruth is a case in point (Ruth 4).

(3) If a man lost his land, a near kin could buy it back, that is, redeem it, thereby keeping it in the family estate (Leviticus 25:25). The scroll on which the official transaction was recorded was rolled up and sealed, and placed in the court of the Tabernacle or Temple. These three things could be redeemed: a servant, a wife, and land.

M. R. DeHaan writes, "At this point in Revelation (chapter 5) the first two have been accomplished. The Church, the Bride of Christ, was caught up in the Rapture spoken of in Revelation 4, and we, His servants, have been fully redeemed, having received our resurrection bodies at the Rapture of the Church. But the earth and the creatures in the earth, both vegetable and animal, are still under the curse. The earth itself is still groaning under the curse of man's sin. These also must be redeemed, for Christ is the perfect Redeemer, and every realm which came under the curse of Adam's sin must also be delivered by the redemption of the Last Adam."

II. THE SCROLL

The meaning of the seven-sealed scroll is alluded to in the Old Testament. The prophet Jeremiah prophesied just prior to the invasion of Jerusalem by Nebuchadnezzar, king of Babylon. He told his people that the enemy would overthrow the city and that they would be carried away captive to Babylon. Moreover, he predicted the length of the captivity. For seventy years they would live in the concentration camps of Babylon, after which time they would be restored to their own land, to build again and possess it (Jeremiah 29:8-14; 30:3).

Jeremiah had a cousin named Hanameel who owned a piece of property. Hanameel concluded that the Babylonian invasion and subsequent captivity would render his land useless, so he was anxious to sell it at once and realize from it as much cash as possible. He conceived a plan of trying to sell it to his cousin, Jeremiah. He reasoned that if Jeremiah's prophecy came true, Nebuchadnezzar would confiscate the land.

At that time Jeremiah had been put in prison for prophesying the Babylonian invasion. As he sat in his prison cell, God told him of Hanameel's plan to visit him there to try to sell Jeremiah his farm. God told Jeremiah to buy the field so that it would be preserved for his heirs when the Jews returned. When Hanameel came to visit him and to present his proposition, the prophet asked the redemption price and agreed to buy the land. The proper court officials were called, the title deed was made out and properly sealed, thus completing the transaction. However, Jeremiah would not enter into possession of it for some time to come. But one day, when the Jews returned, that sealed scroll would be of great value. It would prove that the one who redeemed the land was entitled to possess it. Jeremiah met the conditions of a redeemer, being related to Hanameel, willing to redeem the land, and able to pay the redemption price (Jeremiah 32:6-15).

This historical incident gives meaning to the seven-sealed scroll in Revelation 5. The book that John saw in the hand of Him that sat upon the throne is the title deed to the earth. The earth and the atmosphere around it have been in the hands of an invader. The cruel usurper is Satan. He wrested it from Adam, whom God had given dominion over it (Genesis 1:26-28), so that today the earth is in Satan's power. When the devil offered to give the earth to Christ if He would bow down and worship him, our Lord did not repudiate his claim (Matthew 4:8-9). Three times our Lord called Satan "the prince of this world" (John 12:31; 14:30; 16:11). Paul calls Satan "the god of this world" (2 Corinthians 4:4), and "the prince of the power of the air" (Ephesians 2:2). John wrote, "The whole world lieth in wickedness" [or the wicked one] (1 John 5:19). The scroll that John saw is the title deed to this earth, once committed to man to rule for God, but now in the hands of Satan.

III. THE SEARCH (5:2-3)

> *And I saw a strong angel proclaiming with a loud voice, Who is worthy to open the book, and to loose the seals thereof? And no man in heaven, nor in earth, neither under the earth, was able to open the book, neither to look thereon* (5:2,3).

The strong angel's voice was heard in every place where angels and the souls of men could be found. Who is morally worthy to open this book of justice and destiny? Who qualifies to break the seals and lay claim to the earth? Who has furnished the price of redemption? Who is the rightful heir? Who is worthy to take possession of the earth and govern it in righteousness? The search was begun throughout the entire universe, *"in heaven,"* the dwelling place of God; *"in earth,"* the dwelling place of men; and *"under the earth,"* the dwelling place of other created beings, the underworld of the dead. But neither man nor angel stirred, because none had the right. Not a creature in the celestial and terrestrial universe could claim fitness to execute the designs of God in the earth.

Michael, the guardian angel of the nation of Israel, was there (Daniel 12:1), but he could not qualify. Gabriel, the evangelist, prophet, and chronologist among the angels, was there (Daniel 9:21-27; Luke 1:26-37), but he could not qualify. In addition to these were myriads of angels of various ranks, but there is no kinsman-redeemer among the angelic hosts. Someone greater than angels must be found, someone to whom these created beings must bow in subjection.

What about Adam, to whom God gave dominion over the earth? We have previously pointed out that Adam lost that dominion when he sinned, and in the Fall his entire posterity was disqualified with him. It is useless to search further, for no man from Adam's loins possesses the moral fitness and regal stature to claim the title deed to the earth. Man cannot rescue himself from his own predicament and pit of sin, thus he stands mute at the challenge to take the scroll. History has produced many claimants to world rule and supremacy, but one by one they died before each could realize his dream and desire for world power.

When will man learn that the mortgage deed of this sin-scarred earth was never signed over to him? All the efforts of all the unregenerated and unsanctified men in politics, religion, arts, sciences, philosophy, psychology, and war have forfeited any right to rule the world. Egypt, Babylon, Greece, Persia, Rome, Germany, Italy, Russia, all tried to take over the role of the kinsman-redeemer, and all fell in ignominious ruin.

No man was found worthy to open and to read the book, neither to look thereon (5:4).

IV. THE SOBBING SEER (5:4)

And I wept much, because no man was found worthy to open and to read the book, neither to look thereon (5:4).

I am not passing lightly over this verse. Nor will I trouble myself to answer the silly comments of those men who have told us that John wept because he was disappointed at not having his personal desire for this knowledge gratified. Can you imagine a glorified saint in Heaven troubling himself about something not yet revealed to him?

But how can there be weeping in Heaven? Whatever the correct answer is to this question, it certainly is not revealed fully in the Scriptures. John wept because no man was found worthy to open the scroll, and I only assume that the scroll, unlifted and unopened, brought forth from God's servant tears of concern and compassion over an inheritance unredeemed. Little wonder he gave way to grief, and tears flooded his eyes! Present-day Christianity seems to show little concern over the very thing which caused John to weep. John knew that the finding of a redeemer and the opening of the scroll was necessary before many prophecies of the Old Testament could be fulfilled. There remained to be fulfilled the retribution of the wicked, the restoration of Israel to Palestine, and the reign of Christ over all the earth. These and other prophecies could not be fulfilled as long as the scroll remained sealed.

There was a time in the life and ministry of our Lord when He wept. John wept, and so he might. Jeremiah wept over the fallen city of Jerusalem. When did you and I weep over a world in spiritual darkness, from which men are passing one by one into an eternal eclipse, where there is weeping and wailing and gnashing of teeth? John wept audibly, not because of any weakness, but because of deep concern. Someone has said, "Without tears the Revelation was not written; neither without tears can it be understood."

V. THE SLAIN LAMB (5:5-7)

And one of the elders saith unto me, Weep not: behold, the Lion of the tribe of Juda, and Root of David, hath prevailed to open the book, and to loose the seven seals thereof. And I beheld, and, lo, in the midst of the throne and of the four beasts, and in the midst of the elders, stood a Lamb as it had been slain, having seven horns and seven eyes, which are the seven Spirits of God sent forth into all the earth. And He came and took the book out of the right hand of Him that sat upon the throne (5:5-7).

The sobbing seer is consoled by one of the elders who assures him that One was present to open the sealed scroll and carry out the divine counsels in the earth. Once again the central figure of the book is brought into view. He is the triumphant Christ. John ceased his sobbing to behold Him, the Kinsman-Redeemer who held the crown rights to rule sovereignly over the earth. The hour of Christ's triumph had come.

Christ is described here as *"the Lion of the tribe of Juda."* Dying Jacob uttered the first prophecy which thus describes Him (Genesis 49:8-10). There can be no mistaking who He is. He can be traced throughout the whole of divine revelation. He is the Seed of the woman (Genesis 3:15 cf. Galatians 4:4); of the line of Shem (Genesis 9:26); the seed of Abraham

(Genesis 12:1-3 cf. Galatians 3:7-8,19); of the tribe of Judah (Genesis 49:10). There He stood in the courts of Heaven ready to fulfill the remaining unfulfilled prophecies pertaining to the earth. "Our Lord sprang out of Juda" (Hebrews 7:14), and now as Judah's Lion, which speaks to us of Christ's kingly character, He rises from His throne to rule and reign over the earth. He has every right to open the sealed scroll.

Christ is described further as *"the Root of David."* This identity strengthens His claim to be heir. It was prophesied that Israel's King was to be of the house of David (2 Samuel 7:12-16; Isaiah 11:1-9). He is not only David's greater Son but David's Lord (Matthew 22:41-46 cf. Psalm 110:1). He was the origin and creator of David (Revelation 22:16). He was born in the city of David (Luke 2:11), and before His Birth the angel said, "He shall be great, and shall be called the Son of the Highest: and the Lord God shall give unto Him the throne of His father David: And He shall reign over the house of Jacob for ever; and of His kingdom there shall be no end" (Luke 1:32-33). Most certainly He qualifies to open the seals and claim the title deed to the earth.

And I beheld, and, lo, in the midst of the throne and of the four beasts, and in the midst of the elders, stood a Lamb as it had been slain, having seven horns and seven eyes, which are the seven Spirits of God sent forth into all the earth. And He came and took the book out of the right hand of Him that sat upon the throne (5:6-7).

John turned to see the Lion, but instead he saw a Lamb as it had been slain. The first thing demanding attention is that the Lamb is the central object in Heaven. There is no mistaking the identity of the Lamb. He still bears the death wounds in His body. He is the Lamb of God who takes away the sin of the world (John 1:29), the only acceptable sacrifice for man's redemption (1 Peter 1:18-19). The Lamb that speaks of meekness and sacrifice is He who is about to go forth as the mighty Conqueror of all the earth. John recognized Him at once for he was near the cross to watch Christ die. After Jesus came forth from the tomb He showed the nailprints to His disciples

(Luke 24:40), and again later He displayed those wounds for the benefit of Thomas (John 20:24-28). When we get to Heaven we too will recognize Him, for on His body will still be those marks inflicted upon Him for our redemption. And after the seal judgments are poured out upon the earth and Christ comes back with His redeemed ones to reign, Israel shall recognize Him by those same wounds (Zechariah 13:6), and worship Him as the Lamb of Isaiah's prophecy (Isaiah chapter 53).

If these two symbols, the Lion and the Lamb, seem to be incongruous, I remind you that they do not conflict, but rather complement each other. Christ is about to present Himself as both the Redeemer and the Reigning One. As the Lamb He has the right to claim what He, the Kinsman-Redeemer, has purchased. As the Lion He will go forth, clothed with power and majesty, to overcome all who oppose Him. The rejected One is about to come forth in might and triumph. John saw Him standing. When Christ ascended after His Resurrection, He "sat down" (Hebrews 1:3). But in that day He shall rise to return to the earth which rejected Him. Yes, Christ is standing, alive, upon His feet, in a body recognizable to those who saw Him when He came to earth the first time. There He stands, the Lamb and the Lion, the One who is both Saviour and Sovereign. At present Christ sits with the Father (Ephesians 1:20; Revelation 3:21), but He shall stand again to claim His inheritance in the earth.

When John saw Him He had *"seven horns and seven eyes, which are the seven Spirits of God sent forth into all the earth."* Here again we have the number seven denoting fullness, completion, perfection. The horn stands for authority and imperial power (Deuteronomy 33:17; 1 Samuel 2:10; Psalm 75:10; 89:17,24; Zechariah 1:18-19). Christ possesses it (Matthew 28:18), and now He steps forth to exercise it, perfectly equipped to put down any opposition to His kingdom.

The eyes stand for perception. Christ possesses the essential attributes of deity: power and perception; omnipotence and omniscience. When He exercises His kingly right over the nations of the earth, He shall do so with full authority and full knowledge. He will have the enduement of the Holy Spirit in the plenitude of His power and perception. Three grand qualities, then, are brought before us, qualities of the Kinsman-Redeemer. First, perfection in the Lamb without spot or blemish; secondly, power in the Lion of the Tribe of Judah; thirdly, perception in the Lord of all knowledge and wisdom.

VI. THE SINGERS (5:8-10)

And when He had taken the book, the four beasts and four and twenty elders fell down before the Lamb, having every one of them harps, and golden vials full of odours, which are the prayers of saints. And they sung a new song, saying, Thou art worthy to take the book, and to open the seals thereof: for Thou wast slain, and hast redeemed us to God by Thy blood out of every kindred, and tongue, and people, and nation (5:8-10).

When the Lamb with the death wounds in His body stood up, turned to the throne of Him who held the book in His right hand, and took the book, every redeemed person—millions of them—burst into a song that never had been sung before. This act of the Lion-Lamb guaranteed the subjection of this wicked earth including Babylon, Antichrist, the dragon, and the host of others who spurned the love of God as it was shown in the sacrifice of the Lord Jesus Christ. Because He died the death of the Cross to pay the debt of sin, Christ had every right to take the book and thus complete the work of redemption by rescuing this forfeited earth from the dominion of the devil. He can claim the title deed because He both created the world and redeemed it. Little wonder all the redeemed of all ages took their harps and played and sang the praises of the Redeemer! The odor of this united praise to the Lamb filled Heaven with a sweet fragrance.

The praise and worship of the singers is pure. It is unlike that which goes by the name of worship in many Sunday morning church services. In Heaven all pretense and make-believe will be done away forever. In that day we shall be perfect, like Him whose praises we shall sing. I have no idea what the language will be like, but I know that the singing will be in unison in a language of Heaven that we all will understand. One day I shall be in the company of a great multitude gathered out of every nation in the earth, and together we shall praise the Lamb who redeemed us by His blood. The first expression of praise in Heaven was on the ground of creation (Revelation 4:11), but this song celebrates the glorious work of redemption. It is a worship service unprecedented in all history.

There is nothing of self-praise in this worship. The worshipers recognize that they have been redeemed. Here we see grace reigning. "Thou hast *made us* unto our God kings and priests." On earth the unsaved proudly feel they should do something in order to become saved. And even among Christians there are some who like to receive credit for their faith. But in Heaven all glory goes to the Lamb, for what we are He has "made us." Actually we know this now, and from time to time we testify, "By the grace of God I am what I am" (1 Corinthians 15:10). But here on earth the old nature tends to be proud. At times we speak of our accomplishments, and we proudly listen when we hear someone else speak of them. In Heaven there will be none of this. Without exception, every redeemed heart in Heaven and every redeemed tongue will join in the song.

And hast made us unto our God kings and priests (5:10).

Every redeemed soul becomes a part of God's kingdom in a royal and reigning way. In that day we will not be subjects of the kingdom, but reigning ones with the King of kings (Revelation 1:6; 2:26-27; 3:21; 20:4-6). Jesus promised His own that they would share with Him in the day of His rule over the earth (Matthew 19:28; Luke 22:28-29). Paul also said that those who persevere with Christ "shall reign with Him" (2 Timothy 2:12). The role of the redeemed during the millennium is a regal one.

Then, too, we are made *"priests."* The Apostle Peter said that we are "an holy priesthood" (1 Peter 2:5), "a royal priesthood" (1 Peter 2:9). These are weighty words telling us that all true believers are holy and royal priests. It is not that we are going to be such, but that we are such. This is what

Christ has "made us." Does this sound strange to you? Well, it is true. And do you know the function of a priest? It is "to offer up spiritual sacrifices" (1 Peter 2:5) and "shew forth the praises of Him who hath called you out of darkness into His marvellous light" (1 Peter 2:9). Spiritual sacrifices may take on the form of praise (Hebrews 13:15), material substance (Philippians 4:18; Hebrews 13:16), of the sacrifice of ourselves (Romans 12:1-2). Such sacrifices are said to be "acceptable" to God.

Believers in this dispensation are king-priests. In the Levitical priesthood men were priests only. We are both. As priests we worship in the immediate presence of God; as kings we shall come forth with Him to rule in the earth. This dual role was promised to Israel (Exodus 19:6), but Israel rejected the Chief Cornerstone, and now in Christ believers share both. As holy priests we draw nigh to God in the blessed occupation of praising Him continually; as royal priests we go forth with Him to show forth His virtues.

VII. THE SEVENFOLD DOXOLOGY (5:11-14)

And I beheld, and I heard the voice of many angels round about the throne and the beasts and the elders: and the number of them was ten thousand times ten thousand, and thousands of thousands; Saying with a loud voice, Worthy is the Lamb that was slain to receive power, and riches, and wisdom, and strength, and honour, and glory, and blessing. And every creature which is in heaven, and on the earth, and under the earth, and such as are in the sea, and all that are in them, heard I saying, Blessing, and honour, and glory, and power, be unto Him that sitteth upon the throne, and unto the Lamb for ever and ever. And the four beasts said, Amen. And the four and twenty elders fell down and worshipped Him that liveth for ever and ever (5:11-14).

And now the unnumbered angelic hosts of Heaven join the living creatures and the elders in adoring the Lamb with the death wounds in His body. You will notice that the angels are not singing. We hear much about angels singing, but the Bible does not tell us that they sing. I know of only one place in Scripture where angels are said to sing; it was at the time of creation, "When the morning stars sang together, and all the sons of God shouted for joy" (Job 38:7). The morning stars here are angels, but their song was silenced when sin entered and spoiled the beauty of the original creation. From that time we never again hear of angels singing. Angels speak, as did a host of them at Christ's birth, saying, "Glory to God in the highest, and on earth peace, good will toward men" (Luke 2:14). Now in Heaven John saw and heard them praising the Lamb, but not with singing. At last the Man of Calvary receives universal acclaim.

Two words, *"worthy"* and *"worshipped"* command attention. These words are closely related. Harold Wildish says that worship here is the worthyship of Christ to receive from men and angels this sevenfold doxology.

"Power." Jesus said, "All power is given unto Me in heaven and in earth" (Matthew 28:18). He demonstrated His power in creation (Colossians 1:16); in maintaining an orderly universe (Colossians 1:17; Hebrews 1:3); over demons (Mark 5:1-20); over disease (Mark 5:25-29), and over death (Mark 5:35-43). In Heaven all men and angels yield to His authority. Are we willing to do so now? He is worthy!

"Riches." The Bible says, "He was rich" (2 Corinthians 8:9). And why shouldn't He be, inasmuch as He created all things? "The silver is mine, and the gold is mine, saith the Lord of hosts" (Haggai 2:8). Many a man has learned that he possesses only what he has received, and that "the Lord gave, and the Lord hath taken away" (Job 1:21). "We brought nothing into this world" (1 Timothy 6:7). It is "the living God, who giveth us richly all things to enjoy" (1 Timothy 6:17). In Heaven all men and angels lay their resources at His feet. Are we willing to do so now? He is worthy!

"Wisdom." As I write, word has just been received that the United States has successfully sent her second astronaut into orbit and returned him to earth safely. We boast knowledge and wisdom as we make progress in scientific research, and yet man but discovers what Christ has Himself created. We Christians

know that Christ is made unto us wisdom (1 Corinthians 1:30). Hardly a day goes by without our having to turn to Him for wisdom, and we know that He always gives it to us liberally (James 1:5). In Heaven all wisdom is attributed to Him. Have we yielded our minds to Him now? He is worthy!

"Strength." When He comes to earth the second time it will be as "the King of glory, the LORD strong and mighty" (Psalm 24:8). Satan is strong but Christ is able to bind him (Matthew 12:29) and He will bind him (Revelation 20:2). None but Christ can break the chains of the devil (Luke 8:26-36). He is the Lion of the tribe of Judah. In Heaven all men and angels acknowledge Him as the source of their strength. Do we? Have we laid our physical resources at His feet? He is worthy!

"Honour." Christ is honored in Heaven but dishonored on earth. In Heaven He is praised while on earth He is blasphemed. He is crowned with honor (Psalm 8:5 cf. Hebrews 2:7,9) and clothed with honor (Psalm 104:1). If we are going to give honor to whom honor is due (Romans 13:7) we must turn to Christ and acknowledge Him. In Heaven all men and angels honor Him. Have we? He is worthy! He says, "Them that honour Me I will honour" (1 Samuel 2:30).

"Glory." We are so self-opinionated that the glory which is due to our Lord we take to ourselves. Paul could say, "Not I, but Christ" (Galatians 2:20). When our Lord was here on earth the divine glory was exhibited both in His character and in His acts (John 1:14; 2:11; 11:4,40; 17:5,24). In Heaven all men and angels think more highly of Him than they do of themselves or of each other. Do we ascribe all glory to the Lamb as we will do in Immanuel's land? He is worthy!

"Blessing." To bless means to make happy. Is He happy with every area of our lives? The Psalmist called upon the whole man to make Him happy when he said, "Bless the LORD, O my soul: and all that is within me, bless His holy name. Bless the LORD, O my soul, and forget not all His benefits" (Psalm 103:1-2). Have you ever spent one whole day just concentrating on making the Lord Jesus happy? In Heaven men and angels do this. And the day is coming when "Every creature which is in heaven, and on the earth, and under the earth, and such as

are in the sea, and all that are in them, heard I saying, Blessing, and honour, and glory, and power, be unto Him that sitteth upon the throne, and unto the Lamb for ever and ever" (Revelation 5:13).

To such worship the four living creatures said, "Amen." Is the Lamb the object of our adoration? Do our hearts respond with a ready "Amen"? I consider this page on which Revelation chapter 5 is printed to be one of the most precious in my Bible. I cannot read it and remain silent. I find myself saying "Amen and amen." We should be on our faces with our hearts overflowing with unspeakable adoration for the Lamb. He is worthy!

THE LAMB OPENS THE SEALS

Revelation 6:1-17

The main action of the book of Revelation begins with chapter six. From this point on, as the seals of the book of destiny are opened, the judgment period for the earth is depicted. Christ as the Lion-Lamb, who holds the title deed to the earth by right of creation and redemption, is about to take over. Chapters four and five are scenes in Heaven. Believers have been raptured and have received their crowns or rewards (Revelation 4:10). The giving of the crown belongs to that period after the rapture of the church (2 Timothy 4:8). After the redeemed have received their rewards, earth's official Representative takes command. In Heaven He has been acclaimed "worthy." Now the earth must receive Him, but first the righteous judgment of God must be meted out to the inhabitants of the earth who have rejected Him.

The judgment period takes place in 6:1 to 19:4, the judgment being executed in three series: the seals (6:1 to 8:5); the trumpets (8:6 to 19:21); the vials (16:1 to 19:21).

Actually the seven seals cover the entire judgment period, with the trumpet judgments issuing forth out of the seals, and the vial judgments issuing forth out of the trumpets. This has been illustrated with a telescope comprising three sections, the outer or larger section containing the inner two. Out of the larger section (the seals) issues the second or middle section (the trumpets), and out of the second section issues the inner section (the vials).

Let me say here that these judgments are future; they have not been fulfilled as yet. "The day of vengeance of our God"

153

(Isaiah 61:2) has not yet come upon the earth, but it is drawing near. It cannot be said of any period in the history of mankind that "the kingdoms of this world are become the kingdoms of our Lord, and of His Christ" (Revelation 11:15). But we repeat that the time is drawing near. Up to the present hour God's throne has not been one of judgment but of grace.

Before we look at the text, we should examine a very real problem, namely, whether the details are to be regarded literally or symbolically. This is the question which all students of this book must face. Now I must take issue with the man who says that we must proceed on the principle that either all is literal or all is symbolic. This book must be studied the same as any other book in the Bible. The question of literalness or symbolism must be determined by language and context. Are the horses and the horsemen literal or symbolic? Personally I feel that they are symbolic of the nature of the judgments and calamities which are to come upon the earth. Notice in verse one the phrase, *"as it were."* This phrase indicates the use of symbolic language. The horses are used here in a figurative sense, prophetically of judgment upon the earth in the last days (2 Kings 6:15-18; Zechariah 1:8-11; 6:1-5).

I. THE FIRST SEAL (6:1-2)

> *And I saw when the Lamb opened one of the seals, and I heard, as it were the noise of thunder, one of the four beasts saying, Come and see. And I saw, and beheld a white horse: and he that sat on him had a bow; and a crown was given unto him: and he went forth conquering, and to conquer* (6:1-2).

Judgment is about to fall. All the acts described under the seven seals are acts of judgment. The scene is a judgment scene. The throne is a judgment throne. And now as each seal is opened, God's judicial action is disclosed, one stage at a time. The seventieth week of Daniel's prophecy is about to begin (Daniel 9:27). One of the four beasts [living creatures] is the spokesman. Which of the four speaks first we are not told. We note that when the subject concerns Heaven, the elders speak, and when it concerns the earth, the living creatures speak.

The sound John heard was *"as it were the noise of thunder."* The thundering voice speaks of coming judgment. It is the tone of majesty and might. Thunder portends a coming storm. The first mention of thunder in the Bible is in connection with God's judgment upon Egypt (Exodus 9:23). This voice as a clap of thunder sounds the beginning of the tribulation period, the time of Jacob's trouble (Jeremiah 30:7). Jesus referred to it when He spoke in the synagogue of Nazareth (Luke 4:17-18). The thunder of divine judgment upon the earth rolls with increasing crescendo for seven years until the lightning of Christ's Second Coming to the earth strikes (Matthew 24:27; Revelation 19:11).

I heard . . . one of the four beasts saying, Come and see.

The words *"and see"* should be omitted, according to the Revised Version. The voice is not speaking to John, but rather to the rider on the white horse. Literally he is saying to the rider, "Be going." The command is literally obeyed. This rider who obeys the command of the living creature is not the same rider as the One upon the white horse in Revelation 19:11. Christ is not subject to any such command. In Chapter 19 the Rider is identified as Christ; here he is not named. This rider appears at the beginning of Daniel's seventieth week while the Rider in chapter 19 appears at the end of the week. They cannot be one and the same person. This rider is the Antichrist, the prince of Daniel's prophecy. He is the counterfeit superman, the wicked one to appear after the Church is translated (2 Thessalonians 2:8). The Church of Jesus Christ will not be on earth to see Him. True he wears a crown, but it is the *stephanos*, and not the *diadema* worn by Christ when He rides forth (Revelation 19:12). This rider is Satan's man. His weapon is a bow; Christ's weapon is a sword. He comes imitating Christ and offering peace, but he is as false as is the peace he offers. His golden age is short-lived.

But someone might ask if "white" is not a symbol of purity

or holiness. Does not Christ come forth on a *"white* horse"? The answer to both questions is, *yes.* But when this wicked one appears, "God shall send them strong delusion, that they should believe a lie" (2 Thessalonians 2:11). Then, too, not all that appears white on the surface is pure and holy. Jesus said, "Woe unto you, scribes and Pharisees, hypocrites! for ye are like unto whited sepulchres, which indeed appear beautiful outward, but are within full of dead men's bones, and of all uncleanness" (Matthew 23:27). This man is a whited sepulcher, a false Christ, a pretender.

The Psalmist said, in a prayer to God, "Surely the wrath of man shall praise Thee: the remainder of wrath shalt Thou restrain" (Psalm 76:10). Just as men like Nebuchadnezzar and Hitler were instruments in God's hands, so will it be when the Antichrist appears. God can stir up the heart of a wicked man and impel his fury, and in this way display His own power and glory even as He did in times past (Exodus 14:4 cf. Romans 9:17). No matter what the enemies of God do, at length all will redound to God's praise, inasmuch as they cannot in any degree prevail against Him. An evil man like Khrushchev is to be pitied rather than feared. God is never on the side of might when the mighty are wrong. Men are mere puppets in the hands of Almighty God. When Antichrist appears he shall deceive many (Matthew 24:5), and have all in subjection to himself (Revelation 13), but it will not be for long. He is but acting under the divine mandate. The authority he displays *"was given unto him"* (Revelation 6:2,4). It is by the permissive will of God that he comes forth *"conquering . . . to take peace from the earth."* "For God hath put in their hearts to fulfil His will, and to agree, and give their kingdom unto the beast, until the words of God shall be fulfilled" (Revelation 17:17). It is comforting to know that the true Church will not be here to witness and endure such wholesale deception.

This rider on the white horse sheds no blood. His is a bloodless conquest. He corresponds to the false Christ of Matthew 24:5. His method is that of deception. We shall see as we pursue our study that Matthew 24 is a commentary on Revelation 6. This rider comes with a bow but without an arrow, indicating that he offers a promise of peace. I believe that at this very moment the world would welcome a superman who could unite the United Nations. Jesus said, "I am come in My Father's name, and ye receive Me not: if another shall come in his own name, him ye will receive" (John 5:43). The world that has rejected God's Christ is ready to receive the devil's Christ. After the Church has been translated, this political leader and military strategist will put in his appearance and deceive the entire world. Appearing as a great ruler of men, he will be but a servant of God to carry out the divine purpose in the earth. He will be the last man to attempt to bring peace, but his efforts will only prove that there can be no peace without the presence of the Prince of Peace.

II. THE SECOND SEAL (6:3-4)

And when He had opened the second seal, I heard the second beast say, Come and see. And there went out another horse that was red: and power was given to him that sat thereon to take peace from the earth, and that they should kill one another: and there was given unto him a great sword (6:3-4).

The second of the four living creatures has delegated authority from the Lamb to send forth a red horse and its rider. The red horse represents a bloody warfare. The effort to bring universal peace apart from Christ will fail, and this failure will result in strife, violence, and bloodshed. The devil is called the "great *red* dragon" (Revelation 12:3), and "He was a murderer from the beginning" (John 8:44). The rider on the red horse has a sword. He proceeds to take peace from the earth and to kill. At first the Antichrist seems to be a man of peace, but "When they shall say, Peace and safety; then sudden destruction cometh upon them" (1 Thessalonians 5:3). Keep in mind that the Restrainer, the Holy Spirit, is at that time taken from the earth, so that slaughter is infused into men by satanic power (2 Thessalonians 2:7). *Red* is the appropriate color of communism, and all the world knows what a bloodthirsty lot the Reds are. Their bloody purges in Russia, China, North Korea, and Czechoslovakia are indeed foreshadowings of the red-horse rider. Of those days Jesus said, "And ye shall hear of wars and rumours of wars. . . . For nation shall rise against nation, and kingdom against kingdom" (Matthew 24:6-7). Peace pacts will be meaningless, for in those last perilous days men will be "truce-breakers" (2 Timothy 3:3). The phrase, *"that they should kill one another"* suggests war within each nation, class wars, religious wars, race wars. All the wars that the world has ever known put together will have been mild when compared with the world-wide reign of terror and slaughter of human lives in that day. "Every man's sword shall be against his brother" (Ezekiel 38:21). These Scriptures depict scenes prophetic, not historical.

We are very foolish if we believe that the world can have peace as long as evil, godless men are the heads of nations. Out of World War I came the League of Nations, but it failed because there was no power to prevent a self-seeking nation from withdrawing. Out of World War II came the United Nations Organization, admittedly today a failure, as well as being financially bankrupt. The Nuremberg trial revealed that from 1933 to 1941 Germany violated sixty-nine treaties. All of this foreshadows the awful days that are ahead immediately following the translation of the true Church from earth to Heaven. The rider upon the red horse, most likely the same person astride the white horse, now reveals his identity. He is not the Prince of Peace, but Satan's counterfeit, an impostor. Imagine, if you can, a world without any peace at all.

III. THE THIRD SEAL (6:5-6)

> *And when He had opened the third seal, I heard the third beast say, Come and see. And I beheld, and lo a black horse; and he that sat on him had a pair of balances in his hand. And I heard a voice in the midst of the four beasts say, A measure of wheat for a penny, and three measures of barley for a penny; and see thou hurt not the oil and the wine (6:5-6).*

With the opening of the third seal the same rider appears upon a black horse. This time he holds no weapon of warfare in his hands, but a pair of scales. These balances, like the black horse, suggest scarcity to the extent of famine. Beating plowshares into swords produced no food; it only destroyed the men who produce the food and prevented the soil from being tilled. Famine always follows war. Food rationing of the strictest order is an aftermath of war, particularly in the subjected countries.

Khrushchev, with his tactics, is an example of methods of the Antichrist when he comes. He has infiltrated countries such as China, North Korea, East Germany, Cuba, and others, with his false promise of peace and plenty. Not long after he was accepted in these countries, his peace program collapsed and the food shortage became increasingly critical. In China men, women, and children are starving by the thousands. In East Germany food is rationed. In Cuba the same conditions exist. In most instances the Bible says, "They that be slain with the sword are better than they that be slain with hunger" (Lamentations 4:9). Black follows red; famine follows war. Famine is symbolized in Scripture by the color black. "Our skin was black like an oven because of the terrible famine" (Lamentations 5:10). When our Lord Jesus said that there shall be wars and rumors of wars with nation rising against nation and kingdom against kingdom, He added, "And there shall be *famines*" (Matthew 24:7).

The extent of the famine during the tribulation is suggested by what John saw in that divinely given prophetic vision. *"A measure of wheat for a penny, and three measures of barley for a penny."* In metrology, which is the science of weights and measures, there are linear measures, measures of capacity, measures of weight, measures of value or money. Here the word "measure" is used to denote the amount required to feed a man for one day. The "penny" (*denarius*) was the daily wage of a laborer at that time. Now think of a man working a full day for merely enough food to keep himself alive, and then having to divide that food with his family. The average person passing through such torture would rather be dead. And this condition exists while the war lords enjoy plenty, for *"the oil and the wine"* are the possessions of the few rich who hold the masses in slavery, and therefore they are not to be measured out to the famine-stricken. In communist countries today the poor become poorer and the few rich leaders become richer. The one billion hungry people in the world today, plus the 400,000,000 in danger of starvation, will seem like child's play compared with the famine to come upon the earth in that day predicted by our Lord. The rider with the balances speaks of food conservation. That black day is coming. The day of famine will appear upon the earth. Now we know why this period is called "the tribulation."

IV. THE FOURTH SEAL (6:7-8)

And when He had opened the fourth seal, I heard the voice of the fourth beast say, Come and see. And I looked, and behold a pale horse: and his name that sat on him was Death, and Hell followed with him. And power was given unto them over the fourth part of the earth, to kill with sword, and with hunger, and with death, and with the beasts of the earth (6:7-8).

Following in the wake of the famine comes another horse, still more terrible in its symbolic meaning. It is pale, meaning livid and corpselike. The rider is called Death, the aftermath of war and famine. The fourth living creature is given divine authority to send him forth. Under the three previous seals, a false peace was followed by war and famine in the earth. There have been furious wars, famines, and death-dealing plagues in the past, but nothing comparable to this event which is still future. Its fury is depicted in its widespread effects, killing one-fourth of the earth's population. This is the result of the foregoing judgments, which God calls, "My four sore judgments" (Ezekiel 14:21).

The fourth rider is given the name *Death,* the final claimant and custodian of the body. Hell [or Hades] followed after him to gather the souls of the victims. Hades, the abode of the unregenerated souls that leave the body at death, is an ally of death. Hades is the abode of departed spirits between death and resurrection. It is temporary, in contrast to the lake of fire which is forever (Revelation 20:13-14).

But the Christian can take courage. Because he is in Christ he need not fear. Our Lord said, "I am He that liveth, and was dead; and, behold, I am alive forevermore, Amen; and have the keys of hell and of death" (Revelation 1:18). After all unredeemed men have heard the final word of judgment, "Death and hell were cast into the lake of fire" (Revelation 20:14).

It is interesting to note that the margin of the Revised Version translates "death" to mean "pestilence," a word denoting any deadly infectious malady. This is the order outlined by Christ when He said, "Take heed that no man deceive you. . . . Ye shall hear of wars. . . . There shall be famines and pestilences" (Matthew 24:4,6,7).

Already there are signs indicating that the end might be near. *Your* only hope is a right relation to the Lamb, the Lord Jesus Christ. Accept Him at once, and you can rejoice with the redeemed that we shall be taken out of the earth before that great and dreadful day of the Lord. May God awaken us all to see the horror of the coming tribulation and thereby quicken us to prayer, giving, and a renewed effort to reach the lost with the gospel.

V. THE FIFTH SEAL (6:9-11)

And when He had opened the fifth seal, I saw under the altar the souls of them that were slain for the word of God, and for the testimony which they held: And they cried with a loud voice, saying, How long, O Lord, holy and true, dost Thou not judge and avenge our blood on them that dwell on the earth? And white robes were given unto every one of them; and it was said unto them, that they should rest yet for a little season, until their fellow-servants also and their brethren, that should be killed as they were, should be fulfilled (6:9-11).

The breaking of the fifth seal reveals clearly that some on earth will turn to God after the Church has been translated. There will be those saved during the tribulation, but they will pay with their lives. Following Christ's prophecy of the result of the opening of the first four seals, namely, false Christs offering false peace, war, famine, and pestilences (Matthew 24:5-7), He added, "Then shall they deliver you up to be afflicted, and they shall kill you: and ye shall be hated of all nations for My name's sake" (Matthew 24:9). These are the martyrs of the tribulation days. Having heard the gospel of the kingdom, thousands will believe and receive it, but they will be persecuted by the beast.

We are not told precisely by what means God effects this work of faith in them. Jesus did say, "And this gospel of the kingdom shall be preached in all the world for a witness unto all nations; and then shall the end come" (Matthew 24:14). We do know that the widespread translation and circulation of the Scriptures in eleven hundred languages is being used of God now to prepare the way for a succeeding witness to all nations. God's purpose in the tribulation is to bring about the conversion of Jews who will enter into the blessings of the kingdom. The "good news" of this dispensation and that of the kingdom are not mutually exclusive. Faith in Jesus Christ is essential to salvation in this dispensation of grace as well as in the tribulation.

The tribulation martyrs *"were slain for the Word of God, and for the testimony which they held."* The Scriptures always exalt Christ. He is their theme throughout. Thus in the tribulation there will be a continuing testimony to Him. This will provoke the Antichrist and his followers to hatred, to the extent that they will kill those who hold to the Scriptures and to the Christ of whom they testify. John's own exile on Patmos "for the word of God, and for the testimony of Jesus Christ" (Revelation 1:9), was a foreshadowing of this greater persecution to follow. Yes, the day is coming on the earth when men and women who turn to God through faith in Jesus Christ shall once again seal their testimony with their own blood. They are martyrs, not merely because they were persecuted to death. Millions died under the first four seals who are not martyrs. Those who die under the fifth seal are true martyrs because of the reason for their being slain. The Bible they had in their possession was to them the divinely inspired and infallible Word of God. The prevailing spirit of that time will be one of rebellion against the Bible. This will be a major cause of the world's hatred against them. Thus they are truly martyrs for a righteous cause. They might be spared death if they deny the Book, but they testify faithfully to it; they hold fast to it.

But the death of the tribulation believers is not the end of them. Death never is the end of any man. The word *"souls"* in this passage is not limited to the spiritual part of man in contrast to his body. It is used for the person himself. Jesus used the words "soul" and "himself" interchangeably (Mark 8:36 cf. Luke 9:25). In another passage our Lord admitted that one man can kill the body of another, but He denies that one man can kill the soul of another. He said, "And fear not them which kill the body, but are not able to kill the soul: but rather fear Him which is able to destroy both soul and body in hell" (Matthew 10:28). Stephen used the word "soul" as the figure for a person when he said, "Then sent Joseph, and called his father Jacob to him, and all his kindred, threescore and fifteen *souls"* (Acts 7:14). The point to be made in our study is that the martyred saints were both conscious and fully rational. When God created man, He "breathed into his nostrils the breath of life; and man became a living soul" (Genesis 2:7). The soul, then, is what man is, a rational being, and this is what he will be forever. The body is merely the vehicle to house this conscious, rational being and through which he can express himself. Of course, the intermediate state is not a perfect state. The hope of all saints is to be housed in Heaven in their resurrection bodies (2 Corinthians 5:2-3).

The language in verse 10 sounds strange to the Christian. These martyrs are actually calling for vengeance against their persecutors. How unlike the attitude of Christ and of His followers in this present Church Age! Our Lord prayed for the forgiveness of His murderers (Luke 23:34), as did Stephen (Acts 7:60). The attitude of the tribulation martyrs marks the change of dispensation. We in this dispensation of grace must deal with others in grace as God has dealt with us. The tribulation saints will be living in the dispensation of judgment, thus they pray according to the ruling principle of that period of time in which they find themselves. Their cry for vengeance explains somewhat the imprecatory psalms. The cry, "How long?" is the familiar Jewish cry during the time of Jacob's trouble (Psalm 74:9-10; 79:5; 89:46; 94:3-4). The Christian in this present period of grace is taught that vengeance belongs to God (Romans 12:19), but the persecuted Jews in that day will seek vengeance upon their murderers without any sense of guilt for doing so. It is the time of judgment. The judgment throne is set.

In response to their prayer, *"White robes were given unto every one of them."* The robe is an assuring token that they are God's redeemed ones and that God will care for His own. Then they are told to wait patiently until more of their brethren and fellow-servants are slain for their faith. Chapter 13 describes how severe will be the persecution of Jews by the Antichrist. There can be no response to their cry until the martyred band is complete. Later on God answers the prayers offered here, and His enemies who persecuted His people are dealt with in divine judgment.

VI. THE SIXTH SEAL (6:12-17)

> *And I beheld when He had opened the sixth seal, and, lo, there was a great earthquake; and the sun became black as sackcloth of hair, and the moon became as blood; And the stars of heaven fell unto the earth, even as a fig tree casteth her untimely figs, when she is shaken of a mighty wind. And the heaven departed as a scroll when it is rolled together; and every mountain and island were moved out of their places. And the kings of earth, and the great men, and the rich men, and the chief captains, and the mighty men, and every bondman, and every free man, hid themselves in the dens and in the rocks of the mountains; And said to the mountains and rocks, Fall on us, and hide us from the face of Him that sitteth on the throne, and from the wrath of the Lamb: For the great day of His wrath is come; and who shall be able to stand?* (6:12-17).

The breaking of the sixth seal results in catastrophe on a world-wide scale. This is not the final judgment; it is not the end of the world. There are three great earthquakes mentioned in Revelation (6:12; 11:13; 16:18-19). This is the first of the three. The judgments issuing from the first four seals were at the hands of the Antichrist, but with the opening of the sixth seal, the judgments are supernatural and come from Heaven.

There are those fine teachers of the Word of God who hold that these earthshaking convulsions are to be viewed figuratively, that is, they are moral and political upheavals. Edward Dennett suggests that here we have a violent convulsion of the whole structure of society. C. A. Coates suggests that the sun, moon, and stars are figurative of rule (see Genesis 1:16-18), and that the removal of mountains and islands indicates the unsettling of all that has seemed stable and abiding. Ford C. Ottman says: "The description is figurative, for the heavens do not literally pass away until after the millennial reign of Christ. The great earthquake speaks of the upheaval of human government. Anarchy and riot-rule follow in the path of war, and stable forms of government are overthrown." Dr. Ironside wrote: "It is therefore not a world-wide, literal earthquake that the sixth seal introduces, but rather the destruction of the present order—political, social, and ecclesiastical—reduced to chaos; the breaking down of all authority, and the breaking up of all established and apparently permanent institutions."

I cannot accept all this to be symbolic language. I take it to be literal. Now the application of spiritual lessons from any part of Scripture is certainly not wrong, but I see no reason for departing from the plain terms of Holy Writ when those terms make common sense. Earthquakes have occurred in the past when God acted in judgment. Mount Sinai quaked when God descended upon it in the fire (Exodus 19:18), and the people recognized the quake for what it was (Exodus 20:18-19). In the days of Elijah there was an earthquake which broke rocks in pieces (1 Kings 19:11). When Christ died on the cross of Calvary there was an earthquake (Matthew 27:51-52). Dare we suggest that these recorded incidents were not literal and actual? By what principle of Biblical interpretation may we explain away these historical incidents? I know of none.

The disturbances under this sixth seal judgment were foretold by our Lord when He said, "And there shall be signs in the sun, and in the moon, and in the stars; and upon the earth distress of nations, with perplexity; the sea and the waves roaring; Men's hearts failing them for fear, and for looking after those things which are coming on the earth: for the powers of heaven shall be shaken" (Luke 21:25-26). These words of our blessed Lord mean precisely what they say. The people who will be living on the earth at that time will actually see the fulfillment of the astronomical signs in connection with the heavenly bodies. Christ then added the time element of these happenings, "And then shall ye see the Son of man coming in a cloud with power and great glory" (Luke 21:27). The judgments under the sixth seal occur after the translation of the Church to Heaven and before Christ's Second Coming to earth to reign.

That dreadful day will reveal that God is no respecter of persons. All men:

> *Kings . . . great men . . . rich men . . . chief captains . . . mighty men, and every bondman, and every free man, hid themselves in the dens and in the rocks of the mountains.*

All are gripped with one common terror. All are helpless before *"the wrath of the Lamb."* "The lofty looks of man shall be humbled, and the haughtiness of men shall be bowed down, and the LORD alone shall be exalted in that day. For the day of the LORD of hosts shall be upon every one that is proud and lofty, and upon every one that is lifted up; and he shall be brought low" (Isaiah 2:11-12). The very earth rulers who frightened the people with persecution and death under the fifth seal, are now themselves frightened into helplessness and despair. But there is no place to hide. Even a fall-out shelter cannot provide protection in that day.

"Knowing therefore the terror of the Lord, we persuade men" (2 Corinthians 5:11). There is a Rock to which we can still come for refuge. That Rock is a Person, the Rock of Ages, our Lord Jesus Christ. There is both salvation and security in the cleft of that Rock. Jesus spoke of the day when their cry would go up to the mountains and rocks. "Then shall they begin to say to the mountains, Fall on us; and to the hills, Cover us" (Luke 23:30). But nature's hiding places are inadequate to shield anyone from the wrath of the Lamb. O, you who still reject Him, turn to Christ at once. Receive Him while there is yet time, for the day of His judgment must surely come.

WHO WILL BE SAVED IN THE TRIBULATION?

Revelation 7:1-17

Chapter seven, though a continuation of the description of the tribulation, is nevertheless a parenthesis. In chapter six we saw the opening of the first six seals and the judgments which are to follow. We might naturally look for a description of the seventh seal and its judgment, but the seventh does not follow in order. The Lamb does not open the seventh seal until chapter eight. Were we to omit chapter seven entirely, and continue reading from 6:17 to 8:1, we would have a running narrative and a completed picture of the seal judgments. The omission of chapter seven would not detract in any way from the rest of the picture from man's viewpoint. But the parenthesis is here, and it was put here by our Lord for a reason. What was the reason?

I. THE SUSPENSION OF JUDGMENT (7:1-3)

And after these things I saw four angels standing on the four corners of the earth, holding the four winds of the earth, that the wind should not blow on the earth, nor on the sea, nor on any tree. And I saw another angel ascending from the east, having the seal of the living God: and he cried with a loud voice to the four angels, to whom it was given to hurt the earth and the sea, Saying, Hurt not the earth, neither the sea, nor the trees, till we have sealed the servants of our God in their foreheads (7:1-3).

Chapter six concludes with the statement, "For the great day of His wrath is come; and who shall be able to stand?" (6:17)

The answer is, "No one." So dreadful will His wrath be that all men are seen trying to flee from it, calling on the rocks and the mountains to protect them from it. Chapter seven is included in that period of judgment, but God pauses to answer the prayer of His prophet Habakkuk, "O LORD, revive Thy work in the midst of the years, in the midst of the years make known; in wrath remember mercy" (Habakkuk 3:2). Thus this parenthetical passage is for the purpose of showing mercy. In the midst of wrath, God remembers mercy and suspends judgment. (It is interesting to note that there is a parenthesis between the sixth and seventh trumpets, and another between the sixth and seventh vials).

The judgment winds have been blowing, but now there is a lull in the storm. God stops the storm in order to show mercy to those who will accept it, thereby preparing them for the worst. When God saved me He didn't make this world-system better, but He did equip me to live in a world that is becoming increasingly worse. The world at its worst will always see God at His best. In wrath He remembered mercy on the night of the Passover in Egypt. In wrath He remembered mercy before the flood in Noah's day. In wrath He remembered mercy at Calvary when He cast the world into darkness and shook the earth because of man's sin. In that hour of Christ's death God might have closed the books on man in judgment, but instead He remembered mercy, and salvation shone through the clouds of His wrath. Chapter seven is the mercy chapter of Revelation.

The instruments God uses in suspending judgment are His servants, the angels. It is not uncommon to hear skeptics sneer at the idea of angelic intervention in the affairs of this earth, nevertheless the whole Bible supports it. Angels are God's ministers (Hebrews 1:7,14). Their activity is spelled out clearly in the Scriptures from the creation of man to the ascension of Christ. After the translation of the Church they will become prominent again. Even now we have no idea to what extent God is using them to protect His children and to bridle the forces of evil. Angels seem to appear in times of crises often associated with judgment, as when angels smote that wicked group in

Sodom and delivered Lot from the condemned city (Genesis 19:1-17).

Here we are introduced to four angels standing upon the four corners of the earth. They are commanded to hold back the four winds of the earth, or to halt the process of judgment until God has accomplished some definite purpose. The phrase, *"the four corners of the earth,"* and its equivalent appears frequently in Scripture in passages such as Isaiah 11:12; Jeremiah 49:36; Daniel 7:2; 8:8; 11:4; Zechariah 2:6; Matthew 24:31. The wind as an instrument of judgment in the temporal affairs of man is a prominent idea in the Old Testament as seen in Job 1:19; 38:24; Isaiah 41:16; Jeremiah 4:11-12; 18:17; 49:32,36; Ezekiel 5:2; 12:14; Jonah 1:4,10-12. I take it that "the four corners of the earth" are the four main points of the compass: north, south, east, and west. The Great Tribulation is about to break upon the earth with the opening of the seventh seal, but the fifth angel, ascending from the east [the sunrising], restrains the four from proceeding, and judgment is suspended. The judgments which issue forth from the first six seals are only "the beginning of sorrows" (Matthew 24:8; Mark 13:8). The "great tribulation" referred to by the Lord Jesus (Matthew 24:21), and by Daniel the prophet (Daniel 9:27; 11:31; 12:11), begins with the sounding of the trumpets, which sounding issues forth from the seventh seal.

The angels are told to *"hurt not the earth, neither the sea, nor the trees, till we have sealed the servants of our God in their foreheads"* (Revelation 7:3). The tribulation days are days of hurting, but the sealing angel from the sunrising preserves certain ones from the "hurt." Presently we shall see who they are.

The "great tribulation" (7:14) is held back "till" certain ones are sealed by the sealing angel. The word "till" is a time word indicating that the restraint is temporary. The time is that period within the parenthesis. It answers to another parenthesis recorded by Paul in the Epistle to the Romans, chapters 9-11. Some able students of God's Word refuse to call these chapters in Romans parenthetical, because the great truths of justification by faith and sanctification by faith are set alongside the

Old Testament covenants and promises given to Israel. Granted, these three chapters do harmonize with the whole redemptive plan of God, but we must not overlook the fact that they do refer to the future salvation of Israel in a particular sense. Read Romans 9:1-4; 10:1; and 11:1-2,25-26, and you will see their deep significance in relation to Israel's future restoration. God acts in sovereign grace in a special way for her before the Great Tribulation begins. In her dispersion Israel has gone to the four corners of the earth, a despised and persecuted people, but God will restrain all opposition against her for a season. Judgment will be suspended "till. . . ." This brings us to the second major emphasis in our chapter.

II. THE SEALING OF JEWS (7:4-8)

> *And I heard the number of them which were sealed: and there were sealed an hundred and forty and four thousand of all the tribes of the children of Israel. Of the tribes of Judah were sealed twelve thousand. Of the tribe of Reuben were sealed twelve thousand. Of the tribe of Gad were sealed twelve thousand. Of the tribe of Aser were sealed twelve thousand. Of the tribe of Nepthalim were sealed twelve thousand. Of the tribe of Mannasses were sealed twelve thousand. Of the tribe of Simeon were sealed twelve thousand. Of the tribe of Levi were sealed twelve thousand. Of the tribe of Issachar were sealed twelve thousand. Of the tribe of Zabulon were sealed twelve thousand. Of the tribe of Joseph were sealed twelve thousand. Of the tribe of Benjamin were sealed twelve thousand* (7:4-8).

Judgment is suspended *till* 144,000 Jews are sealed. If language means anything, these sealed ones are literal Israelites. This group cannot be the Church because the Church is in Heaven with her Lord. Moreover the Church is neither Jewish nor Gentile. The Church is a new entity, "one new man" made up of both believing Jews and believing Gentiles (Ephesians 2:11-18). Those who have been baptized into Christ are neither Jews nor Gentiles (Galatians 3:27-28). In this sealed company Israel is plainly and literally before us, twelve thousand from each of the twelve tribes, not present-day adherents of sects or cults. F. L. Brook said, "There is no logical, theological or ety-mological reason for calling Israel anything but the sons of Jacob." If a Seventh Day Adventist, or an adherent to the cult known as "Jehovah's Witnesses," should claim to be a member of the 144,000, let him prove to which tribe he belongs. The 144,000 are all Israelites; not one Gentile is among them. Those who spiritualize the Scriptures, making Israel and the Church one and confusing law and grace, rob the nation of Israel of her promised blessings and in so doing commit a serious evil.

Seiss says: "There is no vice or device of sacred herme-neutics, which so beclouds the Scriptures, and so unsettles the faith of man, as this attempt to read *Church* for *Israel*, and Christian peoples for Jewish tribes. As I read the Bible, when God says '*children of Israel*,' I do not understand Him to mean any but people of Jewish blood, be they Christian or not. And when He speaks of the twelve tribes of the sons of Jacob, and gives the names of the tribes, it is impossible for me to believe that He means the Gentiles, in any sense or degree, whether they be believers or not. I know of no instance in which the descendants of the twelve tribes of Israel include the Gentiles. These sealed ones are one company complete in itself." This sealed remnant of Jews, not having had the gospel explained to them before, will turn to Christ after the rapture of the Church. They will inherit the kingdom under the rule of the Son of Man shortly after they have been sealed. The beast and the Anti-christ will not be able to destroy them.

Dan is not mentioned in Revelation 7. This omission need not create a serious problem for the Bible student. He is omitted because he was guilty of idolatry. God had warned His people that idolaters would be separated from the rest of the tribes (Deuteronomy 29:21). The idolatry of Dan is recorded in Leviticus 24:11; Judges 18:1-2,30-31; and 1 Kings 12:28-30. In the tribulation, when 12,000 from each of the tribes are sealed, the descendants of Dan are not permitted representa-tion. In the tribulation there will not be room for idolaters. Moral weaklings who could not stand in Old Testament times under much less severe opposition, are not included among the chosen and sealed ones. In the place of Dan, Manasseh, Joseph's son, is given a standing. It is possible that the tribe of Dan will be identified with Satan's work carried out by the Antichrist during the tribulation (see Genesis 49:17). William Barclay points out the fact that in Rabbinic symbolism Dan stands for idolatry and that Antichrist is to spring from Dan. This conclusion is based upon Jeremiah 8:16.

And now, a word about the seal. Notice, the seal belongs to *"the living God."* This is a phrase in which the followers of Jehovah have always delighted. It is used in contradistinction to the dead gods of the heathen. The gods which are the figment of the imagination of men, and which are made by hands of men, are all dead. Our God is not a created thing, but the eternal living Creator of all things. Man could not fashion Him; He fashioned man. Isaiah gives to us a picture of the heathen man making a god (Isaiah 44:9-17). Elijah on Mount Carmel proves the power of the living God, while the false prophets of Baal received no response from their dead deity (1 Kings 18). Only in the living God will His followers find strength in their conflicts with their enemies (Joshua 3:10). Only in the living God can a thirsty soul find satisfaction (Psalm 42:2). Hosea reminds Israel that only by the mercy of God did they become children of the living God (Hosea 1:10).

The 144,000 are sealed with *"the seal of the living God."* The seal is the mark of divine possession, protection, and preservation. The seal of Eastern kings was stamped in a signet ring and worn by the one in the place of authority. It was used to identify personal property as well as to preserve and protect it (Genesis 41:42; Esther 3:10; 8:2). Paul speaks about the Holy Spirit as the Seal in the believer, marking him out as God's property (Ephesians 1:13), and assuring him of God's protection and preservation until the redemption of the whole man (Ephesians 4:30 cf. Romans 8:23). Believers in this dispensation are sealed immediately upon being born again, and they are sealed until the day of their resurrection and translation to Heaven, where they shall evermore be with the Lord. The 144,000 of this chapter are sealed with the seal of the living God for protection and preservation through the Great Tribulation that is to come upon all the world, and which will constitute for Israel the time of Jacob's trouble.

III. THE SALVATION OF THE GENTILES (7:9-17)

After this I beheld, and, lo, a great multitude, which no man could number, of all nations, and kindreds, and people, and tongues, stood before the throne, and before the Lamb, clothed with white robes, and palms in their hands; And cried with a loud voice, saying, Salvation to our God which sitteth upon the throne, and unto the Lamb. And all the angels stood round about the throne, and about the elders and the four beasts, and fell before the throne on their faces, and worshipped God, Saying, Amen: Blessing, and glory, and wisdom, and thanksgiving, and honour, and power, and might, be unto our God for ever and ever. Amen. And one of the elders answered, saying unto me, What are these which are arrayed in white robes? and whence came they? And I said unto him, Sir, thou knowest. And he said to me, These are they which came out of great tribulation, and have washed their robes, and made them white in the blood of the Lamb. Therefore are they before the throne of God, and serve Him day and night in His temple: and He that sitteth on the throne shall dwell among them. They shall hunger no more, neither thirst any more; neither shall the sun light on them, nor any heat. For the Lamb which is in the midst of the throne shall feed them, and shall lead them unto living fountains of waters: and God shall wipe away all tears from their eyes (7:9-17).

We learned from the first eight verses that there will be souls saved during the tribulation, and that the first contingent will be Jews. Here we meet another great multitude, but they are Gentiles, *"of all nations, and kindreds, and people, and tongues"* (7:9). This order follows God's plan, namely, "to the Jew first" (Romans 1:16), and then to the Gentile. This redeemed company, then, is neither Israel nor the Church. During this time of Gentile salvation the Church is with the Lord, having been caught away by Him. She is seen *"sitting"* around the throne (4:4); these *"stood before the throne, and before the Lamb"* (7:9). The number of this throng is beyond all counting, as far as man is concerned. The exact number is known to God (2 Timothy 2:19). They are the Gentile converts won to the Messiah as the result of Israel's restoration, and of whom the prophet Isaiah wrote (Isaiah 49:10-12; 60:1-3).

I do not believe that this throng has in it any who reject Christ in this present dispensation of grace. Those who deliberately reject the love of the truth in this age are without hope in the coming age. So it would seem from the message in 2 Thessalonians 2:10-12. This throng heard the good news of the gospel of the kingdom for the first time through the 144,000 redeemed children of Israel. When the disciples asked our Lord what would be the sign of His coming and of the end of the age, He said, "And this gospel of the kingdom shall be preached in all the world for a witness unto all nations; and then shall the end come" (Matthew 24:14). By "the end" I believe Christ meant the end of "the tribulation" (Matthew 24:29 cf. Daniel 7:21-25; 9:24-27). This "great multitude" of Revelation 7:9-17 are the "sheep nations" of whom Christ spoke in Matthew 25:31-40. The 144,000 witnessing Israelites will be persecuted for their testimony. They will be hungry, thirsty, lonely, in need of clothing, and cast into prison. But those Gentiles who believe their message will stand with them and minister to them, so that it is to them Jesus will say, "Inasmuch as ye have done it unto one of the least of these My brethren, ye have done it unto Me" (Matthew 25:40). This throng will be preserved through the tribulation, not kept out of it as the Church will be (Revelation 3:10). I know of no place else in Scripture where these are mentioned. They are an elect Gentile remnant in addition to the elect of the Church and of Israel.

First, notice their *position.* They *"stood before the throne, and before the Lamb"* (verse 9). As was pointed out earlier, the redeemed of this Age of Grace, as typified by the four and twenty elders, are seated on thrones round about God's throne. But this *"great multitude"* is standing. The important fact is that they are in the presence of Him who is seated on His throne. To be permitted to stand before His throne as His redeemed ones is an honor not to be despised. It is a privilege afforded to none but His own willing subjects. It means that they share in the honor of the Lamb. They owe a debt of gratitude to those 144,000 Jewish missionaries, the wise who shall shine because they turned many to righteousness (Daniel 12:3).

Secondly, notice their *purity*. They are clothed in *"white robes"* (verses 9,13), *"made white in the blood of the Lamb"* (verse 14). They appear robed in righteousness and holiness, divinely approved. It is true that they performed good works (Matthew 25:40), but they were not saved by their works (Titus 3:14). Their salvation, like that of all who are saved in every dispensation, is attributed to the sacrifice of the Lord Jesus Christ. God has always had one way of saving people, and that way is through the blood of "the Lamb of God, which taketh away the sin of the world" (John 1:29).

Have *you* been washed in Christ's blood? Have *you* availed yourself of the efficacy of Christ's atoning work at Calvary? If you have, then you are wearing the garment of saints, clothed with the righteousness of the Lord Jesus Himself (Revelation 19:8).

Thirdly, notice their *protection*. John saw *"palms in their hands"* (verse 9). Tucker suggests that the palms may be in celebration of the Feast of Tabernacles which is about to be kept in the land when blessing comes upon both Jew and Gentile (Leviticus 23:39,43; 2 Chronicles 20:19; Ezra 3:11-12). Scott points out that palm branches express the joy of complete deliverance (John 12:12-13). They are celebrating the triumph of having been brought through that awful period of tribulation. Palm branches were used on such occasions. Roman conquerors wore garlands of palm leaves. Greek athletes found a palm branch awaiting the winner at the end of the race. Since the Feast of Tabernacles was preeminently a feast of joy, because of deliverance and protection for the future, I am inclined to apply the same idea here. When the children of Israel returned from captivity, they made booths of palm branches, "and there was very great gladness" (Nehemiah 8:15-17).

Fourthly, notice their *praise*. In their praise they attribute to

God and the Lamb *"salvation"* (verse 10). When our Lord made His triumphal entry into Jerusalem, the people shouted "Hosanna," which was an utterance of prayer and praise for salvation (Matthew 21:9,15; Mark 11:9-10; John 12:13). This multitude that John saw recognized the source of their salvation and victory. Not one of them is silent. And rightly so! When sovereign grace does its mighty work in salvation in any man's life, there is cause for praise to God and the Lamb. The praise of the redeemed ones causes the angelic hosts of Heaven to fall on their faces and worship God, saying:

> *Amen: Blessing, and glory, and wisdom, and thanksgiving, and honour, and power, and might, be unto our God for ever and ever. Amen* (verses 11-12).

These are unfallen angels, therefore they have never known the joy of experiencing salvation; however, they always rejoice in the salvation of sinners on earth (see Luke 15:8-10). They add their *"Amen"* whenever a soul is saved.

In a day such as our own, when there is so little worship, this awe-inspiring scene of men and angels worshiping the Lord stands out as one of the most blessed in the entire Book. Here is true worship indeed! The redeemed ones come before the Lord with all their possessions, and they worship before Him (Deuteronomy 26:10). Our possessions keep us from worship. We call ourselves wise when actually we are stupid. Wise men linger long before the Lamb and present their treasure to Him (see Matthew 2:1-12).

Fifthly, notice their *privilege*.

> *Therefore are they before the throne of God, and serve Him day and night in His temple: and He that sitteth on the throne shall dwell among them* (verse 15).

They engage in one glorious, unbroken ministry. Dr. Ironside writes: "That is, I take it, the millennial temple, which is to be built in the land in that coming day. There will be no day and night in Heaven. The expression can only refer, in this connection, to the temple on earth." This description of their service tells us that they are in their glorified and immortal state. It is a glad, spontaneous, unceasing service. In Old Testament times the privilege of serving God day and night was given to the Levites and priests (1 Chronicles 9:33). In the earthly temple in Jerusalem in that day, no Gentile could serve. But in the new earthly temple in Jerusalem, the privilege of serving God is open to the redeemed of every tongue and every race. What will be true in that day is blessedly true now, namely, he who faithfully works and witnesses for God knows the joy of His presence every moment of every day.

Finally, notice their *provision*.

> *They shall hunger no more, neither thirst any more; neither shall the sun light on them, nor any heat. For the Lamb which is in the midst of the throne shall feed them, and shall lead them unto living fountains of waters: and God shall wipe away all tears from their eyes* (verses 16-17).

The Lamb continues to feed and lead His own. Think of it! The Lamb is the Shepherd graciously providing for every need. There shall be no want. This is a striking contrast from that which they suffer at the hands of the Antichrist when food distribution is all under his control, and the rivers become blood under the vial judgments (Revelation 16:4), and the sun scorches the earth with a great heat (Revelation 16:8-9). The lot of those saved in the tribulation will be one of remarkable deliverance and victory with cessation from all of earth's sufferings. Under the guiding hand of the Lamb every provision will be available to His people. The springs of life with their fountains of living water shall not cease to flow. That which John saw was no invention of his. God had given the prophet Isaiah a similar vision more than seven hundred years before John's time. "They shall not hunger nor thirst; neither shall the heat nor sun smite them: for He that hath mercy on them shall lead them, even by springs of water shall He guide them" (Isaiah 49:10). This Old Testament prophecy finds its perfect fulfillment in the Lord Jesus Christ.

And just think of it—the Lamb is now our Shepherd! He said, "Blessed are they which do hunger and thirst after righteousness: for they shall be filled" (Matthew 5:6). "Whosoever drinketh of the water that I shall give him shall never thirst; but the water that I shall give him shall be in him a well of water springing up into everlasting life" (John 4:14). "I am the bread of life: he that cometh to Me shall never hunger; and he that believeth on Me shall never thirst" (John 6:35). In Jesus Christ there is satisfaction for the hunger and thirst of the human soul. To the Christian He is the Good Shepherd who provides "green pastures" and "still waters" for His sheep (Psalm 23:2). Indeed He is the Shepherd and Bishop of our souls (1 Peter 2:25).

Now to the final word concerning them.

God shall wipe away all tears from their eyes (7:17).

Life had been filled with tears as they took their place in that hour of judgment. Loved ones were killed before their very eyes. But now they are comforted as God wipes the tears from every eye. They will know then that their past sorrows were not worthy to be compared with the glory into which they have entered (see Romans 8:18). The closing words of our chapter are unequalled in depth and tenderness.

God shall wipe away all tears from their eyes.

Sorrow shall not always have the upper hand. The day is coming on earth when God will have removed every semblance of the cause of tears.

SILENCE IN HEAVEN

Revelation 8:1-13

Chapter eight records the opening of the seventh and final seal. Here we pick up the next event in order following the opening of the sixth seal in chapter six. The period prophesied here is still the tribulation, Daniel's seventieth week. With the opening of the seventh seal we are introduced to the sounding of the seven trumpets. The seventh seal includes the seven trumpets. The parenthesis between the sixth and seventh trumpets includes 10:1 to 11:14. The sounding of the seventh trumpet appears at 11:15. This entire period of the tribulation is one of a series of judgments. Not until after the judgments are there voices heard saying, "The kingdoms of this world are become the kingdoms of our Lord, and of His Christ; and He shall reign for ever and ever" (11:15).

The chapter before us may be divided into four sections.

I. THE SILENT PAUSE (8:1)

And when He had opened the seventh seal, there was silence in heaven about the space of half an hour (8:1).

Notice that the silence is in Heaven, not on earth. The Bible tells us of a coming day when all the earth (Habakkuk 2:20), and all islands (Isaiah 41:1), and all flesh (Zechariah 2:13) will be called upon to be silent before God. Presently this is not the day of silence on the earth. There are many voices and varied noises which well-nigh prevent men from hearing the Word of God, but that day when all creation remains silent before God will surely come. The silence in Heaven of which our text speaks precedes the silence on earth. In chapters five and six all of Heaven resounds with the praises of redeemed men and of angels, giving glory to the Lamb. Here there is a stillness and a silence. No voice is heard; no motion is seen. Subsequent to the silence God will speak. "Then shall He speak unto them in His wrath, and vex them in His sore displeasure" (Psalm 2:5). Now it is man's turn to speak. God has spoken. "God . . . spake in time past unto the fathers by the prophets," and He "Hath in these last days spoken unto us by His Son" (Hebrews 1:1,2). But the next time His voice is heard throughout all the earth, judgment will fall upon the unbelieving world of men.

II. THE SOLEMN PREPARATION (8:2)

And I saw the seven angels which stood before God; and to them were given seven trumpets (8:2).

The continued ministry of angels is seen. The seven before us in this verse hold the prerogative to announce the execution of judgment through the sounding of the trumpets. But they are restrained for the space of about half an hour. This interlude is the preparation for that judgment. Now "half an hour" is not a long period of time when one is engaged in some pleasantry, but thirty minutes of intense suspense can be well-nigh nerve shattering. These are solemn moments because of the judgment which is to follow. This is the silent, solemn preparation for the most awful judgments ever to come upon the world. They are the judgments prophesied by Enoch (Jude 14), expected by the Psalmist (Psalm 96:13), and verified by the Apostle Paul (Acts 17:31). Indeed the wrath of God will be revealed from Heaven against all ungodliness and unrighteousness of men (Romans 1:18).

And the seven angels which had the seven trumpets prepared themselves to sound (Revelation 8:6).

Here are the executors of God's will prepared for judgment. Each of the seven angels holds a trumpet. Trumpets in Scripture are used in various ways. Their sounding was a summons to worship (Numbers 10:3,7; 23:15-24; 1 Chronicles 16:42) and warfare (Numbers 10:5-9; Judges 3:27,30; Nehemiah 4:9-20). The idea of the trumpet originated with God and He controlled its use (Numbers 10:1). Priests only were qualified to blow them (Numbers 10:8). There were different sounds for each occasion, thus it was important that the priest blow with accuracy. How important it was that the summons to warfare be not confused with that which called the people to worship (1 Corinthians 14:8)! The sound of the trumpet in Israel indicated the intervention of God in the affairs of men on earth.

The seven trumpets before us tell of the great final intervention of God in judgment. These trumpets will not be calling men to work or to worship. They are warlike in character and they tell us that divine judgment is about to fall upon the wicked ones who dwell on the earth.

III. THE SAINTS' PRAYERS (8:3-5)

> *And another angel came and stood at the altar, having a golden censer; and there was given unto him much incense, that he should offer it with the prayers of all saints upon the golden altar which was before the throne. And the smoke of the incense, which came with the prayers of the saints, ascended up before God out of the angel's hand (8:3,4).*

Here is an angel with priestly prerogatives. Exactly who he is we are not told. Some teachers hold to the idea that this angel is the Lord Jesus Christ, because he ministers both Godward and manward, serving as both Priest and Judge. This is a possibility, but it does not really matter who the angel is.

The point for emphasis here is that the prayers of saints are given efficacy through the incense added by the angel. Who are these saints, and for what are they praying? Under the fifth seal the souls of the martyred saints cried for just judgment (6:9-10). It seems that their petition is being taken up here by the Jewish remnant on earth. Apparently their prayers of imprecation, like those in the imprecatory psalms, meet with divine approval, for they are furthered and benefited by the angel. At once it is made clear that their prayers have a profound connection with the sounding of the trumpets and the coming judgment. The prayers of the saints in that day will be for vengeance, and God will answer without delay.

And the angel took the censer, and filled it with fire of the altar, and cast it into the earth: and there were voices, and thunderings, and lightnings, and an earthquake (8:5).

Immediately after the prayers ascend, the judgment descends. The altar from which the angel filled the censer with fire represented the place of judgment. The fire represented the judgment of God upon sin as seen in the Levitical offerings. Scott writes: "As the altar was the expression of His holiness and righteousness in dealing with the sin of the people of old, so that same holiness and righteousness will search the earth and judge and punish it accordingly."

The fire from the altar was emptied upon the earth and at once there followed voices, and thunderings, and lightnings, and an earthquake. These convulsions causing disorder in the earth are but the beginning of terrible calamities which follow the sounding of the trumpets. Those on the earth in that day will have rejected the all-sufficient Sacrifice, therefore "There remaineth no more sacrifice for sins, but a certain fearful looking for of judgment and fiery indignation, which shall devour the adversaries" (Hebrews 10:26-27). The Saviour has become the Judge. The casting of the fire into the earth is merely a token judgment indicating that the sound of the trumpets will follow.

IV. THE SINNERS' PUNISHMENT (8:7-9:21)

The trumpet judgments appear to occur just before the second coming of Christ in power and great glory as King, for when the seventh trumpet sounds, "the mystery of God should be finished" (10:7). In this connection we read further, "And the seventh angel sounded; and there were great voices in heaven, saying, The kingdoms of this world are become the kingdoms of our Lord, and of His Christ; and He shall reign for ever and ever" (11:15). C. Ernest Tatham writes: "On the last day of ancient Jericho's existence the army of Israel compassed the city seven times as the priests blew their trumpets. At the seventh blast the walls fell flat, and the destruction of the city followed immediately (Joshua 6). There seems to be a strong suggestion that this Old Testament event provides a forecasting shadow of these final trumpet judgments."

A. *The First Trumpet*

The first angel sounded, and there followed hail and fire mingled with blood, and they were cast upon the earth: and the third part of trees was burnt up, and all green grass was burnt up (8:7).

Take the language as you find it. There is nothing in this verse to indicate symbolism. The plagues in Egypt, similar to these, were literal (Exodus 9:22-25). There is one major difference, however. Then the plagues were to save Israel; in the tribulation they will trouble her. At the sounding of this first trumpet, one-third of all vegetation will be destroyed. This leaves a bleak picture of desolation caused by hail and fire. The widespread character of God's judgment under the first trumpet is potent.

B. *The Second Trumpet*

And the second angel sounded, and as it were a great mountain burning with fire was cast into the sea: and the third part of the sea became blood; And the third part of the creatures which were in the sea, and had life, died; and the third part of the ships were destroyed (8:8-9).

Now this is not a literal mountain. Whatever it was, it looked like a mountain, *"as it were* a great mountain." This immense meteoric mass resembled a mountain ablaze. As the waters in Egypt were turned into blood and the fish did die, we accept this prediction of forthcoming judgment as literal (Exodus 7:19-21 cf. Psalm 105:29). Included in the sounding of the second trumpet is the serious effect upon commerce, the third part of the world's ships being destroyed. In our missile age this devastating judgment does not appear incredulous. This prophecy given to John resembles closely those utterances which the Holy Spirit gave to Old Testament prophets (Hosea 4:1-3; Zephaniah 1:3; Isaiah 2:16).

C. *The Third Trumpet*

And the third angel sounded, and there fell a great star from heaven, burning as it were a lamp, and it fell upon the third part of the rivers and upon the fountains of waters; And the name of the star is called Wormwood: and the third part of the waters became wormwood; and many men died of the waters, because they were made bitter (8:10-11).

Here is another meteoric phenomenon. A literal star, or meteor, soaring through space, approaches the earth. In its sweep along the surface it turns one-third of the water in the earth into a deadly liquid. It affects rivers, springs, and wells. There is a striking prophecy of this in the Old Testament (Jeremiah 9:14-15; 23:15). We should not think it strange that a great burning star could communicate a poisonous bitterness to the waters upon which it fell. On March 21, 1823, a volcanic explosion in the Aleutian Islands caused the water to become bitter so as to be unfit for use. God will use that which He created to effect His ends. He put the stars in their place (Genesis 1:14-16); He knows how many there are (Psalm 147:4); and He has called each one by name (Job 9:9-10). The name of this star is "Wormwood" (bitterness). (See Deuteronomy 29:18; Proverbs 5:4; Jeremiah 9:15; 23:15; Amos 5:7).

When our Lord hung upon the cross, His enemies "Gave Him vinegar to drink mingled with gall" (Matthew 27:34). But at the sounding of the third trumpet, many wicked men will die from water made bitter by the Divine Judge. How wonderful that in this day of grace God makes available to men the soul-satisfying water of life! (John 4:14; 7:37-39)

D. *The Fourth Trumpet*

And the fourth angel sounded, and the third part of the sun was smitten, and the third part of the moon, and the

> *third part of the stars; so as the third part of them was darkened, and the day shone not for a third part of it, and the night likewise. And I beheld, and heard an angel flying through the midst of heaven, saying with a loud voice, Woe, woe, woe, to the inhabiters of the earth by reason of the other voices of the trumpet of the three angels, which are yet to sound!* (8:12-13).

Here is a prophecy, the fulfillment of which will baffle all scientists who have made a study of the heavenly bodies. The events recorded here are similar to those under the sixth seal (6:12-14). They are predicted clearly by Christ Himself (Luke 21:25-28). No scientific answer will be able to explain adequately these astronomical effects. Apart from the intervention of the sovereign Creator of all things, there can be no explanation. These are the judgments of God going forth in the earth. On the fourth day He brought the sun, moon, and stars into view in order to provide light for man; under the fourth trumpet He shall withdraw the light He Himself created. All of this will affect seriously the health and well-being of people on the earth at that time. This will disturb the seasons and hinder the growth of fruits and vegetables.

And yet these judgments are merely preliminary to still greater woes to follow. Three more trumpets are yet to be heard. These are called the "woe" trumpets, indicating the severity of the consummation of God's judgment at the end of the tribulation. Men have been finding false comfort in the lie that "All things continue as they were from the beginning of the creation" (2 Peter 3:4). But the day will come when the so-called fixed laws of nature will be changed by Him who is the Source of all things. And the tragedy in that day will be in the fact that men will not repent and turn to God.

Oh, there is now full salvation offered to all men everywhere if only they will turn to God through faith in Jesus Christ! Are you who read this trusting Him for deliverance from the wrath to come? If you are not, then receive Him at once as your Saviour and Lord.

HELL ON EARTH

Revelation 9:1-21

The verses which occupy us in our present study contain prophecies of dreadful diabolical activity to take place on the earth. The fifth and sixth trumpets sound, and the next in order of the judgments are unleashed upon a rebellious and unrepentant race of men. These are referred to respectively as the first and second "woe" judgments (8:13). This added description of the three trumpets yet to sound suggests the seriousness and solemnness of those judgments which are to follow. There will be "woe" on earth when these trumpets sound.

The phrase, *"the inhabiters of the earth"* (8:13), I do not understand to mean all people living on the earth at that time. Edward Dennett writes: "The 'inhabiters of the earth' is a moral expression, as in chapter 3:10, indicating a class; those whose hearts and hopes are set upon earth, those who, in the language of the Apostle Paul, 'mind earthly things' (Philippians 3:19)." Earth dwellers are those persons who, in their utter rejection of Jesus Christ, live for this life on earth only, caring not at all about Heaven and the life to come. It is to all such that the judgments issuing from the sounding of the fifth and sixth trumpets are directed.

The Fifth Trumpet

And the fifth angel sounded, and I saw a star fall from heaven unto the earth: and to him was given the key of the bottomless pit. And he opened the bottomless pit; and there arose a smoke out of the pit, as the smoke of a great furnace;

187

and the sun and the air were darkened by reason of the smoke of the pit. And there came out of the smoke locusts upon the earth: and unto them was given power, as the scorpions of the earth have power. And it was commanded them that they should not hurt the grass of the earth, neither any green thing, neither any tree; but only those men which have not the seal of God in their foreheads. And to them it was given that they should not kill them, but that they should be tormented five months: and their torment was as the torment of a scorpion, when he striketh a man. And in those days shall men seek death, and shall not find it; and shall desire to die, and death shall flee from them. And the shapes of the locusts were like unto horses prepared unto battle; and on their heads were as it were crowns like gold, and their faces were as the faces of men. And they had hair as the hair of women, and their teeth were as the teeth of lions. And they had breastplates, as it were breastplates of iron; and the sound of their wings was as the sound of chariots of many horses running to battle. And they had tails like unto scorpions, and there were stings in their tails: and their power was to hurt men five months. And they had a king over them, which is the angel of the bottomless pit, whose name in the Hebrew tongue is Abaddon, but in the Greek tongue hath his name Apollyon. One woe is past; and, behold, there come two woes more hereafter (9:1-12).

I. THE UNNAMED PERSONALITY (9:1)

At the sound of the trumpet, John writes, "*I saw a star fall* [R.V. *fallen*] *from heaven unto the earth.*" This star I have referred to as "the unnamed personality" is definitely a personage. This is made clear in the use of the masculine pronouns "*him*" and "*he.*" But who is the star? The tense of the verb "*fallen*" (R.V.) tells us that the star had already fallen from heaven. John was not told when or how the star had fallen, but he was given to see that the star is an intelligent being to whom acts are ascribed which could not be said except of a living being. Jesus said to the seventy disciples, "I beheld Satan as lightning fall from heaven" (Luke 10:18). By this He meant, I feel certain, the fall of Lucifer from Heaven, through which he became Satan (Isaiah 14:12-15). If we are interpreting Scripture reference with Scripture reference correctly, then there seems to be little doubt that the "star" is Satan, the great enemy of God and man, and that the reference in Revelation 9:1 is to his original fall.

II. THE UNVEILED PIT (9:2)

The fallen star is given the key to the bottomless pit and permission to open the pit. We learn from Luke's account of our Lord's visit to the country of the Gadarenes that the pit of the abyss was dreaded by demons. It was one place they feared to go (Luke 8:31). And yet it is their place of which Jude wrote, "And the angels which kept not their first estate, but left their own habitation, He hath reserved in everlasting chains under darkness unto the judgment of the great day (Jude 6). Deciding against the glorious estate in which they were created, they abandoned their holy abode, the rank they had been given in the order of creation. As the apostate angels in Heaven did not escape the judgments of God (2 Peter 2:4), surely apostate men on earth will not escape divine judgment. Whether God's creature be an angel in Heaven or a man on earth, He will not spare in the day of judgment. He "spared not" the world in Noah's day (2 Peter 2:5); He "spared not His own Son" (Romans 8:32) when He delivered up Christ to die on the cross, therefore let not the unrepentant, Christ-rejecting sinner expect that God will spare him. We may be certain that the pit is a literal place, inasmuch as beings can go there. Moreover, Christ has authority over the abyss (Revelation 1:18), so it must have been our Lord who gave the key to Satan.

The locality of the abyss is said to be in "the lower parts of the earth" (Ephesians 4:9), the place into which Christ went at death when He paid the full price of redemption from the penalty of sin. It is a place that is sealed tight, from which there is no release except by divine permission. There is, then, a day coming upon the earth when the prison house of demons will be opened, and evil spirits who prefer to inhabit human bodies, but who have been imprisoned, will be released to inflict torment upon unrepentant men. In that day men will experience a sample of hell on earth. Ordinarily the abyss is "the place of no return," but for a brief season Satan will be permitted, by divine authority of course, to lead forth to the earth some who have been held captive there. This world of "outer darkness," upon which man has never looked, a place where "there shall be weeping and gnashing of teeth" (Matthew 25:30), a place originally "prepared for the devil and his angels" (Matthew 25:41), will release many strange and wicked things upon the earth.

III. THE UNPRECEDENTED PUNISHMENT (9:2-6)

As soon as the bottomless pit is opened, a cloud of obnoxious smoke is emitted. Like the cloud of a great atomic blast, or a mighty volcanic eruption, a strange and awesome blackness fills the air and blots out the sun from view. These terrors are more than human; they are demonic. Out of the darkness from the pit of the abyss come demons to do their fearful work of tormenting the souls and bodies of those who have wilfully rejected the Son of God. The plague of darkness that God sent to Egypt, "even darkness which may be felt" (Exodus 10:21-22), and which lasted only three days, was mild compared with the darkness of hell let loose on the earth during the time of the Great Tribulation. Because men are sinners by nature they hate the light and prefer the darkness of superstition, error, and ignorance (John 3:19). Not until they feel the darkness of hell itself will they have any desire to flee from it, but by that time it will be too late.

Coming out of the blackness of hell is seen a host of locusts shaped like horses. They come to inflict punishment, to torment as a scorpion's sting would leave its victim in torture. These demons from hell, who have been imprisoned for centuries, are prepared for battle. These infernal cherubim have combined in them the horse, the man, the woman, the lion, and the scorpion. These are not ordinary locusts such as plagued Egypt (Exodus 10:12-15), for these had no king over them (Proverbs 30:27), but they are intelligent beings who take orders from

Satan (Revelation 9:11). The duration of the torment is "five months" (9:5,10). No reason is given as to the duration of the punishment.

The nature of the punishment these demons inflict upon men can be seen from the following verse.

And in those days shall men seek death, and shall not find it; and shall desire to die, and death shall flee from them (9:6).

The victims become so weary of the agony that they long to die in order to get release from it, but death eludes them. Death has always been the enemy of men (1 Corinthians 15:26). Unsaved men are ever trying to evade it, except in cases where the mind fails. But in the time of the Great Tribulation, due to the severity of the agony and suffering, men will seek it only to discover that they cannot die. J. J. Van Gorder has said: "It may be that suffering men will plunge into lakes or seas to seek death by drowning, only to find for some unknown reason that their bodies will not sink. Poison may be swallowed only to find it has been neutralized to impotency." The day when men shall choose death rather than life is predicted by God through Jeremiah the prophet (Jeremiah 8:3). Oh, the misery of waiting for death when it cometh not! (Job 3:21) Such will be the state of men that even death would be a relief. What mercy in our present dispensation of grace that these demons are locked up in the abyss! What mercy that God prevented fallen man from eating of the tree of life and living forever in a body ridden with incurable and painful disease! (Genesis 3:22-24). What mercy that believers shall escape this invasion of the underworld! The prophecy of Joel seems to coincide with this prophecy of John (Joel 2:1-11).

IV. THE UNSCRUPULOUS PRINCE (9:11)

And they had a king over them, which is the angel of the bottomless pit, whose name in the Hebrew tongue is Abaddon, but in the Greek tongue hath his name Apollyon (9:11).

The king over these demons is Satan, who is described in both Hebrew (*Abaddon*) and Greek (*Apollyon*). Both words mean "destroyer." The name being given in both Hebrew and Greek indicates that the judgment will come upon both Jew and Gentile, the only ones escaping being those who have the seal of God in their foreheads (9:4). Paul stated clearly that the gospel of Christ is for both Jew and Gentile (Romans 1:16), but that either who reject God's Son must suffer (Romans 2:8-9). The purpose of Satan, namely to destroy, is the opposite of God's purpose in Christ, which is to save. This unscrupulous prince of the demons is called by our Lord "the prince of this world" (John 12:31; 14:30; 16:11). After the Church has been caught up to be with her Lord, both apostate Jews and apostate Gentiles will suffer at Satan's hands.

> *One woe is past; and, behold, there come two woes more hereafter* (9:12).

I have not exaggerated the horrors of the coming judgment upon the earth, which judgment is but a foretaste of an eternal hell to follow. Oh, trust the Lord Jesus Christ at once!

The Sixth Trumpet

> *And the sixth angel sounded, and I heard a voice from the four horns of the golden altar which is before God, Saying to the sixth angel which had the trumpet, Loose the four angels which are bound in the great river Euphrates. And the four angels were loosed, which were prepared for an hour, and a day, and a month, and a year, for to-slay the third part of men. And the number of the army of the horsemen were two hundred thousand thousand: and I heard the number of them. And thus I saw the horses in the vision, and them that sat on them, having breastplates of fire, and of jacinth, and brimstone: and the heads of the horses were as the heads of lions; and out of their mouths issued fire and smoke and brimstone. By these three was the third part of men killed, by the fire, and by the smoke, and by the brimstone, which issued out of their mouths. For their power is in their mouth, and in their tails: for their tails were like unto serpents, and had heads, and with them they do hurt. And the rest of the men which were not killed by these plagues yet repented not of the works of their hands, that*

they should not worship devils, and idols of gold, and silver,
and brass, and stone, and of wood: which neither can see,
nor hear, nor walk: Neither repented they of their murders,
nor of their sorceries, nor of their fornication, nor of their
thefts (9:13-21).

The fifth and sixth trumpet judgments are successive without any overlapping. The fifth is completed before the sixth commences. Now we are not to be surprised at the increased woe to be poured out upon unbelievers in the day being described here. We are assured that "evil men and seducers shall wax worse and worse" (2 Timothy 3:13), and that "in the last days perilous times shall come" (2 Timothy 3:1), therefore we can expect that God will step up the tempo of divine judgment commensurate with the wickedness in men's hearts.

The voice that is heard when the sixth angel sounds the trumpet emanates:

> *From the four horns of the golden altar which is before*
> *God* (9:13).

It was to that same golden altar that the prayers of the saints ascended for vengeance upon those who martyred their brethren (8:3). It seems now that the cry for vengeance is being answered. The horns of the altar were always available for the sinner's sacrifice, but in those days which John saw there is no more room for a sacrifice. The "one sacrifice for sins" was offered by Jesus Christ (Hebrews 10:12,13). Now His enemies must be made His footstools. God will speak to men in His wrath and vex them in His sore displeasure (Psalm 2:5). The altar of divine mercy will one day put forth divine judgment.

V. THE UNLOOSED PERSONAGES (9:13-15)

When the angel sounded the sixth trumpet, a voice was heard to say:

> *Loose the four angels which are bound in the great river*
> *Euphrates.*

The four angels are bound, therefore they are fallen angels who followed Lucifer in his rebellion and revolt against God (Isaiah 14:12-14). Good angels are not bound, but are free to serve God's children. In this present age of grace certain demons who would torment and kill all men are kept bound by God. But after the Church has been raptured God will release four of them at the sounding of the sixth trumpet just as a host will be released when the fifth trumpet sounds.

These infernal creatures are let loose in the area of the Euphrates River. Why this visitation of judgment commences in this particular part of the world we are not told. But we do know that the Euphrates was one of four tributaries which flowed from the river in Eden (Genesis 2:10-14). It was here that Satan began his first diabolical work against our first parents which resulted in our fallen human race. Here the first murder was committed (Genesis 4:8), and here man's first organized rebellion against God took place (Genesis 11).

Earlier in our study we saw four unfallen angels restraining judgment until God's servants were sealed for protection (7:1). Now four fallen angels are loosed for the purpose of executing judgment, and their activity commences at the very seat of Satan's empire. But we must remember that all of this is the judicial acting of God. It is all under divine control. God uses Satan's own hosts to bring to nought the powers of evil.

There is something else we know about the Euphrates River, namely, that one day God made an unconditional covenant with Abraham, saying, "Unto thy seed have I given this land, from the river of Egypt unto the great river, the river Euphrates" (Genesis 15:18). The Euphrates was the ideal boundary of the territory which God gave to Israel. This coveted land of inestimable wealth is the desire of nations, but God has promised it to His people, and He will protect it for them (Exodus 23:31; Deuteronomy 1:7; 11:24; Joshua 1:4). It is likely that greedy hands will be prepared to seize Palestine about the time of these predicted judgments, but God will intervene in behalf of the Jews.

These four demonic personages go about to slay the third part of the human race. If the population of the earth should total three billion, this terrible scourge will reduce it one billion, assuming there is no limit to the extent of the territory included in this judgment. Just as vegetation and water will be reduced one-third (8:7-10), here also the human population will be reduced one-third. A remarkable thing about this judgment is that it will take place at an exact time known only to God, that is, the date of the event is already scheduled. Even now the four angels are being prepared for "the" (R.V.) hour, day, month, and year (9:15). God has a program, and it is being carried out on schedule. Christian, give God time! He will bring His plan to pass. The world's mightiest armies, with godless men at their head, will be puppets in the hands of Almighty God. God holds the reins of governments in His own hand.

VI. THE UNRESTRAINED POWER (9:16-19)

An immense army of 200,000,000 horsemen appears. It is the combined power of the devil and men acting in their own interest, and yet, at the same time, they are ignorantly carrying out God's judicial will. Everything is under satanic control, but God is behind the scenes moving these very scenes. There is no power on earth able to restrain these hellish horsemen.

It is difficult to classify this unrestrained power. However, Clarence Larkin has given us an illuminating paragraph: "Supernatural armies are not unknown to Scriptures. Horses and a chariot of fire separated Elijah from Elisha in the day when Elijah was taken up by a whirlwind into Heaven (2 Kings 2:11). When Dothan was besieged by the army of Syria, God opened the eyes of Elisha's servant, and he saw the mountains around the city full of horses and chariots of fire (2 Kings 6:13-17). When the Lord Jesus Christ shall come to take 'The Kingdom,' He will be attended by the armies of Heaven riding on white horses." Just as horses have been associated with supernatural activity in the past, they will be also in these days of divine judgment on the earth.

The weapons of this mighty power are fire, smoke, and brimstone (9:17-18). While they are the weapons of hell, they are nevertheless the emblems of God's judgment. Brimstone is a gas with a sulphurous smell. It was this stifling and strangling gas that God sent down from Heaven upon the city of Sodom when He destroyed it (Luke 17:29). The coming judgment upon Babylon will take on a similar form (Revelation 14:10), as will the judgment against the beast and the false prophet (Revelation 19:20), Satan (Revelation 20:10), and eventually all unbelievers (Revelation 21:8). What a ghastly place this earth will become when hell is let loose! It is but a sample of the torment that unbelievers must endure in hell forever. And to think that in those days there will be no one to help. If this message has reached anyone who is not yet saved, I urge upon you to receive Jesus Christ at once as your Lord and Saviour.

VII. THE UNREPENTANT PEOPLE (9:20-21)

Notice that there are those who *"were not killed."* God will suffer only one-third of the race to die under this tremendous woe. He will spare two-thirds of mankind, not because they deserve to be spared, but because in wrath He remembers mercy. God has never delighted in the death of the wicked. In the midst of His visitations of severest judgments, He delights to be gracious to the guilty. But alas, the death of one billion people in the earth, with the accompanying grief and the confusion which must follow such a disaster, finds the residue of people not willing to repent. Such is the human heart, deceitful above all things and desperately wicked. After two world wars, and one hundred lesser wars in the past fifty years, the world is more wicked than ever. Instead of repentance, sin increases.

In those last days immediately preceding the second coming of Christ to earth, punishment will not of itself lead men to repent. The severest of God's judgments upon guilty men do not soften rebellious hearts. Even in hell itself men and women will manifest bitter defiance against all that is holy. While it is true that in hell there will be "wailing" (Matthew 13:42,50) and "weeping" (Matthew 22:13; 24:51; 25:30), there shall be also "gnashing of teeth," an expression of the hatred in the unregenerate heart of man. God's judgment upon Pharaoh did not soften his heart, but rather did the Eygptian monarch become more defiant.

Here God permits us to look into the future and see to what extent wickedness will prevail. More people than ever before will *"worship devils."* Such idolatry has been in the world ever since the fall of man. Worship was sought after by Satan in our Lord's temptation (Matthew 4:8-10). It was denounced by the Apostle Paul (1 Corinthians 10:20-21). These invisible, wicked spirit beings, unholy in character, and belonging to Satan's evil kingdom, seek to control the minds and bodies of living men. When all restraint is taken from the earth after the rapture of the Church, and man has had an opportunity to repent, we can well imagine the staggering world-wide influence of demons over men.

There will be the revival of idolatry. People will cling to their "idols of gold, and silver, and brass, and stone, and of wood: which neither can see, nor hear, nor walk." Idol worship prevails today even among the most enlightened and religious people in our own country. Attached to such worship is crass materialism. Millions of images made of stone, wood, metal, and plastic have flooded our nation. People wear them around their necks, display them on the dashboards of automobiles, erect them in their front yards. From the sale of these metals and materials, which men worship, the Roman Catholic Church has grossed huge sums of money.

Next there follows a list of evil practices which correspond to the heathen character of the world's dominant religion during the period of the tribulation. The first of these is *"murder,"* which, ever since Cain killed Abel, is looked upon as a common crime! The free and flagrant taking of human life will be on the increase. God's absolute and eternal law which says, "Thou shalt not kill" (Exodus 20:13), will be totally ignored.

Then there follows that which is here designated *"sorceries."* J. A. Seiss refers to this as "Impure practices with evil agencies, and particularly with poisonous drugs. The word specially includes tampering with one's own or another's health, by means of drugs, potions, intoxications, and often with magical arts and incantations, the invocation of spiritual agencies. We have only to think of the use of alcoholic stimulants, of opium, of tobacco, of the rage for cosmetics to increase sex attraction."

The *"fornication"* mentioned here is the flagrant disregard for the sacred institution of marriage. Today there is a limited restraint placed upon the violation of marriage vows. But in the day described in our text restraint will be withdrawn and human passion will break loose. Society will be deluged with the sins of fornication and adultery, the institution of legal and sacred wedlock will be denounced, and the teaching of free love will prevail. As we see even the morals of Christians degenerating in our day, we shudder to think of our human race in the days ahead of us.

The list of sins concludes with *"thefts."* Honesty will be obliterated. There will be no regard for another's rights. Since fraud, deceit, and theft are common today, we see no hope for the world of tomorrow. The wickedness of the days here described are almost too appalling to contemplate. Little wonder we read, "Behold, the Lord cometh with ten thousands of His saints, To execute judgment upon all, and to convince all that are ungodly among them of all their ungodly deeds which they have ungodly committed, and of all their hard speeches which ungodly sinners have spoken against Him" (Jude 14-15).

May God grant that these solemn and inspired words from the Holy Scriptures shall call sinners to repentance and summon Christians to a life of total dedication to Jesus Christ. All evil must produce its bitter fruit. May this terrible picture of the moral state of the world in the coming days turn many hearts to God at once in true repentance.

How blind men are who say that the world is getting better!

THE MIGHTY ANGEL FROM HEAVEN

Revelation 10:1-11

If you have been expecting the seventh angel to sound the seventh trumpet at this point, you are going to be disappointed. Between the breaking of the sixth and seventh seals we met with a sort of interlude. That interlude (chapter 7) described how God remembers mercy in the midst of wrath and seals a host of Jews and Gentiles. We mentioned in that earlier study that another such parenthesis would appear between the sixth and seventh trumpets. The passage before us (10:1-11:14) is that parenthesis. The sixth trumpet has already sounded, but the seventh trumpet does not sound until later (11:15). These interludes, or parentheses, are parts of the whole. They are not unconnected segments.

I. THE APPEARANCE OF THE MIGHTY ANGEL (10:1)

And I saw another mighty angel come down from heaven, clothed with a cloud: and a rainbow was upon his head, and his face was as it were the sun, and his feet as pillars of fire (10:1).

The "mighty angel" here is not named. However, there are a number of things about Him which have led some teachers of the Bible to identify Him as Jesus Christ. The idea that Christ should be called an angel need not trouble us. "Angel," like "Son of Man," is a title, and neither implies that the One who bears the title is a created being. Frequently in the Old Testament we meet with "the Angel of Jehovah." These pre-incarnate appearances of Christ are called theophanies or

Christophanies. He is called "the angel of His [Jehovah's] presence" (Isaiah 63:9), "the angel of the LORD (Exodus 3:2). Read Exodus 3, and you will see that the claims and actions of the Angel of Jehovah pertain only to Deity. Here in the apocalyptic vision John saw Him "come down from heaven." When our Lord was on the earth He said, "I came down from heaven" (John 6:38). After His Resurrection He was taken up into Heaven. But the day is coming when this same Jesus, the Mighty Angel of Jehovah, will appear on the earth again.

His face was as it were the sun (10:1).

John says that "His countenance was as the sun shineth in his strength" (1:16). On the Mount of Transfiguration, "His face did shine as the sun" (Matthew 17:2). It was thus that Saul of Tarsus met Him on his way to Damascus (Acts 9:3 cf. 26:13). It would seem that the Mighty Angel is He whom the prophet described as "the Sun of righteousness" (Malachi 4:2).

His feet as pillars of fire (10:1).

John saw "His feet like unto fine brass, as if they burned in a furnace" (1:15). These are the feet of majesty set for the judgment of the earth.

II. THE ATTIRE OF THE MIGHTY ANGEL (10:1)

John saw Him *"clothed with a cloud"* (10:1). The cloud was of old the garment of the divine presence and was associated with divine movements. The Lord directed Israel by day in "a pillar of cloud" (Exodus 13:21). When Israel murmured, "the glory of the LORD appeared in the cloud" (Exodus 16:10). At Sinai He descended in "a thick cloud" (Exodus 19:9,16). When the tables of stone were renewed to replace the broken ones, "The LORD descended in the cloud" (Exodus 34:4-5). When the tabernacle was completed, "Then a cloud covered the tent of the congregation, and the glory of the LORD filled the tabernacle" (Exodus 40:34). This cloud was designated "the cloud of the LORD" (Exodus 40:38). God had said, "I will appear in the cloud upon the mercy seat" (Leviticus 16:2). The cloud was associated with direction as well as with Deity (Numbers 9:15-22). The Psalmist states that the cloud is characteristic of the Almighty, "Clouds and darkness are round about Him" (Psalm 97:2). On the Mount of Transfiguration, when the effulgence of Christ's deity shone forth, "A bright cloud overshadowed them: and behold a voice out of the cloud, which said, This is My beloved Son, in whom I am well pleased; hear ye Him" (Matthew 17:5). When Christ ascended to Heaven, "a cloud received Him" (Acts 1:9). Before He left the earth He said, "They shall see the Son of Man coming in a cloud with power and great glory" (Luke 21:27). "Behold, He cometh with clouds" (Revelation 1:7). Clouds, then, belong to the attire of Deity. The cloud-clothing suggests that the Mighty Angel is Christ.

And a rainbow was upon His head (10:1).

In chapter four the rainbow was "round about the throne" (4:3); here it is upon the head of the Mighty Angel. We know that the rainbow is the symbol of God's everlasting covenant with the earth (Genesis 9:12-13), therefore we would not expect any one other than the Divine Person to wear it upon His head. Ezekiel saw the rainbow as part of the glory of the throne of God (Ezekiel 1:28). Just as the cloud is indicative of the coming storm of wrath in divine judgment, so the rainbow is indicative of divine mercy in the midst of judgment, an evident symbol of security for the believing ones. God protects His own when conditions in the earth are at their worst.

III. THE ACTIONS OF THE MIGHTY ANGEL (10:2)

He set His right foot upon the sea, and His left foot upon the earth (10:2).

The full significance of this action is nowhere stated in Scripture. We do know that the sea and the land stand for the sum total of the material universe. I take it that the action of planting the feet down, one foot on the earth and the other on the sea, is equivalent to claiming both the earth and the sea as His own possession. "For the earth is the Lord's, and the fulness thereof" (1 Corinthians 10:26,28). I am reminded of the reference in which God said to Joshua, "Every place that the sole of your foot shall tread upon, that have I given unto you, as I said unto Moses" (Joshua 1:3; Deuteronomy 11:24). The Mighty Angel is "the Lord of all the earth" (Joshua 3:11), for "all things were created by Him, and for Him" (Colossians 1:16). When He shall set His feet upon the land and the sea He will express His intention of taking possession of that which is His. Seiss says, "It is an act befitting the character and office of Christ, but hardly a created angel." Christ came to have dominion over all creation, so then all things must be put under His feet (Psalm 8:6; Hebrews 2:8). Satan will assert his claim to the earth, but when Christ puts His foot down He will take possession of His own property and subdue all assaults of the enemy.

IV. THE ASSERTION OF THE MIGHTY ANGEL (10:3-4)

And cried with a loud voice, as when a lion roareth; and when He had cried, seven thunders uttered their voices (10:3).

He cried as when a lion roars. Here is the mighty voice of the Lion of the Tribe of Judah (Revelation 5:5 cf. Hebrews 7:14). He is asserting Himself prior to the exercise of judgment. Elsewhere in Scripture the lion's roar was a symbol of imminent judgment. Hosea prophesied, "They shall walk after the Lord: He shall roar like a lion: when He shall roar, then the children shall tremble from the west" (Hosea 11:10). Joel added his prophecy, "The Lord also shall roar out of Zion, and utter His voice from Jerusalem; and the heavens and the earth shall shake: but the Lord will be the hope of His people, and the strength of the children of Israel" (Joel 3:16). Amos said, "The Lord will roar from Zion, and utter His voice from Jerusalem; and the habitations of the shepherds shall mourn, and the top of Carmel shall wither" (Amos 1:2). "Their roaring shall be like a lion, they shall roar like young lions: yea, they shall roar, and lay hold of the prey, and shall carry it away safe, and none shall deliver it" (Isaiah 5:29). The lion roars when he is about to make his last leap upon his victim. In a loud voice to be heard over all the earth Christ asserts His right to rule and His intention of accomplishing it.

> *And when He had cried, seven thunders uttered their voices* (10:3).

Thunder is a recognized type of God's voice in judgment (1 Samuel 7:10; Psalm 18:13). The detailed substance of these awesome peals of thunder is not indicated. The number seven is suggestive of the completeness and finality of the Angel's mighty sayings. We see these seven thunders in Psalm 29 where "the voice of the LORD" goes forth seven times as thunder. When the Father spoke from Heaven to the Lord Jesus on earth, "The people therefore, that stood by, and heard it, said that it thundered" (John 12:28-29). Here in Revelation 10 the seven thunders are the judgment thunders of God.

John heard what the thunders said, and when he was about to put into writing what he heard, a voice from Heaven said:

> *Seal up those things which the seven thunders uttered, and write them not* (10:4).

The command was clear and absolute, and John obeyed it. Therefore what the seven thunders said is not known by any of us, so it is foolish to speculate. As far as I understand the book of the Revelation, the seven thunders are the only part of this book which has been sealed. Concerning the rest of what John saw and heard, the Lord said to him, "Seal not the sayings of the prophecy of this book" (22:10). But John is not alone in having been forbidden to write all that he saw and heard. Paul was not permitted to speak or write about all the things he heard in Paradise (2 Corinthians 12:4). God knows with whom He can trust His secrets. "God thundereth marvellously with His voice; great things doeth He, which we can not comprehend" (Job 37:5).

V. THE AFFIRMATION OF THE MIGHTY ANGEL
(10:5-7)

After the sound of the seven thunders, the Mighty Angel lifted His hand toward Heaven and swore, or uttered an oath. The vision is most solemn! It is not inherently wrong for Christ to take an oath. Keep in mind that the scene before us does not occur during the dispensation of grace. Under the law God swore, and here Christ swears to attest the authority and finality of His own statements. There may be limitations on swearing during the gospel period (Matthew 5:33-37; James 5:12), but here we have moved on to another period of time after the Church has been caught up to Heaven.

We have it stated that God attested His promise to Abraham by an oath, "For when God made promise to Abraham, because He could swear by no greater, He sware by Himself" (Hebrews 6:13). When God made a promise to Abraham, He pledged Himself to carry it out (Genesis 22:16). The attestation that God gave to Abraham was the greatest that God could give. God had actually staked His very existence on the carrying out of His promise. In other words, it is as though He were saying, "I will cease to be God if I fail to keep My promise." The fulfillment of the promise was as certain as God's existence. To make an oath, one must swear by someone or something greater than himself, else the oath is of no more value or veracity than a mere statement. But the Almighty could not swear by a person greater than Himself, for there is none greater. One man may not accept the assertion of another because men do not trust one another, but if a man would swear by one greater, then his assertion would be considered binding. So in order to condescend to a weakness in man's nature, God confirmed His promise with an oath. The great events yet to happen in the earth, as announced by God, must surely come to pass. These events have to do with judgment. Christ has staked His very existence on their fulfillment. (For a similar oath which God made to David see Psalm 89:3,35).

What did the Mighty Angel affirm? To what did he swear?

That there should be time no longer (10:6).

Examine the marginal note in your Bible, or consult the Revised Version, and you will have a literal and more accurate translation of the text. It reads, *"That there should be no more delay."* The very next verse explains the meaning.

But in days of the voice of the seventh angel, when He shall begin to sound, the mystery of God should be finished, as He hath declared to His servants the prophets (10:7).

Christ is saying in the midst of the tribulation that there is one more trumpet judgment. Time will continue long after this event, but what He says is that when the seventh trumpet sounds, all evil in the earth will be put down without further delay. Sin has been reigning, and righteousness has suffered throughout man's day on the earth, but now things must change. There must be a reversal of this order. The Mighty Angel's affirmation means that the hour has struck.

The mystery of God should be finished (10:7).

This phrase indicates that all the counsels and covenants of God concerning His governmental dealings over man and the earth, made known through the penmen of Holy Scriptures, will be consummated. When Christ comes to reign, there will be no longer mystery, but manifestation. "The earth shall be full of the knowledge of the LORD, as the waters cover the sea" (Isaiah 11:9). When the Mighty Angel asserts His rightful claim to the earth, the program of God in judgment will reach its completion without delay. For centuries men have been saying, "My Lord delayeth His coming" (Matthew 24:48), while others have scoffingly said, "Where is the promise of His coming?" (2 Peter 3:4) But God is not slack concerning any of His promises.

The great mystery of our age has been the so-called silence of God in the face of prevailing wickedness. Sin has stalked around the earth unashamed without much divine intervention. But one day the judgment of the Almighty will be laid upon the world. Then we shall know why He permitted Satan and sin. The mystery of the struggle between light and darkness, good and evil, will be made known in that day. I confess that at times I have been baffled, and even troubled, by questions in my own mind as to the strange providential ways and dealings of God. But I know that I must wait in patience until that day when the mystery will be made known. That which is now unknown will then be revealed.

Here we must exercise care so as not to confuse the coming judgments of God with the mysteries of Christ (Matthew 13) and of Paul (Romans 11:25; 1 Corinthians 15:51; Ephesians 1:9; 5:32; 6:19; Colossians 2:2; 2 Thessalonians 2:7; 1 Timothy 3:16). The secret here in the Revelation refers to what had already been made known by God to the Old Testament prophets. The great secrets concerning Christ and His Church were confined to the New Testament prophet, the Apostle Paul. But all will be fulfilled in their respective times.

VI. THE AGENCY OF THE MIGHTY ANGEL (10:8-10)

And the voice which I heard from heaven spake unto me again, and said, Go and take the little book which is open in the hand of the angel which standeth upon the sea and upon the earth. And I went unto the angel, and said unto him, Give me the little book. And he said unto me, Take it, and eat it up; and it shall make thy belly bitter, but it shall be in thy mouth sweet as honey. And I took the little book out of the angel's hand, and ate it up; and it was in my mouth sweet as honey: and as soon as I had eaten it, my belly was bitter (10:8-10).

When the Mighty Angel appeared, "He had in His hand a little book" (10:2). What does the little book contain? Nothing short of divine revelation. It is the Word of God. Its message is that portion of divinely-revealed truth which pertains to the final judgments and the second coming of Christ to reign. This little book might be the same seven-sealed book described in chapter five. Some teachers believe it to be the writings of Daniel, which God told him must be sealed up until "the time of the end" (Daniel 12:9). At any rate, we know it is God's Word, the mighty agent He uses in disclosing His sovereign purposes.

John was commanded to take the little book, and when he did so, the Angel said:

> *Take it, and eat it up; and it shall make thy belly bitter, but it shall be in thy mouth sweet as honey* (10:9).

What are we to understand from this command given to John? The Word of God is compared with food. Jesus said, "Man shall not live by bread alone, but by every word that proceedeth out of the mouth of God" (Matthew 4:4). Jeremiah wrote, "Thy words were found, and I did eat them; and Thy word was unto me the joy and rejoicing of mine heart: for I am called by Thy name, O LORD God of hosts" (Jeremiah 15:16). The Psalmist read, "How sweet are Thy words unto my taste! yea, sweeter than honey to my mouth!" (Psalm 119:103) "As newborn babes, desire the sincere milk of the word, that ye may grow thereby" (1 Peter 2:2). "For every one that useth milk is unskilful in the word of righteousness: for he is a babe. But strong meat belongeth to them that are of full age, even those who by reason of use have their senses exercised to discern both good and evil" (Hebrews 5:13-14). Eating the Word is, in its more general application, appropriating and assimilating God's truth; it is meditating in it (Psalm 1:2). No child of God will deny that the truth of the Scriptures is sweet to know. "It is sweet to know as we onward go: the way of the Cross leads home." It is sweet to know that Satan will not hold sway over the earth forever. The prophetic Word is sweet because it talks of the blessing and glory that are on ahead. Ezekiel had an experience quite similar to that of John (Ezekiel 2:9-3:4).

But why did that Book which tasted so sweet leave God's servant with the feeling of inward bitterness? I believe that the prophecies of coming judgment leave the child of God with great heaviness of heart and bitter anguish of soul. It was so with the Apostle Paul (Romans 9:1-3). The future will be glory for the saint but grief for the sinner. God's Word is a two-edged sword. It contains the sweet message of deliverance and the bitter message of damnation (Hebrews 4:12). He who appropriates the Book cannot escape its mixture of sweet and bitter. There is nothing sweeter than the gospel to a believing soul, but, on the other hand, there is nothing more bitter than the divine pronouncement of forthcoming doom upon the unbeliever. Scott said, "Prophecy both gladdens and saddens, as it contains announcements both of joy and grief." A proverb says, "Pleasant words are as an honeycomb sweet to the soul, and health to the bones" (Proverbs 16:24). But words of doom and damnation are not pleasant words. In Isaiah's day the truth was bitter to the people, so they did not want it (Isaiah 30:8-11). Nevertheless God's Word is His agent in salvation and in condemnation.

VII. THE ASSIGNMENT OF THE MIGHTY ANGEL (10:11)

And he said unto me, Thou must prophesy again before many peoples, and nations, and tongues, and kings (10:11).

After partaking of the Book, John was assigned the task of ministering to many more people that which he himself had received. The believer who receives God's truth is solemnly obligated to pass it on to others. The minister who fails to preach the whole counsel of God will be held accountable by God (Ezekiel 33:7-9). It is not easy for the minister to deal with matters of sin and judgment, but he has no choice. There are "peoples and nations and tongues and kings" who must hear God's message of salvation. John was faithful, for in the chapters which follow he prophesies of the final overthrow of the nations, the Great White Throne judgment and hell. The message may not be what the people want, but it is what God wants them to have.

Many years ago I promised God that I would preach His Word exactly as He revealed it to me. This is not an easy task. I have found those persons in attendance who were resentful of truth that exposes sin and pronounces judgment.

No man who faithfully proclaims God's Word can escape persecution at the hands of his hearers. The truth is always unwelcome when it strikes at the sin and immorality of those who hear it. The faithful Elijahs usually trouble the Ahabs (1 Kings 18:17). But I must warn you who are continuing in your sin, that, unless you repent, you must suffer the judgment of the Almighty. Receive Christ as your Saviour and Lord, and do it at once.

THE TWO WITNESSES

Revelation 11:1-19

The chapter before us is admittedly a difficult one. Seiss calls this chapter "one of the most difficult in the whole Apocalypse." Barclay says, "This chapter is at one and the same time the most difficult and the most important chapter in the *Revelation*." If you have read it you know for yourself that conclusions cannot be arrived at hastily. Much prayer and study are required. But we cannot be deterred by the difficult. We must press on in our pursuit of the understanding of these great prophecies.

I. THE TEMPLE WORSHIP (11:1-2)

And there was given me a reed like unto a rod: and the angel stood, saying, Rise, and measure the temple of God, and the altar, and them that worship therein. But the court which is without the temple leave out, and measure it not; for it is given unto the Gentiles: and the holy city shall they tread under foot forty and two months (11:1-2).

We observe at once that the language is peculiarly Jewish. This whole chapter is anticipation in character, looking ahead to the rebuilt temple in Jerusalem during the tribulation. None of the details have been fulfilled. There is nothing in history to which we can point; it is all prophetic. That there will be a temple built at Jerusalem for the worship of Jehovah is proved by several passages.

There were at least three temples built in Jerusalem: Solomon's temple described in 1 Kings 8 and destroyed by Nebuchadnezzar in 583 B.C. (2 Kings 24-25); Zerubbabel's temple, described in Ezra 3 and destroyed by Antiochus Epiphanes in 168 B.C.; Herod's temple, referred to by our Lord in John 2:20 and destroyed by Titus in 70 A.D.

God's temple in this present dispensation of grace is His Church, made up of each true believer in the Lord Jesus Christ (Ephesians 2:21 cf. 1 Corinthians 6:19). But the verses before us (Revelation 11:1-2) cannot be applied to the Church. Those who make this temple the Church are wrong in their interpretation. The worship here is Jewish, not Christian. There is neither an earthly temple nor an altar associated with Christian worship (Hebrews 10:19-22).

This temple is to be built in the "holy city." This takes us to Jerusalem, for there is no other city so designated in the Scriptures. (See Nehemiah 11:1,18; Isaiah 52:1; Daniel 9:24; Matthew 4:5; 27:52-53.) We understand the "holy city" to be what the Scriptures always mean, namely, Jerusalem. God is not finished with the Jews. A magnificent temple will be erected at Jerusalem and many worshipers will gather. A system of priesthood and sacrifices will be set up in the midst of an ordered service of worship. Some of the details of the temple and its system of worship is doubtless to be found in Ezekiel 40-48.

In that temple the personal Antichrist will appear and claim the right to be worshiped. "Who opposeth and exalteth himself above all that is called God, or that is worshipped; so that he as God sitteth in the temple of God, shewing himself that he is God" (2 Thessalonians 2:4). This is the abomination of desolation spoken by Daniel (Daniel 9:2) and attested by our Lord (Matthew 24:15). The religious system of the man of sin will be connected with the temple at Jerusalem. The mass of the people will accept him who will come in his own name (John 5:43).

The outer court of this temple is not included in the measurement but is to be rejected. The reason for this is given. It is the court of the Gentiles. Notice that these verses speak of

Jews and Gentiles. The Church is not mentioned, for in Christ, the Head of the Church, "there is neither Greek nor Jew circumcision nor uncircumcision, Barbarian, Scythian, bond nor free: but Christ is all, and in all" (Colossians 3:11).

The temple in Jerusalem was divided into four courts. One of these was the court of the Gentiles, into which Gentiles might come, but beyond which they dare not pass under penalty of death. If the measuring here indicates the idea of an impending claim (see Ezekiel 40; Zechariah 2; and Revelation 21:15), then there is to be no portion staked out for the Gentiles. The reason for this is obvious: *"the holy city shall they tread under foot forty and two months."* The Gentiles are not being favored by God above the Jews, but rather God is using them for the chastisement of Israel (Zechariah 14:1-2).

The "rod" which in the book of the Revelation is an instrument of chastisement (see 2:27; 12:5; 19:15), will be laid upon Israel at the hand of the Gentiles for a limited time only— *"forty and two months."* This is the famous phrase prophesied by Daniel as "a time, times, and an half" (Daniel 7:25; 12:7), meaning one year plus two years plus half a year. The duration of Israel's trouble is computed then in literal months, the equivalent of *"a thousand two hundred and threescore days"* (11:3), the exact time the beast is permitted to thunder forth his blasphemies (13:5). This is the period of the exile of the woman clothed with the sun (12:6). These three-and-one-half years are the last half of Daniel's seventieth week (Daniel 9:25-27 cf. Revelation 12:14), the Great Tribulation which will come to a close with the personal return of Christ to the earth, when He shall subdue all evil and establish His reign. "Then shall the LORD go forth, and fight against those nations [Gentiles], as when He fought in the day of battle. And His feet shall stand in that day upon the mount of Olives, which is before Jerusalem on the east, and the mount of Olives shall cleave in the midst thereof toward the east and toward the west, and there shall be a very great valley; and half of the mountain shall remove toward the north, and half of it toward the south" (Zechariah 14:3-4). Our Lord said that "Jerusalem shall be trodden down of the Gentiles, until the times of the Gentiles be fulfilled" (Luke 21:24). The "times of the Gentiles" will end at the second advent of our Lord, when the armies of the beast are destroyed by Him as recorded in Revelation 19:17-19.

II. THE TWO WITNESSES (11:3-12)

Now read carefully every word of this passage:

> *And I will give power unto My two witnesses, and they shall prophesy a thousand two hundred and threescore days, clothed in sackcloth. These are the two olive trees, and the two candlesticks standing before the God of the earth. And if any man will hurt them, fire proceedeth out of their mouth, and devoureth their enemies: and if any man will hurt them, he must in this manner be killed. These have power to shut heaven, that it rain not in the days of their prophecy: and have power over waters to turn them to blood, and to smite the earth with all plagues, as often as they will. And when they shall have finished their testimony, the beast that ascendeth out of the bottomless pit shall make war against them, and shall overcome them, and kill them. And their dead bodies shall lie in the street of the great city, which spiritually is called Sodom and Egypt, where also our Lord was crucified. And they of the people and kindred and tongues and nations shall see their dead bodies three days and an half, and shall not suffer their dead bodies to be put in graves. And they that dwell upon the earth shall rejoice over them, and make merry, and shall send gifts one to another; because these two prophets tormented them that dwelt on the earth. And after three days and an half the spirit of life from God entered into them, and they stood upon their feet; and great fear fell upon them which saw them. And they heard a great voice from heaven saying unto them, Come up hither. And they ascended up to heaven in a cloud: and their enemies beheld them* (11:3-12).

These two witnesses, though not named, have been the topic of much discussion, study, and speculation.

A. *They Are Persons*

The two witnesses are not the law and the gospel, or the Old Testament and the New Testament. They speak. They have mouths. They are heard, handled, and hated. They are individuals, for after their martyrdom John sees their "dead bodies" (11:9). By no stretch of the imagination can we regard these witnesses as other than real persons. In the New Testament the noun "witness" refers to a person who testifies to what he has seen or heard or knows. These witnesses wear clothing of "sackcloth," a word used for a garment worn when one is expressing mourning or declaring the need for repentance (Matthew 11:21; Luke 10:13).

These two witnesses are called *"the two olive trees, and the two candlesticks standing before the God of the earth"* (11:4). What John saw here is explained in Zechariah's vision. Read Zechariah, chapters 4 and 5, where the two olive trees represent two individual persons, Joshua and Zerubbabel, men who were the media whereby the Word of God was transmitted to the people. They are men who have enjoined upon them a position of responsibility in service before the Lord of all the earth. Joshua is mentioned in Zechariah 3:1,3,6,8,9. The two together, Zerubbabel and Joshua, are mentioned also by the Prophet Haggai as standing together in a united witness for Jehovah (Haggai 1:1; 2:2,4). Thus we see that the phrase "two olive trees" is explained by Scripture and means two persons.

B. *They Are Prophets*

They shall prophesy . . . *in the days of their* prophecy . . . *these two prophets* (11:3,6,10).

Notice that the Lord calls them, *"My two witnesses"* (11:3), meaning they are forthtellers and foretellers of Christ and His message. They preach to men on earth God's message sent from Heaven. We are not told expressly why there are two, but we do know that both the law and the gospel, whether the gospel of grace or the gospel of the kingdom, is established by at least two witnesses (Deuteronomy 17:6; 19:15; Matthew 11:2-3; 18:16; 21:1; Mark 6:7; John 8:17).

But who are these two prophets? I have nothing new to offer my readers. But for the benefit of any who have not had the opportunity to hear or read the different views, we shall examine two of them now. Most students who do not attempt to spiritualize these verses and who believe that the two witnesses are persons, are agreed that one of them is Elijah. There are several facts on which this view rests. (1) Elijah did not experience physical death (2 Kings 2:9-11), "and as it is appointed unto men once to die" (Hebrews 9:27), this Old Testament prophet could return and experience death as the two witnesses will (11:7-8). (2) It is predicted in Malachi 3:1-3 and 4:5-6 that Elijah would appear on the earth to prepare the way for the Messiah's Second Advent. (3) The witnesses are given power to perform the same miracle that Elijah performed, namely, that of withholding rain from the earth for the space of three-and-one-half years (1 Kings 17:1 cf. Luke 4:25; James 5:17-18).

Those who object to Elijah being one of the two witnesses say that John the Baptist fulfilled all that was predicted of Elijah. This objection is based upon the clear statements of Christ in Matthew 11:14 and 17:12 that John was the Elijah of the prophecy. But the objectors to Elijah being one of the witnesses have evidently failed to see that Christ's statement that John was Elijah was based on a contingency, namely, "if ye will receive it" [the kingdom] (Matthew 11:14). But they rejected the offered kingdom (Matthew 17:12), therefore John is excluded from being the one to fulfill the prophecy. The angel told Zacharias that John "shall go before Him in the spirit and power of Elias" (Luke 1:17), but he did not say that John would be the literal Elijah. John denied that he was Elijah (John 1:21). I take the passage in Malachi literally. Elijah means Elijah. "The great and dreadful day of the LORD" (Malachi 4:5) is the day of Christ's Second Advent to the earth when He shall rule the nations with a rod of iron.

Now concerning the other of the two witnesses, I am inclined to agree with those teachers who identify him as *Enoch*. (1) Enoch, who lived before the flood, was translated without seeing death (Genesis 5:24). (2) Inasmuch as Christ is the only Person ever to put on immortality (1 Timothy 6:16), and Enoch, like Elijah, was translated without experiencing immortality, both must return to die. (3) Like Elijah, Enoch was a prophet of judgment (Jude 14-15), and this is consistent with the ministry of the two witnesses who prophesy judgment. I believe that these two prophets, Enoch and Elijah, fit the case in Revelation 11 more accurately than any others.

C. *They Are Powerful*

The Lord said:

> *I will give power unto My two witnesses. . . . These have power* (11:3,6).

They are given supernatural power to defend themselves by sending forth fire out of their mouths to slay any who would hurt them (compare 2 Kings 1:7-14). Because they are Christ's witnesses, they are immortal until their work is done. The whole earth is against these two, but they continue to display divine power to hold back rain, turn water into blood, and smite the earth with plagues (Luke 4:25).

Keep in mind that the day in which they prophesy and display such power is not the present dispensation of grace. Today God's true witnesses do not kill, torment, and mete out judgments upon their enemies. We do not render evil for evil. The keynote of the gospel in our age is grace. Like Stephen and Paul and Peter, Christians do not avenge themselves. The two witnesses, however, are sent to the earth in judgment times. The third woe and the seventh trumpet are ready to send forth their judgments, therefore these are special witnesses for an extraordinary work. Because they are judgment prophets they are given judgment powers.

Paul had his enemies who hated and persecuted him, but he was not given the power nor the right to retaliate. He wrote, "The weapons of our warfare are not carnal, but mighty through

God to the pulling down of strong holds" (2 Corinthians 10:4). "Finally, my brethren, be strong in the Lord, and in the power of His might. Put on the whole armour of God, that ye may be able to stand against the wiles of the devil. For we wrestle not against flesh and blood, but against principalities, against powers, against the rulers of the darkness of this world, against spiritual wickedness in high places. Wherefore take unto you the whole armour of God, that ye may be able to withstand in the evil day, and having done all, to stand. Stand therefore, having your loins girt about with truth, and having on the breastplate of righteousness; And your feet shod with the preparation of the gospel of peace; Above all, taking the shield of faith, wherewith ye shall be able to quench all the fiery darts of the wicked. And take the helmet of salvation, and the sword of the Spirit, which is the word of God: Praying always with all prayer and supplication in the Spirit, and watching thereunto with all perseverance and supplication for all saints" (Ephesians 6:10-18). James and John would have liked to duplicate the acts of Elijah, but our Lord rebuked them (Luke 9:54-56).

D. *They Are Persecuted*

> *And when they shall have finished their testimony, the beast that ascendeth out of the bottomless pit shall make war against them, and shall overcome them, and kill them* (11:7).

These two witnesses, like all true witnesses of Jesus Christ, are immortal until their work is done. Do not overlook the fact that they were not killed until after they had *"finished their testimony"* (11:7). The beast who comes up out of the abyss cannot harm them until they accomplish their divinely-ordered mission. Satan is unable to silence or slay them. Their lives and their labors stand together. God will not allow anything to interfere with their witness-bearing as long as they are in His will. Early attempts were made on the life of our Lord, but none were successful. Not until He said, "It is finished" (John 19:30), did He surrender His Spirit to the Father. Attempts were made to kill Paul, one of those such efforts meeting with apparent success (2 Corinthians 12:1-4), but God raised him up and spared him to finish his testimony. Paul knew that when the time of his departure had come, he had finished his course (2 Timothy 4:6-7). How these two witnesses will be actually preserved, we do not know. Coming from Heaven to earth as they will, the question has been asked as to whether or not they will partake of earthly food. The Word of God does not discuss these details. We know that Elijah was supernaturally fed when he was on the earth the first time (1 Kings 17). But such details in relation to his coming again need not bother us now.

So significant will be the testimony of the two witnesses that their death at the hands of the beast shall cause an international stir. Their dead bodies go unburied and lie in the streets of Jerusalem for three-and-one-half days. It is quite possible that these scenes in John's vision on Patmos were predicted by David in Psalm 79:1-3,10-11. Notice that the place where the witnesses die, *"the holy city"* (11:2) is here called *"the great city, which spiritually is called Sodom and Egypt, where also our Lord was crucified"* (11:8). Here we have our Lord's own description of spiritual and moral conditions in Jerusalem in that day. As it was in the days of Lot in Sodom, and in the days of the idolatrous Pharaohs in Egypt, so it will be in the "holy city" where our Lord was crucified. And just as God sent fire and brimstone from Heaven upon Sodom, and judgment plagues upon Egypt, He will send awful judgments upon the *"holy city . . . forty and two months"* (11:2). How sad that the religious center of the earth, the place of our Lord's birth, life, crucifixion, resurrection, and ascension, set apart for holy purposes, retrogresses morally so as to reach its darkest age!

The bodies of the two witnesses become a spectacle to all the world.

> *The people and kindreds and tongues and nations shall see their dead bodies* (11:9).

As far back as 1935 the scoffers made sport of this verse, but today international television has silenced all such. When the news spreads concerning the death of Christ's witnesses, there is jubilation and the sending of gifts (11:10). Their corrupting bodies are exposed to the view of all, an act contrary to divine law and human decency (Deuteronomy 21:22-23). Every method of communication will be used to spread the news that the two witnesses are dead at last. The world's superman, the beast, will become the new world's champion and the hero in the eyes of a morally degenerating mass of humanity. This will be the world's most ungodly period. It is described in Jude 14-15. As we think of how near to our own day the fulfillment of these prophecies might be, we are amazed at the blindness of the leaders of society. Many are still clinging to the ridiculous idea that man will improve the world by his own efforts. Even today, to silence the heralds of the gospel of Christ, and get rid of the "old-fashioned and outworn message of historic Christianity" is considered by many to be a mark of progress.

But the end of the two witnesses is not yet.

E. *They Are Preserved*

And after three days and an half the Spirit of life from God entered into them, and they stood upon their feet; and great fear fell upon them which saw them (11:11).

The enemies of God are about to witness a demonstration of divine power that the beast cannot equal. Imagine, if you can, the fear and consternation that will grip the peoples of the world as they actually view the dead coming back to life. And then more excitement and drama are added to the scene as Christ's vindicated witnesses are seen ascending alive to Heaven. No intercontinental ballistic missile can prevent their escape from earth. Here is a re-enactment, as it were, of Elijah's and Enoch's first departure to Heaven, the former's being described for us in 2 Kings 2:11. Never before in the history of the world have so many people witnessed such a sight. The modernists and liberals who reject a literal resurrection and rapture will witness both. The death, resurrection, and ascension of the witnesses harmonize in some details with that of our Lord. The tomb of Christ was watched and guarded by men who were overjoyed at His death, but they could not prevent His Resurrection and Ascension. He went back to Heaven from whence He came. And so do all of God's own. God preserves all who come to Him through Jesus Christ.

The miracle of the preservation of the two witnesses is accompanied by other activity of supernatural origin. To add to men's terror,

> *The same hour was there a great earthquake, and the tenth part of the city fell, and in the earthquake were slain of men seven thousand* (11:13).

The earthquake is not symbolic but literal, an actual visitation of judgment from God. An earthquake attended both the death and resurrection of our Lord (Matthew 27:51; 28:2). The marginal reading in the Bible says there were seven thousand "names of men." Robert Govett says that this expression denotes "persons of distinction" or "celebrated men." We have a modern idiom whereby they would be called "name men," or "men of name," called in the Old Testament "men of renown" (Genesis 6:4). The preservation of God's witnesses is followed by the prosecution of the devil's witnesses.

The miraculous preservation of the two witnesses produced one good effect.

> *The remnant were affrighted, and gave glory to the God of heaven* (11:13).

I am not suggesting that these are saved. Most likely they are compelled by force to recognize divine power in the earth as in Philippians 2:9-11. There is no evidence of godly sorrow and genuine repentance. As Seiss points out, "When true repentance shows itself, judgment delays or lingers, but there is no postponement (of judgment) here." Pharaoh and Saul and Judas acknowledged that they had sinned, but in not one case are we assured of genuine repentance and real conversion to God. Demons were terrified and confessed Christ's deity when they recognized His power, but no change was wrought in them. Temporary impressions sometimes are made upon men's minds during a period of great catastrophe, but the same men will lapse back to their former way of life just as soon as the pressure is removed. The stony ground hearers receive the Word with joy, yet they soon fall by the way (Matthew 13:5-6,20-21). Many became Christ's disciples but they soon forsook Him (John 6:66). Felix trembled at the preaching of Paul but he did not receive Jesus Christ (Acts 24:25). When the scribes and Pharisees saw Christ perform a miracle on the paralytic, "They were all amazed, and they glorified God, and were filled with fear" (Luke 5:26), but there is no ground to believe that they ever became saved. The very ones who glorified Christ were soon anxious to take His life (Luke 4:15,29). That crowd in the Great Tribulation in John's vision was terror-stricken; they were not praising and blessing God, else we would not have the following words, *"The second woe is past; and, behold, the third woe cometh quickly"* (11:14).

III. THE THIRD WOE (11:15-19)

With the translation of the two witnesses from earth to Heaven, the seventh trumpet sounds.

> *And the seventh angel sounded; and there were great voices in heaven, saying, The kingdoms of this world are become the kingdoms of our Lord, and of His Christ; and He shall reign for ever and ever* (11:15).

Verse 14 marks the end of the parenthetical portion of the vision between the sixth and the seventh trumpets (10:1-11:14).

A. *The Anticipation of the Kingdom*

The Revised Version substitutes, "The kingdom of the world." There will not be more than one kingdom nor more than one king. Christ's kingdom will be one universal kingdom with every knee bowing to Him and every tongue confessing that He is Lord to the glory of God the Father. The whole earth shall be filled with His glory. The sounding of the seventh trumpet is the official proclamation of the coming coronation of the King of kings and Lord of lords. He is the King of Psalms 2 and 24, and His kingdom is described in Daniel 2:44; 4:3,34;

6:26; 7:13-14, as well as by the angel in Luke 1:32-33. His government will be a righteous government, the kind that human laws and religions can never produce. Christ's coming again to the earth will result in a radical change in the government and religion of this world.

The language in Revelation 11:15 might sound as though the prophecy was already fulfilled as soon as the seventh trumpet sounds. Concerning this, Seiss says, "The tense of the expression is that peculiar to prophetic language, which fixes upon a result yet future, or only beginning to be, as if already accomplished." Actually the change of rule, with Christ as King over all the earth, does not occur until the events recorded in chapters 12-18 have been fulfilled.

B. *The Acclaim of the King*

And the four and twenty elders, which sat before God on their seats, fell upon their faces, and worshipped God, Saying, We give Thee thanks, O Lord God Almighty, which art, and wast, and art to come; because Thou hast taken to Thee Thy great power, and hast reigned (11:16-17).

No sooner do the voices in Heaven announce the coming kingdom than the elders fall on their faces to worship God and give thanks that the Almighty has at last assumed His sovereign right in the earth. Presently the kingdoms of this world are in Satan's control (Matthew 4:8-9). Our Lord never said that they were not. On the contrary He called Satan "the prince of this world" (John 12:31; 14:30; 16:11), and admitted that the world was his kingdom (Matthew 12:26). But the hour will come when God shall resume His power, and the Angel Gabriel's words to Mary shall be fulfilled (Luke 1:31-33). There are many details about the coming kingdom which we cannot now take time and space for. But I must remind all who cannot accept the fact that God is capable of anger and vengeance, to believe the inspired writings. Do not be deceived because God's wrath has been postponed for so long a time. God gave the sovereignty of the earth to His Son, and though men will not acknowledge Him now, the time will come when they will be forced to do so. The world kingdom that has been in Satan's hands must come to an end.

C. *The Anger of the Creation*

And the nations were angry, and Thy wrath is come, and the time of the dead, that they should be judged, and that Thou shouldest give reward unto Thy servants the prophets, and to the saints, and them that fear Thy name, small and great; and shouldest destroy them which destroy the earth (11:18).

Those things which cause rejoicing in Heaven stir up anger on earth. The two places and their inhabitants have nothing in common. The earth dwellers who lived for the things of this earthly life must now relinquish all to the Creator and Owner of all. "The earth is the LORD's, and the fulness thereof" (Psalm 24:1; 1 Corinthians 10:26,28). Christ is merely taking over what is rightfully His own. We are not surprised at the anger of men. Interrupt the plans and pursuits of any man who has as his goal the accumulation of wealth, and you will arouse his anger. Now take from him all that he possesses, and he will become wrathful and fiercely hostile. "Why do the heathen [or *nations*] rage?" (Psalm 2:1) You have a partial answer right here. The unbelievers in the earth must stand by as God's servants receive their rewards.

In this life we never see full justice meted out, but when Christ returns to take over, then all will receive their due deserts. The losers will rage in vain, for they will have had their opportunity to join the heavenly family. Read our Lord's parable on rewards in Luke 19:11-26. When Christ comes again there will be winners and losers. His *"servants the prophets,"* those to whom a revelation was given and who spoke and wrote for Him, will be first to receive their reward. They were first in point of time. And what a price some of them paid! Think of Elijah in the wilderness; Isaiah in his shameful appearance; Jeremiah in the dung and the dungeon; Daniel in the lions' den. Then there were the saints, Paul, Peter, James, and John. These are the "greats," but notice our text says, *"small and great.*" The "small" are listed first. When our Lord spoke of the reward of the tribulation saints, He emphasized the importance of faithfulness in small things (Matthew 25:31-46). Here is a challenge to us all to test our ways. Will our works survive the fire (1 Corinthians 3:5-8)? May God help us to be faithful (1 Corinthians 4:1-2).

D. *The Ark of His Testament*

And the temple of God was opened in heaven, and there was seen in His temple the ark of His testament; and there were lightnings, and voices, and thunderings and an earthquake, and great hail (11:19).

The chapter division here is unfortunate because verse 19 seems to introduce chapter 12. But we shall examine it in the order that we have it here, as it is included in chapter 11. Actually we have in the verse before us an entirely new prophecy which continues on through chapter 14. It is one which is related chiefly to Israel. The ark of the covenant had to do with Israel, not with the Gentiles or the Church.

It is stated that *"the temple of God was opened in Heaven."* The Revelation is the book of the unveiling, the book of the opening. Seven great openings characterize it which are not depicted elsewhere in Scripture:

> In 4:1—a Door is opened in Heaven
> In 6:1-8:1—the seals are opened
> In 9:2—the abyss is opened
> In 11:19—the temple of God is opened
> In 15:5—the tabernacle of testimony is opened
> In 19:11—the Heaven is opened
> In 20:12—the books of judgment are opened.

There is a heavenly temple after which the tabernacle and temple of the Jews were patterned. When God instructed Moses concerning the building of the tabernacle, He said, "And look that thou make them after their pattern, which was shewed thee in the mount" (Exodus 25:40). The writer to the Hebrews refers to the tabernacle and its ministries as "patterns of things in the heavens" (Hebrews 9:23). The earthly worship was copied after the heavenly. But sin has marred the earthly worship so that the two are no longer alike.

When the New Jerusalem comes down from Heaven, it is called "the holy city" (Revelation 21:2), and John states expressly, "I saw no temple therein" (21:22). When the scenes in chapter 21 are fulfilled there will be no need for a temple as a place of worship. If all were holy on earth now, there would be no need for a place of worship. Jesus said, "God is Spirit: and they that worship Him must worship Him in spirit and in truth" (John 4:24). True worship is a matter of the heart. However we dare not overlook the exhortations in Scripture which call God's children together (see Hebrews 10:25).

The fact that John sees the temple of God and the ark indicates that Israel is coming into view and that God will once more renew His dealings with Israel nationally. Now we know the prophecy in the book of Jeremiah, which says, "And it shall come to pass, when ye be multiplied and increased in the land, in those days, saith the LORD, they shall say no more, The ark of the covenant of the LORD: neither shall it come to mind: neither shall they remember it; neither shall they visit it; neither shall that be done any more" (Jeremiah 3:16). I believe this verse means that when the millennial kingdom is established, Jerusalem shall be the throne of the Lord, and Christ Himself shall be recognized as the fulfillment of all the Old Testament types, including the ark. Then they will not miss the ark. But here the ark is mentioned as John saw it in the temple of God.

The ark, made with acacia wood and overlaid with gold, was the only piece of furniture in the holy of holies. It was two-and-one-half cubits long, one-and-one-half cubits in height (Exodus 25:10-16).

There are five names given to it in the Old Testament.

It is called *the ark of the covenant,* possibly because it contained the two tables of the law, which constituted the basis of the Old Covenant (Numbers 10:33).

It is called *the ark of testimony* because by means of it God testified of His own holiness and man's sin, and of Christ in His deity and humanity as the Mediator between God and man (Exodus 25:22).

It is called *the ark of God,* because it was the only visible throne of God (1 Samuel 3:3). At this point it should be noted that when the instructions were given for the erection of the tabernacle and its furnishings, God began with the ark and concluded with the gate (Exodus 25:10—26:37). This is simply saying that God began from within, with Himself, and worked out toward man. Salvation is of the Lord (Jonah 2:9). God's way of salvation is the grace way (Ephesians 2:8-9); it is not the way of the sinner's self-effort (Titus 3:5).

It is called *the ark of God's strength* because of the miracles and mighty works associated with it (Psalm 132:8).

It is called *the holy ark* because it was God's throne (? Chronicles 35:3), the place where He dwelled between the two cherubims (Exodus 25:10-22 cf. Psalm 80:1), where Moses could meet with Him and commune with Him.

One of the special purposes of the ark was to protect and preserve its contents, the same being true of Noah's ark and the ark in which Moses' mother put him. The ark contained the golden pot that had manna, Aaron's rod that budded, and the tables of the covenant (Hebrews 9:4). We shall not go into greater detail at this time concerning the ark and its contents. Suffice it to say that the ark, which speaks of God's covenant with Israel, is in the midst of a judgment scene described in terms of *"lightnings, and voices, and thunderings, and an earthquake, and great hail."* The judgment is coming, but Israel will be saved.

WAR IN HEAVEN

Revelation 12:1-17

I am discovering this book of the Revelation to be one of the most wonderful in all the Word of God, and the chapter before us is one of the most picturesque in the book. It is the great "sign" chapter. The word "wonder" in verses 1 and 3 is *semeion*, translated "sign" in the Revised Version, and used here for the first time in the Revelation. There are two "wonders" (or signs) in this chapter, the first being a "great wonder" and the second called "another wonder."

This is a chapter of "great" things. Note "a great wonder" (verse 1); "a great red dragon" (verse 3); "great wrath" (verse 12), and "two wings of a great eagle" (verse 14). Before us is a most dramatic scene. In order to understand it the signs must be interpreted correctly. However, the signs are only a part of the chapter, for in addition to the *signs* there is the *struggle,* the *salvation,* and the *safety.*

I. THE SIGNS (12:1-6)

First, there is the sign of the woman clothed with the sun.

> *And there appeared a great wonder in heaven; a woman clothed with the sun, and the moon under her feet, and upon her head a crown of twelve stars: And she being with child cried, travailing in birth, and pained to be delivered (12:1-2).*

This is the second of four representative women mentioned in the Revelation. (1) Jezebel who represents paganism (2:20); (2) Israel (12:6); (3) the scarlet woman who represents the apostate church (17:1); and (4) the Lamb's Wife, the true Church (19:7).

The woman before us as a "sign" is symbolical. But of whom is she a symbol? The Roman Catholic Church has made the woman to be the Virgin Mary. The Spanish artist, Murillo, has produced some famous scenes on canvas in support of this view. In fact, one of the canvases depicts her body great with child. At the same time the scene is supposed to portray her assumption into Heaven and her glory as its queen. But such a view is untenable. In the first place, there is not a shred of evidence that the body of Mary ever ascended into Heaven. And in the next place, it is utterly ridiculous to show Mary in Heaven, about to deliver her child, after the birth, death, resurrection, and ascension of Christ. This is not a vision of the Virgin Mary.

There are those among Protestants who tell us that the woman here symbolizes the Church. Now it is a part of Scripture symbolism to speak of the Church as a woman (2 Corinthians 11:2; Ephesians 5:23-32; Revelation 19:7). But we do not read far into our chapter before discovering that the woman gave birth to a child, and that the child was the Lord Jesus Christ. Now we know that the Church did not give birth to Christ, but rather Christ founded His Church (Matthew 16:18). This is not a vision of the Church.

Then there is the blasphemous teaching of Mary Baker Glover Patterson Eddy, who was conceited enough to claim that this woman of Revelation 12 represented herself. She added that the "man child" that she brought forth is Christian Science; that the "dragon" is "mortal mind" (whatever that is) attempting to destroy her new religion. I shall not go beyond Dr. Ironside's answer to Mrs. Eddy's interpretation: he said that with such a theory "I need not take up the time of sane people."

There is a passage of Scripture in which the sun, moon, and stars are discussed in a way which, I believe, sheds light on our present passage in Revelation 12:1. Please notice some of the details in Joseph's dream. "And he dreamed yet another dream, and told it his brethren, and said, Behold, I have dreamed a dream more; and, behold, the sun and the moon and the eleven

stars made obeisance to me. And he told it to his father, and
to his brethren: and his father rebuked him, and said unto him,
What is this dream that thou hast dreamed? Shall I and thy
mother and thy brethren indeed come to bow down ourselves to
thee to the earth? And his brethren envied him; but his father
observed the saying" (Genesis 37:9-11). From verse 10 I would
conclude that Jacob understood these symbols to represent his
entire family, Israel, "of whom as concerning the flesh Christ
came" (Romans 9:5). In this connection observe a prophecy of
Isaiah, "Before she travailed, she brought forth; before her
pain came, she was delivered of a man child. Who hath heard
such a thing? who hath seen such things? Shall the earth be
made to bring forth in one day? or shall a nation be born at
once? for as soon as Zion travailed, she brought forth her children" (Isaiah 66:7-8). Most expositors have seen clearly that
this woman represents Israel, and with this view I concur.

But should we stop with this simple identification? Back in
the year 1933 I came across some notes on the Apocalypse by
the well-known Lutheran minister, the late J. A. Seiss. I learned
later that these notes in an expanded form were in Seiss' book
of fifty-two lectures on *The Apocalypse*. Dr. Seiss saw that the
woman symbolized Israel, but not Israel exclusively. His interpretation of the woman is that she represents both Israel and
the Church. I wanted to accept this view, but I could not see it
altogether as Dr. Seiss presented it.

Some years later, the late Donald Grey Barnhouse ran a
series of studies on the Apocalypse in his magazine *Revelation*.
I quote in full his comments on this part of our text:

"Most expositors have seen clearly that this woman represents Israel, but have stopped with that simple identification.
We believe that there is something more in view here. The
rest of this chapter is going to reveal to us that there is war
in the spiritual realm, and that this war is a great controversy,
ages long, for the control of the universe. The war began with
the fall of Satan, and will continue until the great and terrible
day of the Lord shall bring this war to a close. The woman,
then, represents not merely Israel, 'of whom as concerning
the flesh Christ came' (Romans 9:5), but is that spiritual body

of the elect from the very beginning of the history of man, by whom God had eternally purposed to bring to naught the revolt of Satan. All of the symbols mentioned in these verses are found in the earliest chapters of the book of Genesis. The woman, the sun, the moon, the stars, the man-child, the seed, the dragon, 'that old serpent which is the devil and Satan'; all of these are to be found in the opening paragraphs of the Bible.

"Those who know the book of Genesis well, realize that Satan must have existed before he appeared in the third chapter. The rest of the Bible presents to us this malignant figure as having once been among the angels of God. When did he fall? There is a mass of evidence which has been collected in G. K. Pember's *Earth's Earliest Ages* which demonstrates beyond doubt that there was a long interval between the first creation, described in the first sublime sentence of the Bible and the chaos of the second verse. It was during this interval that the war in Heaven was begun by Lucifer's rebellion. God's next revealed move was the creation of man to whom were committed all of the symbols of authority. The sun, moon, and stars, as we have seen in other passages, are symbols of authority. God purposed eternally that all authority should be gathered together in Christ. He proceeds to this end, however, by way of the garden of Eden, the cross of Calvary, and the return of the Lord in glory.

"As soon as Satan had intruded into the new creation which God had made, thinking to have gained a great victory by accomplishing the fall of the man and the woman, God proceeded to announce in prophecy that which is here portrayed in Revelation as a great drama in the spiritual warfare in the heavenly places. The great curse upon Satan was announced in terms which included the promise of the Redeemer and the triumph of God. 'And the LORD God said unto the serpent, Because thou hast done this, thou art cursed above all cattle, and above every beast of the field; upon thy belly shalt thou go, and dust shalt thou eat all the days of thy life. And I will put enmity between thee and the woman, and between thy seed and her seed; it shall bruise thy head, and thou shalt bruise His heel' (Genesis 3:14-15).

"That which we read in these terms in the book of Genesis as referring to the earthly struggle involving Adam, Eve, and Satan, is presented to us in the twelfth of Revelation as being a part of the spiritual warfare which we shall some day realize is but a tiny corner of the whole battlefield, though the scene of the decisive struggle and the victory of God. God created the woman who represents the elect of the race in order that she might become the channel of His redemption. We must look beyond mere Israel to the greater vision of the whole plan of redemption. This is revealed in Galatians in a beautiful way. Speaking of the inviolability of the covenants of God, St. Paul says, 'Now to Abraham and his seed were the promises made.' He does not say, 'And to seeds, as of many'; but 'as of one, and to thy seed, which is Christ' (Galatians 3:16). Here God definitely takes the promises out of the realm of the mere literal progeny of Abraham and back to the third of Genesis, where we see that Jesus Christ was in view. Why was there a chosen people? In order that there might be a line for the Lord Jesus Christ. Why was there a holy land? In order that there might be a place to erect the cross to crucify the Lord Jesus. These were the chief elements in the divine strategy.

"So the identification of this woman, clothed with all the authority of God, is certain. She represents that spiritual Israel that is more than Israel. It goes backward through the line of the seed to Eve and forward through the line of the seed to Mary and the Lord Jesus. We must not forget that the enmity of Satan came against this people because they have been chosen as the channel of the power and blessing of God. It may have seemed for a moment that the fall of man caused the plans of God to be frustrated, but the great promise which we have seen brought the matter clearly out into the realm of a promise of victory. God has promised, and what He has promised He will fulfill. Between the second and third verses of our chapter we see that the woman who was clothed with all authority is presented as crying with great travail. The entrance of sin into the human race, the fall, has taken place between the two verses, nevertheless, the promises of God are sure and certain in Christ, and He will bring His victory in His own time, even though the following verse in Genesis announces that the woman shall bring forth her children in sorrow. Many verses speak of the sorrows of Israel under the figure of a woman in travail."

I have passed on these thoughts for the benefit of my readers and I leave each to draw his own conclusions. However, I feel strongly that the woman in John's vision does represent Israel, but that the comments by Dr. Barnhouse are worthy of careful consideration.

And she being with child cried, travailing in birth, and pained to be delivered (12:2).

Only of Israel can it be said that she brought forth this "child" who is none other than the Lord Jesus Christ, "For verily He took not on Him the nature of angels; but He took on Him the seed of Abraham" (Hebrews 2:16). This is He of whom the prophet wrote, "Therefore the Lord Himself shall give you a sign; Behold, a virgin shall conceive, and bear a son, and shall call His name Immanuel" (Isaiah 7:14 cf. Matthew 1:23). He is the Seed of the woman (Genesis 3:15); the Son of Abraham (Matthew 1:1); of the Tribe of Judah (Genesis 49:8-10 cf. Micah 5:2; Revelation 5:5); the Star and Scepter of Jacob (Numbers 24:17-19 cf. Genesis 49:10). He is the descendant of David with whom God made a covenant (2 Samuel 7:11-16), which four generations later Jeremiah declared could never be broken (Jeremiah 33:17-18,20-22). The same covenant was confirmed by other of the prophets in words which forbid fulfillment in David, or in any mere son of David (see Ezekiel 34:23-24; 37:24-25). Indeed it was from the chosen people, the Israel of God, that Jesus Christ sprang in His human lineage. God's great purposes in bringing Israel into being were to make that nation a repository for His Word and a nation out of which Christ should come.

In John's vision there are interesting facts stated about the Man Child.

And she brought forth a man child, who was to rule all nations with a rod of iron: and her child was caught up unto God, and to His throne (12:5).

This verse contains a remarkable summary of three significant events in Christ's life, namely, His Incarnation, Ascension, and Second Coming to earth to rule. No other person in history fits into the details here. When we compare Scripture reference with Scripture reference we learn that of Christ only is it said,

"He shall rule all nations with a rod of iron" (Psalm 2:8-9; Revelation 19:15). There are two time lapses in verse 5: the first, a period of thirty-three years, from our Lord's birth to His ascension; the second, a period of almost 2,000 years, from His ascension to the end of the Great Tribulation, those last three-and-one-half years described as *"a thousand two hundred and three score days"* (12:6). We are not to be concerned about the total omission of detail of the earthly life of Christ. The vision here has to do with those crises in His life which bear directly upon His triumph over the hostile powers of darkness. The first prophecy concerning Christ, as recorded in Genesis 3:15, likewise omits His earthly life but includes the fact of His death. The interest in the Revelation is not in the human Jesus, who walked the roads in and about Palestine, but in the exalted and victorious Christ.

We have examined the primary interpretation of the Man Child. Before we leave this portion of our chapter let us consider a secondary application. I see in the Man Child, by way of application, the Church of Christ. The Church is Christ's Body of which He is the Head (Ephesians 1:22-23; Colossians 1:18,24). Of believers also it is stated that they shall rule the nations with a rod of iron (Revelation 2:27). The Church too shall be caught up to Heaven. It is interesting to note that the word which is used here for the Child's being *snatched* or caught up is the same word as is used in 1 Thessalonians 4:17 to describe the rapture of the Church to meet the Lord in the air, and also to describe Paul's experience of being caught up into the third Heaven (2 Corinthians 12:2).

The second sign is a *"great red dragon."*

> *And there appeared another wonder in heaven; and behold a great red dragon, having seven heads and ten horns, and seven crowns upon his heads. And his tail drew the third part of the stars of heaven, and did cast them to the earth: and the dragon stood before the woman which was ready to be delivered, for to devour her child as soon as it was born* (12:3-4).

There is no problem in identifying the dragon. He is:

*That old serpent called the Devil, and Satan, which de-
ceiveth the whole world* (12:9).

He is seen by John as having *"seven heads."* Seven speaks of
completeness, and the head of wisdom. Of him it is written,
"Thou sealest up the sum, full of wisdom" (Ezekiel 28:12).
Our Lord said, "Behold, I send you forth as sheep in the midst
of wolves: be ye therefore wise as serpents, and harmless as
doves" (Matthew 10:16). The devil is a master strategist and
deceiver. His past is recorded in Isaiah 14:12-15. His present
activity is seen in part in 2 Corinthians 4:3-4; 11:13-15. His
"ten horns and seven crowns upon his heads" speak of his
usurped authority. Our Lord called him "the prince of this
world" (John 12:31; 14:30; 16:11). Indeed the whole world
lieth in the wicked one (1 John 5:19). Whole governments are
in his power, and through them he operates. Jesus said that "he
was a murderer from the beginning" (John 8:44), and Peter
adds that "Your adversary the devil, as a roaring lion, walketh
about, seeking whom he may devour" (1 Peter 5:8).

The dragon is seen here standing before *"the woman which
was ready to be delivered, for to devour her child as soon as it
was born"* (12:4). The devil has been at war with God's Son
ever since the divine pronouncement in Genesis 3:15. The history of the human race is a record of war between the seeds,
the "seed of the serpent" and the "Seed of the woman." God
Himself declared this war. The devil is determined to obliterate
God's witness in the world, while God is determined that He
shall have a witness to Jesus Christ. Satan hates any testimony
to the truth about the Son of God, and he will resort to any
method to silence such a witness, whether by murder, as when
Cain killed Abel; or through mixture, as in the unholy alliance
between the sons of God and the daughters of men in Genesis 6;
or through the decree of Herod to destroy the woman's Child
(Matthew 2:13); or by infuriating a mob to throw Him over a
cliff (Luke 4:28-29); or by tempting Christ to cast Himself
down from the pinnacle of the temple (Matthew 4:6). The
Man Child survived every attack of the dragon upon Him. He
went to the cross and died, but He conquered death and as-

cended back to Heaven. Now we await His return to finish the work and establish His sovereign rule in the earth.

II. THE STRUGGLE (12:7-9)

And there was war in heaven: Michael and his angels fought against the dragon; and the dragon fought and his angels, And prevailed not; neither was their place found any more in heaven. And the great dragon was cast out, that old serpent, called the Devil, and Satan, which deceiveth the whole world: he was cast out into the earth, and his angels were cast out with him (12:7-9).

This entire twelfth chapter is one of conflict. Here we see events to take place during the final half of the tribulation, the last three-and-one-half years of Daniel's seventieth week. This period actually begins with the blowing of the seventh trumpet in 11:15-19 and concludes at the end of chapter 19. It brings Israel to the forefront in God's plans.

Between verses 5 and 6, however, there is a prophetic gap. All of the present Age of Grace is omitted. Now there are reasons for this. The war spoken of here is a series of conflicts with the dragon persecuting the woman, who is Israel. The events in verse 7 do not begin until after the Church has been raptured. In fact, it is possible that the Rapture occasions this conflict.

Herman Hoyt suggests that while there is no direct statement of Scripture, except that that the word "war" usually refers to a series of conflicts, it seems legitimate to assume that this phase of the war started at the time of the Rapture. He cites Daniel 12:1,2 in support of the idea that the rapture of the Church through the domain of Satan, which is the aerial and stellar heavens, arouses Satan to hinder the Rapture if possible. Satan is the hinderer of all that God would accomplish through His own people (see Daniel 10:13; 1 Thessalonians 2:18). At the moment when Satan interferes with the Rapture, Michael and his angels, who are ministers to the saints (Hebrews 1:7,14), rush to the rescue—and the battle is on. This may explain "the voice of the archangel" at the time of the Rapture (1 Thessalonians 4:16). Michael is not a messenger-angel but a warrior. He is the divinely appointed commander-in-chief of the heavenly hosts who engages in conflicts with Satan and his army of fallen angels.

The first recorded conflict in which Michael engages was over the body of Moses. The long journey of Israel, which lasted forty years, was ended. The Land of Promise was almost reached. At Moab Moses had delivered his orations and pronounced his prophetic blessings. The land was spread before him, but this mighty servant of Jehovah was not permitted to enter because of his hasty action of smiting the rock twice (Numbers 20:7-11). But he did see the land from a distance. And there he died. "So Moses the servant of the LORD died there in the land of Moab, according to the word of the LORD. And He buried him in a valley in the land of Moab, over against Beth-peor: but no man knoweth of his sepulchre unto this day" (Deuteronomy 34:5-6).

But there is more to the story than appears in the Pentateuch. The brief Epistle of Jude adds an important statement. "Yet Michael the archangel, when contending with the devil he disputed about the body of Moses, durst not bring against him a railing accusation, but said, The Lord rebuke thee" (Jude 9). A. C. Gaebelein concludes that Michael was present on that mountain to supervise the burial of Moses. The devil came to claim the body of Moses, but that was one funeral service over which he did not preside. Had the devil succeeded, he could have prevented Moses' appearing on the Mount of Transfiguration, or we might have a shrine containing the bones of Moses where miracles would be reported to have happened. Dead bones are only one of Satan's many deceptive devices which lure large crowds to worship. But we know that the worship of dead bones is one of the worst forms of idolatry. I can just imagine that lifeless body of Moses in the hands of Satan's ministers being brought into the camp of Israel as an object of adoration and worship as was the serpent of brass (2 Kings 18:4).

We must turn to the book of Daniel for further light on the

ministry of the Archangel Michael. His name appears for the first time in chapter ten of Daniel's prophecy. We find Daniel giving himself to prayer and deep exercise of soul for a period of three weeks (Daniel 10:2). When he prayed he received a direct answer immediately through the Angel Gabriel (9:21-23). But here there is no direct answer, rather a delayed answer. After the expiration of three full weeks, a messenger appeared to Daniel and said, "Fear not, Daniel: for from the first day that thou didst set thine heart to understand, and to chasten thyself before thy God, thy words were heard, and I am come for thy words. But the prince of the kingdom of Persia withstood me one and twenty days: but, lo, Michael, one of the chief princes, came to help me; and I remained there with the kings of Persia" (10:12-13). Here we have unveiled one of the mysteries of delayed answers to our prayers, but with it the blessed assurance that God has heard us.

But who is "the prince of the kingdom of Persia"? Since Michael the archangel is called "one of the chief princes" (10:13), we dare assume that the prince of Persia is likewise an angel, however a fallen wicked angel assigned by Satan, who is "the prince of the devils [demons]" (Matthew 9:34; 12:24) and "the prince of this world" (John 12:31; 14:30; 16:11).

Paul uses the word "principalities" not less than eight times (Romans 8:38; Ephesians 1:21; 3:10; 6:12; Colossians 1:16; 2:10,15; Titus 3:1). This word may be translated "governments." In some smaller countries the ruler is called a "prince" and the area over which he rules a "principality." In Persia an evil spirit-being was delegated by Satan to influence the Persian monarch. The plurality of the "principalities" in Paul's writings suggest that there may be many of them, and the evil princes over them are called "the rulers of the darkness of this world" (Ephesians 6:12). In Daniel 10:20 we see that there is "a prince of Grecia." So then why not a prince for Russia, China, France, the United States, and one for every country? Satan is out to control the affairs of all the kingdoms of this world.

Now let us observe another important verse in Daniel's prophecy. "Now I am come to make thee understand what shall befall thy people in the latter days: for yet the vision is for many days" (10:14). This statement makes it clear that in the latter days there will be activity against Daniel's people, the Jews, and that Michael will be prominently active against the enemy who attacks them. This is supported further by Daniel 12:1: "And at that time shall Michael stand up, the great prince which standeth for the children of thy people: and there shall be a time of trouble, such as never was since there was a nation even to that same time: and at that time thy people shall be delivered, every one that shall be found written in the book." I understand the time of the fulfillment of this prophecy to be the Great Tribulation, the same period of which John wrote in Revelation 12.

The war is decisively won by Michael and his angels. So complete is the victory that, after the war is over, Michael and his hosts supervise the mopping up exercises. Every inch of the aerial and stellar heavens is searched thoroughly to make certain that none of Satan's demons remain (Revelation 12:9). This marks the end of Satan's rule in the air. The prince of this world is cast out of the heavens. The first and second heavens were part of his kingdom. He had access to all the heavens, though limited (Job 1:6). Now his access to them comes to an end.

III. THE SALVATION (12:10-12)

And I heard a loud voice saying in heaven, Now is come salvation, and strength, and the kingdom of our God, and the power of His Christ: for the accuser of our brethren is cast down, which accused them before our God day and night. And they overcame him by the blood of the Lamb, and by the word of their testimony; and they loved not their lives unto the death. Therefore rejoice, ye heavens, and ye that dwell in them. Woe to the inhabiters of the earth and of the sea! for the devil is come down unto you, having great wrath, because he knoweth that he hath but a short time (12:10-12).

All Heaven rejoices over the victory won by Michael and his angels. Never again will Satan cross the threshold of

Heaven. Little wonder there is spontaneous outburst of praise. Scott suggests that the insertion of the definite article before each of the subjects named gives definiteness and force. "*The* salvation" is not that of the soul now, nor even of the body at Christ's coming, but is a wide and comprehensive thought embracing the overthrow of the enemy and the deliverance of creation from its present thraldom and agony (Romans 8:21). "*The* power" refers to the irresistible might which shall crush all opposing authority—whether satanic in the heavens or human on the earth. "*The* kingdom" must be understood here in its largest extent, as embracing the heavens and the earth. This is the final phase of God's great plan of salvation. While it has not already "come," the end is in sight. In that day there will be no occasion to pray, only praise.

A word must be added about the weapons used in this war.

> *And they overcame him by the blood of the Lamb, and by the word of their testimony; and they loved not their lives unto the death* (12:11).

There are no planes, bombs, missiles, nor atomic submarines. The destruction of bodies is not the goal.

Michael's first weapon was "*the blood of the Lamb.*" The blood of the Lamb is ever the fortress of saints and of angels. Justified and forgiven men, who have no hope but in the merit of their Saviour's blood, are on the victory side. Men on earth may ridicule Christ's blood, but in Heaven much is made of it. They recognize that victory did not come by means of personal merit or might. Without the atoning blood Satan's accusations would have no refutation. Christ's blood gave them standing before God. And so it gives us standing even now. The devil has access to God today for the purpose of accusing us (Zechariah 3:1). He does this whenever we sin. But our Advocate, the Lamb slain from the foundation of the world, is there to plead our cause. Praise God for the Blood!

> *And by the word of their testimony* (12:11).

This is God's Word, the Sword of the Spirit, forever settled in Heaven. They who believe it, identify themselves with it, and testify to it are assured of victory. This Word is authoritative against demons. It will work wonders in the heart and hand of the weakest saint. John adds a testimony in full agreement with this (1 John 2:13-14). The believer who would resist Satan cannot afford to neglect the Word of God.

And they loved not their lives unto the death (12:11).

The one who yields all to God cannot possibly lose a battle. For the sake of the truth they resigned all that man counts dear. Battles are fought and won by blood, by the Word of God, and by surrendering our lives to the Lord Jesus Christ.

IV. THE SAFETY (12:13-17)

A great deception in the minds of many is that Satan is in hell. The fact of the matter is he never has been in hell. He is going there, and he knows it, for hell was "prepared for the devil and his angels" (Matthew 25:41). Just as Heaven is a prepared place for Christ's own (John 14:3), so hell is a prepared place for our Lord's enemies. The present abode of the devil and his demons is the atmospheric and stellar heavens, but he operates chiefly on earth through unregenerated men.

The prophetic scene before us depicts his complete expulsion from the air, after which the full force of his diabolical work will be against those on the earth at that time.

Therefore rejoice, ye heavens, and ye that dwell in them. Woe to the inhabiters of the earth and of the sea! for the devil is come down unto you, having great wrath, because he knoweth that he hath but a short time (12:12).

The result of that war in Heaven is blessing in Heaven but "woe" on earth. This woe is the last in the predicted series of three (8:13; 9:12; 11:14; 12:12). The word "woe" is used as a divine denunciation. Whenever God pronounces a woe there is judgment ahead. This third woe upon the earth, aimed first at Israel, is more severe than any of the former. The reason is obvious. *"He* [the devil] *knoweth that he hath but a short time."*

As soon as he is cast down to the earth, he at once proceeds
to make war against the woman (Israel).

> *And when the dragon saw that he was cast unto the earth,*
> *he persecuted the woman which brought forth the man child*
> (12:13).

The Jew has always been a target for Satan's bitter attack.
There is no nation in history whose people have been hated
and persecuted as has been the Jew. When God called Abraham
He let it be known that he would be the object of cursing
(Genesis 12:3). But why should this be so? For no other
reason than that Abraham was chosen by God. When a man
answers the call of God and casts his lot on the side of righteousness, he can expect to be hated by the enemies of God.
(Read John 17:14-16; 1 John 3:1-2). Israel was chosen by
God to be the repository for His Word and the nation through
whom God's Son and the world's Redeemer should come. Little
wonder that Satan hates the Jew. After his final defeat in
Heaven his wrath against the Jew will be great, for he knows
that he has only three-and-one-half years remaining before
he is bound and cast into the abyss.

> *And to the woman were given two wings of a great eagle,*
> *that she might fly into the wilderness, into her place, where*
> *she is nourished for a time, and times, and half a time, from*
> *the face of the serpent* (12:14).

Verse 14 resumes the narrative where it was interrupted at
verse 6. What is now added to the statement of verse 6 is that
God provides an airlift for Israel's escape from the dragon.
Those who are protected are the Jews who are loyal to God.
The eagle's wings suggest the miraculous swiftness with which
God will help them to escape. After Israel's exodus from Egypt,
God reminded the people, saying, "Ye have seen what I did
unto the Egyptians, and how I bare you on eagles' wings, and
brought you unto Myself" (Exodus 19:4). (See also Deuteronomy 32:11-12). This expression is probably a metaphor
for the divine provision afforded to God's people once again
when another flight from her enemy becomes necessary. This

prophesied flight is doubtless the one to which Christ referred in Matthew 24:15-21.

The period of time that these believing Jews are protected is referred to as *"a time, and times, and half a time."* This period is further described as "a thousand two hundred and threescore days" (12:6), or "forty and two months" (11:2; 13:5). The phrase "time, and times, and half a time" equals three-and-one-half years (cf. Daniel 7:25; 9:27; 12:7).

> *And the serpent cast out of his mouth water as a flood after the woman, that he might cause her to be carried away of the flood* (12:15).

The words *"as a flood"* indicate symbolic language. Possibly this is a flood of evil propaganda issuing from his mouth. This propaganda against the Jew will spread throughout the world. There might be some organized effort on the part of the Antichrist to locate the Jews with the view to destroying them. As the water of life proceeds from the mouth of the Lord Jesus Christ (Matthew 5:2), so the water of death proceeds from the mouth of the Antichrist. This figure of a flood is used elsewhere in Scripture to represent overwhelming powers of destruction against the people of God (see Psalm 124). But we have the assuring promise that "When the enemy shall come in like a flood, the Spirit of the LORD shall lift up a standard against him" (Isaiah 59:19). Isaiah was prophesying this very event in Revelation 12, for verse 19 is immediately followed by a prophecy of the Advent of Christ, "And the Redeemer shall come to Zion" (Isaiah 59:20). This view is supported by the divinely inspired words through the Apostle Paul in Romans 11:26.

> *And the earth helped the woman, and the earth opened her mouth, and swallowed up the flood which the dragon cast out of his mouth* (12:16).

By divine intervention God raises up a standard against the enemy of His people. There was a flood in Noah's day which threatened to destroy the royal seed, but God designed an ark and Shem was preserved, and in him the Jewish race.

Pharoah would have destroyed that race, but God preserved the baby Moses in an ark. Later God used that same Moses to lead His people across the Red Sea to freedom and preservation. Pharoah, in mad pursuit of Israel, was swallowed up by the sea, and the people along with Moses sang, "Who is like unto Thee, O LORD, among the gods? who is like Thee, glorious in holiness, fearful in praises, doing wonders? Thou stretchedst out Thy right hand, the earth swallowed them" (Exodus 15:11-12).

Seiss writes: "In this same wilderness, when God's anger was visited upon Korah, Dathan, and Abiram, for their rebellion against Moses and Aaron, 'the ground clave asunder that was under them, and the *earth opened her mouth, and swallowed them up,* and their houses, and all the men that pertained unto Korah, and all their goods: they and all that pertained to them, *went down alive into the pit,* and the earth closed upon them, and *they perished!'* (Numbers 16:31-33). It is the region and time of miracles when there is to be a renewal of wonders, 'like as it was to Israel in the day that he came up out of the land of Egypt' (Isaiah 11:15-16). It is the region and time of great earthquakes and disturbances in the economy of nature (Zechariah 14:4; Luke 21:25-26; Revelation 11:13,19). And there is reason to think that it is by some great and sudden rending of the earth that these pursuing hosts are arrested in their course, if not *en masse* buried up in the convulsion. At least, the object of their bloody expedition is thwarted. They fail to reach the woman in her place of refuge. The very ground yawns to stop them in their hellish madness."

Verse 6 is closely related to verse 14. God has a wilderness, a place of safety and security for His people in the time of their calamity. History shows that every nation has been frustrated in attempts to wipe out the Jew. Even in the Great Tribulation, when Satan puts forth his supreme effort to destroy the Jew, he is powerless to accomplish his evil desire. To the very end God frustrates the efforts of the dragon.

Baffled at every turn, Satan turns against a small remnant of faithful Jews in an attempt to exterminate them.

> *And the dragon was wroth with the woman, and went to make war with the remnant of her seed, which keep the commandments of God, and have the testimony of Jesus Christ* (12:17).

There will be, then, an attack upon the large body of Jews and also upon the remnant who are left behind by those who fled. This remnant may be the witnessing ones of the 144,000 mentioned in chapter 7. But they are destined to survive the attacks upon them, having been sealed for this very purpose (7:2-4).

It is said that they *"keep the commandments of God, and have the testimony of Jesus Christ."* This is what God expects of His people at all times. As we approach the end of this present Age of Grace, an age characterized by lawlessness and opposition to God and His Son, we Christians, even as those saints in the tribulation, must be loyal to God's Word and to our Lord Jesus Christ. A battle is raging today, and no man can remain neutral in the conflict. You are either on the side of the Saviour or on the side of Satan. And be certain that the devil is not resting in his all-out effort to damn the souls of men. Oh, how we need to watch and wait and work as we look for the coming of our Lord! We dare not be indifferent in the light of the lateness of the hour. Let us publish abroad the gospel of grace while we have opportunity.

THE WORLD'S LAST DICTATOR

Revelation 13:1-18

In chapter 12 the conflict in Heaven ended with Satan's defeat and his final overthrow from Heaven. He was cast out of Heaven into the earth. In Revelation 13 we have a detailed description of his all-out effort in the earth just prior to his being cast into the bottomless pit. It is his last drive to defeat the program of God and establish his own kingdom.

Now we know that Satan is a spirit-being and that he cannot operate effectively on earth except as he does through the passions and personalities of men. Thus he embodies himself in men in order to get what he wants. He knows his time is short, so he comes in rage and fury to do as much damage as he possibly can. In chapter 12 we saw the fact of Satan's hostility; here in chapter 13 we see the means of that hostility. The two worst rebels in all of human history appear on the scene. They are called "beasts." They are not animals, but men. They are called beasts because of the cruelty of their reign.

The Lamb who holds the title deed to the earth is to come shortly and take over His possession. Satan knows this, therefore this is his last all-out effort to throttle the divine plan. It is "woe" time for the world, the day of Satan's greatest miracles. Demonism at its height will produce a reign of terror throughout the earth. This is the period prophesied by Paul in 2 Thessalonians 2:7-11, when that wicked one shall be revealed, "whose coming is after the working of Satan with all power and signs and lying wonders."

The chapter before us prophesies the activity of the two

beasts on the earth after the Church has been caught up to Heaven to be with her Lord. The first Beast appears out of the sea (13:1-10), while the second comes up out of the earth (13:11-18). Both are Satan-controlled men, so that actually there is in this chapter a trinity of evil, the dragon and his two associates. Satan always has been a clever imitator, a device he has used successfully to deceive men. Here in the dragon, the beast, and the false prophet, we see the satanic trinity, Satan's imitation of the divine trinity (see Revelation 16:13).

The majority of commentators whose books I have read identify the Antichrist with one of these two beasts, opinions being divided as to which one is the Antichrist. If he must be identified with either, it would seem to be the first. William R. Newell has written well on this matter, giving nine reasons why he believes the first beast is the Antichrist (*The Book of the Revelation*, pages 195-200). While the word *Antichrist* appears only in the Epistles of John (1 John 2:18,22; 4:3; 2 John 7), it would seem that the particular characterization of Antichrist, namely, opposition to Christ along with imitation of Christ, culminates with the beasts in their combined deeds.

I. THE WONDER OF THE BEAST (13:1-2)

And I stood upon the sand of the sea, and saw a beast rise up out of the sea, having seven heads and ten horns, and upon his horns ten crowns, and upon his heads the name of blasphemy. And the beast which I saw was like unto a leopard, and his feet were as the feet of a bear, and his mouth as the mouth of a lion: and the dragon gave him his power, and his seat, and great authority (13:1,2).

The King James Version reads, "And *I* stood upon the sand of the sea." The American Standard Version reads, "And *he* stood upon the sand of the sea." This latter reading is probably correct when linked with the last verse of the previous chapter, *"And the dragon was wroth with the woman. . . . And he stood upon the sand of the sea."* It is not John who stands upon the sand of the sea, but the dragon. He has already been identified as "that old serpent, called the Devil, and Satan" (12:9). He is the one who introduced all sin, sorrow, and suffering into the world (Genesis 3).

The phrase "the sand of the sea" indicates Satan's position as usurper of the earth and of his power over its people. The "sand" pictures the many people who make up the nations, "the number of whom is as the sand of the sea" (20:8). Satan sees the sea of the nations in their restlessness and political agitation (Isaiah 17:12; 57:20; Revelation 17:15), and so he stands upon the earth about to proceed in his final struggle for supremacy.

The first beast has *"seven heads and ten horns, and upon his horns ten crowns, and upon his heads the name of blasphemy"* (13:1). It is clearly stated that he is a man (verse 18), but it is also affirmed twice that he comes out of the abyss (11:7; 17:8), which means that he is in league with Satan and energized by Satan. The heads speak of wisdom, the horns of confederated power, and the crowns represent ruling authority. The restless world will be desperate for a leader, and this man will represent to the unregenerated mass of humanity what will appear to be the solution to the world's ills. But all of his genius and ability only combine in blasphemy against God. This is exactly what one would expect inasmuch as *"the dragon gave him his power, and his seat* [i.e., throne], *and great authority"* (13:2).

The description of this emerging dictator in verse 2, namely, *"like unto a leopard . . . a bear . . . and a lion,"* compares with the great prophecies of Daniel. King Nebuchadnezzar had a dream in which he saw a "great image." "This image's head was of fine gold, his breast and his arms of silver, his belly and his thighs of brass, his legs of iron, his feet part of iron and part of clay" (Daniel 2:32-33). The four metals represented four world empires which were to arise in succession until the second coming of Christ to earth when He shall rule the world. Christ is the "Stone" cut out without hands in Daniel 2:34. The names of the four empires in the order of their succession are given. The first is the Babylonian (Daniel 2:38). The second is the Medo-Persian (Daniel 5:30-31).

The third is the Grecian (Daniel 8:20-21). The fourth we know to be the Roman, for it was the Romans under Titus in 70 A.D. who destroyed Jerusalem (Daniel 9:26).

Those same four kingdoms are depicted again in Daniel 7 where they appear as a lion, a bear, a leopard, and an indescribable monster, the latter representing the feet of iron and clay in Nebuchadnezzar's image. The "little horn" (Daniel 7:8) might well be the first beast in Revelation 13. Notice that the beast is a composite of the previous world powers, like a leopard, a bear, and a lion. He combines in himself the abilities and characteristics of the leaders of the three world empires preceding the Roman, the swiftness of the leopard, the overpowering tyranny of the bear, and the wild ferocity of the lion.

However, there is a point of difference not to be overlooked. The two visions of the same three beasts are in reverse order. Daniel saw first the lion, then the bear, and last the leopard. John saw first the leopard, then the bear, and last the lion. Daniel saw the kingdoms from the beginning of the times of the Gentiles; thus he saw Babylon first, then Persia, after that Greece, and finally Rome. John, however, looks back after those kingdoms have run their course. How remarkably infallible are the prophetic Scriptures! Both Daniel and John beheld the same end-time visions.

II. THE WOUND OF THE BEAST (13:3)

And I saw one of his heads as it were wounded to death; and his deadly wound was healed: and all the world wondered after the beast (13:3).

Three times in this one chapter the wound of the beast is mentioned, and in all three verses it is made clear that the wound brought death but that the beast was restored to life again (verses 3,12,14). Some teachers see here the political death in the fall of the Roman Empire, which will be restored again. Others see in the Antichrist a man who has been here on the earth before and has died, but whom Satan will raise from the dead. Both views are tenable. I believe that we will see a revival of the Roman Empire. Actually Rome has never been destroyed completely. This political-religious combination has continued to smolder from underneath the ruins of the old Roman Empire. The Roman Catholic Church will play an important role in both the political and religious activity in the end times. We must bear in mind that the beast, though a man, is likewise representing a kingdom (Revelation 17:3,9,10), and I understand this kingdom to be the revived Roman Empire. This forthcoming Roman Empire, being revived before our very eyes, will be resurrected through the genius and personality of a human being.

Now is it possible that the Antichrist will be a man who had died and whom Satan will raise up again? Yes, it is possible. Satan's masterpiece of deception will be a clever imitation of Christ. Christ, the Seed of the woman, is God incarnate. Antichrist, the seed of the serpent, might well be Satan incarnate. As God raised Jesus from the dead, Satan could raise his representative from the dead, for he does have a certain power over death (Hebrews 2:14). By reading carefully Revelation 11:7; 17:8,11, it seems that the beast goes into the place of departed spirits, and then is raised up out of that place. In Revelation 17:8 four things are said of him: "The beast that thou sawest *was,* and *is not;* and *shall ascend out of the bottomless pit,* and *go into perdition.*" This indicates quite clearly that the Antichrist has been on the earth before.

Is it possible to identify the Antichrist? Yes, it is possible. There is a striking similarity between the Antichrist and Judas Iscariot. These two only are called "the son of perdition" (John 17:12; 2 Thessalonians 2:3). Judas is the only man whom Christ ever called *diabolos* (devil) (John 6:70). Judas is the only man of whom it is said that Satan himself entered into him (Luke 22:3).

The Antichrist is not a system, but a person. When the prophetic Scriptures speak of Antichrist, the masculine pronoun "he" is used. While he is the head of the final apostate system, he is nevertheless a man, the man who is being looked for by many and whose advent seems to be drawing near. After the Church has been raptured, and the restraining power of the Holy Spirit has been removed, this coming one will become earth's dictator.

We are moving toward "one world," that is, a unified political system and a unified religious system. The first beast will be the head of a great confederation of nations. A world-wide dictatorship under which all nations shall be consolidated into one great empire is inevitable. It will be the final form of the last great Gentile world power prior to Christ's second coming to the earth. Daniel saw that the power of this beast "shall devour the whole earth" (Daniel 7:23). Rome in her previous history controlled parts of Africa, Europe, and the Mediterranean, but never the "whole earth." It is this one great world ruler on whom Daniel focuses attention in the last six chapters of his prophecy. He is the "little horn" in Daniel 7:8, the "king of fierce countenance" in Daniel 8:23, the Roman "prince" in Daniel 9:26, and the "willful king" in Daniel 11:16. This one seems to be Satan incarnate, the first beast in Revelation 13.

III. THE WONDERING AFTER THE BEAST (13:3)

And all the world wondered after the beast (13:3).

A world which has been denying the resurrection of Christ for centuries now accepts the fact that here is a man who has conquered death. After having denied the One who is the Truth, the world in amazement believes a lie. "And for this cause God shall send them strong delusion, that they should believe a lie: That they all might be damned who believed not the truth, but had pleasure in unrighteousness" (2 Thessalonians 2:11-12). Some of the very persons who denied Christ's miracles and rejected Him will believe in the devil's miracles and accept his false Christ. Under such a man we see the world power in its final consummation just prior to the return of Christ to the earth.

He will possess an attractive and fascinating personality. His exceptional qualities of wisdom, daring, and leadership will draw to himself the highest admiration from people all over the world. He will be admired for his military prowess, for many shall say, *"Who is like unto the beast? who is able to make war with him?"* (13:4) Conceive, if you can, the most attractive features of the great world leaders combined in one man. Satan has such a man, and when he comes the leaders of nations will yield their thrones to him. Men will not flee from him but instead will idolize him. How sad that his fame does not lie in any moral greatness, but in astuteness and sheer brute force! Satan has produced his best as he approaches the last great conflict between God and himself.

IV. THE WORSHIP OF THE BEAST (13:4,12,15)

And they worshipped the dragon which gave power unto the beast: and they worshipped the beast, saying, Who is like unto the beast? who is able to make war with him?

And he exerciseth all the power of the first beast before him, and causeth the earth and them which dwell therein to worship the first beast, whose deadly wound was healed.

And he had power to give life unto the image of the beast, that the image of the beast should both speak, and cause that as many as would not worship the image of the beast should be killed (13:4,12,15).

The wondering is followed by worship. Spiritism, which is a form of demon worship and which has advanced with rapid strides in the last century, will reach its zenith during the latter half of the tribulation. While the eternal triune God is being blasphemed by the Antichrist, millions will worship Satan who controls the man of sin. This is he of whom Paul wrote, "Who opposeth and exalteth himself above all that is called God, or that is worshipped; so that he as God sitteth in the temple of God, showing himself that he is God" (2 Thessalonians 2:4).

The worship of the first beast is enforced by another beast who is called three times "the false prophet" (Revelation 16:13; 19:20; 20:10). Like the first beast, he is a real person, a man who is subordinate to and dependent upon the first beast, as the first beast is subordinate to and dependent upon Satan.

This second beast is seen *"coming up out of the earth"* (13:11), or, more accurately, out of *"the land,"* meaning the ancient land of Palestine where Christ was born and died. In appearance he is *"like a lamb,"* imitating the Lamb of God and Israel's Messiah. This clever deception arises in the same land where Jewish prophets announced that the Messiah would appear. I believe that our Lord included these beasts in His prophecy in Matthew 24:11,24.

We see in this chapter a world religion under one head with all worship controlled by him.

> *And he doeth great wonders, so that he maketh fire come down from heaven on the earth in the sight of men, And deceiveth them that dwell on the earth by the means of those miracles which he had power to do in the sight of the beast; saying to them that dwell on the earth, that they should make an image to the beast, which had the wound by a sword, and did live. And he had power to give life unto the image of the beast, that the image of the beast should both speak, and cause that as many as would not worship the image of the beast should be killed* (13:13-15).

In order to procure results in getting people to worship the first beast, he performs miracles thereby demonstrating that he possesses supernatural ability. We should bear in mind the fact that a miracle is not necessarily of God.

We need not be surprised at reading of the forthcoming worship of demon-possessed men. It was Satan's original sinful ambition to be higher than the other angels, and therefore to be worshiped (Isaiah 14:12-14). Through his servants he attracted to himself the worship of heathen (Deuteronomy 32:16-18). Satan's final assault against Christ in the wilderness temptation was an attempt to get our Lord to worship him (Matthew 4:8-10; Luke 4:5-8). In pursuance of his goal he has incited his servants to demand worship as in the case of Nebuchadnezzar (Daniel 3). In the same book, Daniel prophesied of the Antichrist, "He shall exalt himself, and magnify himself above every god, and shall speak marvellous things against the God of gods, and shall prosper till the indignation be accomplished: for that that is determined shall be done"

(Daniel 11:36). The worship of the Antichrist in the tribulation will be forced upon the people even as it was in Nebuchadnezzar's day. And at last Satan finds a man who will accept what Christ rejected, and through him will direct the worship of the entire inhabited world. It is shocking to tell about, but nevertheless true, that the end of the age will be characterized by the worship of the devil. Even now Satan has his forerunners of the Antichrist leading many to worship him (2 Corinthians 11:13-15).

V. THE WARFARE OF THE BEAST (13:7)

And it was given unto him to make war with the saints, and to overcome them: and power was given him over all kindreds, and tongues, and nations (13:7).

The beast makes war with the saints. Now the "saints" here are not the believers of this present dispensation which make up the Church. Not all saints are in the Church. There were saints in Israel before the Church came into being, and there will be saints on earth during the tribulation after the Church has been taken up to Heaven. Israel and the Church are not the same, nor does God deal in the same way with each. The saints mentioned in our verse are saved during the tribulation (Revelation 7).

For some time the beast is quite popular. His personality, military prowess, great intellect, and ability to express himself will capture the hearts and the worship of the masses. But suddenly he turns against the Jewish saints at Jerusalem. Now remember that he has made a covenant with the Jews, but in the middle of the tribulation he will break that covenant (Daniel 9:27). When he comes he will promise them peace in the land of Palestine. The nation will accept him as the promised Messiah and the fulfillment of the Abrahamic covenant. But the peace he offers the Jews is a false peace. Daniel prophesied that he "by peace shall destroy many" (Daniel 8:25). He will move into Palestine, desecrate the restored temple (2 Thessalonians 2:4; Revelation 11:1-2), and institute a religious system that will become the worship of Palestine and of the entire earth. He will recognize no religion other than the worship of Satan through himself. Because the people refused to bow to God's Christ, they must in that day bow to the devil's Antichrist. His subordinate, the second beast, called the "false prophet" (16:13; 19:20; 20:10), will assist the Antichrist in enforcing his false religious system. Through force the deification of Satan is accomplished and the desire of his proud heart is at last realized. For a more complete description of the Antichrist, the student should read Daniel 11:36-45.

VI. THE WONDERS OF THE SECOND BEAST (13:13-15)

And he doeth great wonders, so that he maketh fire come down from heaven on the earth in the sight of men (13:13).

This second beast is the false prophet who works to support the Antichrist. He is an administrator of the affairs of Satan. As a means of impressing the people favorably, he performs miracles. This is a means of accomplishing his purposes. He substantiates his claims by demonstrating supernatural control over the forces of nature.

These signs are religious in character. There is the sign of fire from Heaven. This has been one way that God revealed Himself in history. He sent fire from Heaven upon Sodom and Gomorrah (Genesis 19:24). He sent fire from Heaven to slay Nadab and Abihu (Leviticus 10:1-2). He sent fire from Heaven to Mount Carmel in answer to the prayer of Elijah (1 Kings 18:38). Similar miracles will have been performed by the two witnesses (Revelation 11:3-6), so that the false prophet's duplication of such wonders will serve as an aid in causing the citizens of earth to worship the beast. You will recall that it was by the calling of fire from Heaven that Elijah authenticated himself and his message as from God (2 Kings 1:10,12). Now consider the last words spoken by God in the Old Testament just prior to the 400 silent years: "Behold, I will send you Elijah the prophet before the coming of the great and dreadful day of the LORD: And he shall turn the heart of the fathers to the children, and the heart of the children to their fathers, lest I come and smite the earth with a curse" (Malachi

4:5-6). Here is a promise that Elijah would come before the second coming of Christ to the earth. I believe that Elijah is one of God's two witnesses in Revelation 11. Now I believe we can learn from all of this the reason why the false prophet calls down fire from Heaven. The devil and his representatives know the prophetic Scriptures. So, by imitating the miracles of Elijah through the false prophet, Satan hopes to convince the nation Israel that the false prophet is Elijah, and that the man to whom this Elijah is pointing is none other than Israel's Messiah, who ought to be worshiped. Oh, the cleverness of Satan's wiles!

Look now at verse 14.

> *And deceiveth them that dwell on the earth by the means of those miracles which he had power to do in the sight of the beast; saying to them that dwell on the earth, that they should make an image to the beast, which had the wound by a sword, and did live* (13:14).

Here we see the purpose for the miracle of the false prophet. The real purpose for the miracle was to prepare the minds of the people for the announcement in verse 14. The false prophet will attempt to lead the people to finance the erection of a great image in Jerusalem, thereby making Jerusalem the center of a world-wide religious system. Once again Satan is imitating what is predicted in the prophetic Scriptures. He knows that Jerusalem was the center of Christ's activities when He came to earth the first time, and that it will be His capital city when He comes again to reign on the earth. When one reads our Lord's prophecies in Matthew 24, he can see that Christ was referring to these same events (Matthew 24:15-24). Moreover our Lord identifies the time period when the false prophet and the Antichrist appear on the scene as the "great tribulation" (Matthew 24:21).

> *And he had power to give life unto the image of the beast, that the image of the beast should both speak, and cause that as many as would not worship the image of the beast should be killed* (13:15).

How the image is made to speak, or what it says, is not

revealed. Some have ventured to guess that the image is made to speak through some electronic device. Others have thought it might be through ventriloquism. And still others believe that it will be nothing short of a supernatural miracle performed by Satan. One thing is certain. When the image speaks, Jews and Gentiles, Roman Catholics and Protestants, wherever they are, will worship the image or be killed if they refuse.

VII. THE WORLD MARKET UNDER THE BEAST (13:16-17)

And he causeth all, both small and great, rich and poor, free and bond, to receive a mark in their right hand, or in their foreheads: And that no man might buy or sell, save he that had the mark, or the name of the beast, or the number of his name (13:16-17).

Here is the mark of the beast. It is an identifying mark indicating that the one bearing it both worships the beast and submits to his rule. To be without the mark will label one as a traitor to government. Such an one will be killed instantly or else starved to death slowly. All men must eat if they will live. Therefore in order to remain alive one must be able to buy and sell, and these things he will be permitted to do only if he can show the mark of the beast.

There are forerunners today of this intricately planned system which will control world commerce, the latest of these being the European common market. It is not impossible that modern labor unions could be closely tied in with such a world dictatorship. Of recent date one union was able to stop all exports and imports from and to the entire Eastern seacoast of our own country. Merchandise which is manufactured in union shops often has the union's stamp on it. Members of labor unions carry cards which give them preference both commercially and socially. These things I have mentioned may have nothing whatever to do with the mark of the beast and the coming world market, but certainly they have made the world "mark" conscious. The day will surely come when the producer and the consumer, the seller and the buyer, will be powerless under the control of the Antichrist. Capital and labor are struggling for control now, but then both will be controlled by the beast. Anyone who is outside of his vast control will be ruthlessly boycotted. No one else will employ or be employed. All classes of society are included. No exceptions will be made. All will worship the beast or die.

> *Here is wisdom. Let him that hath understanding count the number of the beast: for it is the number of a man; and his number is Six hundred threescore and six* (13:18).

I have an idea you are expecting me to tell you what the number 666 means. I wish I knew, but I must confess that I do not. It is interesting (and amusing) to see what some minds have conceived. Someone has said that A = 100, B = 101, C = 102, D = 103, and so on, and then came up with the following:

$$
\begin{array}{l}
H = 107 \\
I = 108 \\
T = 119 \\
L = 111 \\
E = 104 \\
R = \underline{117} \\
666
\end{array}
$$

Another has suggested the following. In Greek numbers, E = 5, U = 400, A = 1, N = 50, TH (the Greek letter *theta*) = 9, A = 1, S = 200, and so he came up with the name:

$$
\begin{array}{l}
E = 5 \\
U = 400 \\
A = 1 \\
N = 50 \\
T = 9 \\
H \\
A = 1 \\
S = \underline{200} \\
666
\end{array}
$$

These illustrations only show how far man's mind can carry him in weird speculation. The Word of God says, *"It is the number of a man."* We know that man was created on the sixth day. We know further that seven is the number of completion or perfection. Six then is short of seven, so that man at his zenith is still imperfect. We know that the Antichrist will be the fullest manifestation of man at his best, but any man at his best is a poor imitation of Jesus Christ.

What the world needs is Jesus Christ, not the Antichrist. If you have not received God's Son, do so at once. Trust Him now for eternal life.

THE WINE OF THE WRATH OF GOD

Revelation 14:1-20

When one has read through chapter 14, it is seen to stand out in bold contrast to chapter 13, in which was seen the Antichrist ruling the earth. Dreadful gloom for those on the earth was depicted under the rule of the satanic trinity. The devil's man *"like* a lamb" (13:11) was seen thrusting his sickle into the earth. But here in chapter 14, the Lamb of God (14:1) is seen reaping the earth with His sickle (14:14-16). Just as the blackest night will show the brightest stars, so the darkest period in the world's history has its Light shining on the horizon. The darkness in chapter 13 is relieved by refreshing scenes of a magnificent sunrise which now appears.

In chapter 14 there is a series of seven separate visions, each complete in itself. They are disconnected pictures, however, and are not intended to present a chronological sequence of events. By now you probably have observed that from time to time the Holy Spirit sets forth in outline a panoramic view of things to come, and then He goes on later to fill in the details. Chronologically, the events in chapters 15 and 16 occur before the reaping and harvest visions in chapter 14. For example, in chapter 14, verse 8, a brief announcement, or vision, shows the judgment of Babylon, but her actual doom is described under the seventh vial of wrath and judgment in chapter 16, verses 17 to 21.

Let us say that chapter 14 is like a table of contents. It takes the reader back to the beginning of the tribulation week and carries him forward to the end of the week. It contains anticipative visions which set forth the end, for the comfort of the saints. In place of the wicked beasts, the Lamb comes into view. In place of a multitude of people worshiping the Antichrist, there appears a host of redeemed ones praising and following Christ.

I. THE FIRST VISION (14:1-5)

> *And I looked, and, lo, a Lamb stood on the mount Sion, and with Him an hundred forty and four thousand, having His Father's name written in their foreheads. And I heard a voice from heaven, as the voice of many waters, and as the voice of a great thunder: and I heard the voice of harpers harping with their harps: And they sung as it were a new song before the throne, and before the four beasts, and the elders: and no man could learn that song but the hundred and forty and four thousand, which were redeemed from the earth. These are they which were not defiled with women; for they are virgins. These are they which follow the Lamb whithersoever He goeth. These were redeemed from among men, being the firstfruits unto God and to the Lamb. And in their mouth was found no guile: for they are without fault before the throne of God* (14:1-5).

A. *The Saviour*

And I looked, and, lo, a Lamb.

This Lamb is no other than the Jews' Messiah and Deliverer, our Lord and Saviour Jesus Christ. It is refreshing to have Him appear when almost all of the people in the earth are worshiping Satan. Thus far we have met the Lamb frequently in the Revelation. The Lamb is *crucified*, "as it had been slain" (5:6); *glorified*, as He is worshiped (5:8,12,13); *justified*, as He opens the seals (6:1,16); *magnified*, as He is recognized (7:9,10,14,17); and, here, *rectified*, when He comes to earth and all wrong against Him will be amended.

B. *The Site*

The site of His appearing is *"Mount Sion."* This is an earthly scene, a picture of Christ's return to reign, the selected place from which He shall rule gloriously. This is not "the heavenly Jerusalem," sometimes called "Mount Sion" (Hebrews 12:22). Speaking prophetically of Christ's second coming to the earth, the Father said through the Psalmist, "Yet have I set My King upon My holy hill of Zion" (Psalm 2:6). The Lamb seen standing on this mount is also a prophetic forecast of Christ's return to the earth as recorded in Zechariah 14:4 and Revelation 14. Mount Zion is Jerusalem, Israel's earthly capital. (See also 2 Samuel 5:7; Psalm 48:2; Isaiah 24:23).

C. *The Sealed*

The Lamb is . . .

With an hundred forty and four thousand.

Who are these? I believe that the 144,000 in this chapter are the same group of 144,000 in chapter 7. I see no reason for making the number 144,000 symbolical in this chapter. They are the saved and the sealed, 12,000 from each of twelve tribes, and they have been faithful to the trust committed to them from the time they were called. During the reign of the Antichrist they are God's witnesses, preaching the gospel of the kingdom and heralding the coming King.

D. *The Seal*

Having His Father's name written in their foreheads.

In chapter 7 we are told that they are sealed in their foreheads (7:3). Here we are told what that seal is and why they are sealed. This company is clearly identified with Jesus Christ and the Father. It seems that the seal is visible to the eye, not the invisible seal of the Holy Spirit, as is the case with Christians in this dispensation (Ephesians 1:13; 4:30). In chapter 13 the mark of the beast is upon each of his worshipers. In chapter 14 God puts His mark upon them who worship Him. The seal proclaimed their ownership, character, and loyalty to the Lamb. The name of the Father, which is the Jewish mark, is further indication that the 144,000 are the same as those Jews in chapter 7.

E. *Their Song*

And I heard a voice from heaven, as the voice of many waters, and as the voice of a great thunder: and I heard the voice of harpers harping with their harps: And they sung as it were a new song before the throne, and before the four beasts, and the elders: and no man could learn that song but the hundred and forty and four thousand, which were redeemed from the earth (14:2-3).

Herman Hoyt says of these two verses, "Out of heaven a voice with tremendous range, like that of many waters, is heard. It rolls and peals and echoes like that of thunder, and, gathering volume, it finally individualizes into the voice of many harpers harping with their harps." Their song is a redemption song, exclusively and peculiarly their own. This is not a heavenly choir, but an earthly choir of redeemed Jews. John also had seen and heard a much larger chorus in Heaven, the redeemed of this present dispensation, singing their song of redemption (5:8-10). The words of their song are recorded, but here in Revelation 14 we are not told the words of this song. Regardless of the dispensation in which a man has lived, if he has been redeemed by God, he has something worthwhile to sing about.

It is possible that the voices are to be accompanied by harps. More than forty times this musical instrument is mentioned in the Old Testament, and always it is associated with joy. When sorrow replaces joy, the harp ceases (Isaiah 24:8). When the people were in captivity because of their sins, their song ceased as well as the playing of their harps (Psalm 137:1-4). But at the end of the tribulation, the 144,000 shall take up their harps again, and sing and play once more to the glory of God.

F. *Their Sanctification*

These are they which were not defiled with women; for they are virgins.

This is not easy to interpret. Are we to assume that these are all men because they "were not defiled with women"? Or are we to assume that they are all women because they "are virgins"? Frankly, I do not believe that either assumption would be absolutely correct. I believe the meaning of this first sentence in the verse is explained to some extent by the sentence which follows, namely:

These are they which follow the Lamb whithersoever He goeth.

The 144,000 were a truly *separated* and *sanctified* group of people. They were free from spiritual fornication, that spiritual adultery of which the Apostle James wrote, "Ye adulterers and adulteresses, know ye not that the friendship of the world is enmity with God? whosoever therefore will be a friend of the world is the enemy of God" (James 4:4). This is one of the gross sins of apostate Christendom in the last days, as indicated in Revelation 18:9. In the Old Testament spiritual adultery is associated with the worship of idols and the evil practices attached to such worship (Exodus 34:15; Deuteronomy 31:16; Judges 2:17; Hosea 9:1). Throughout the tribulation the 144,000 will refuse to take part in those idolatries and fornications of the masses who worship the image of the beast. You will recall that under the sixth trumpet this is one of the open sins against God (Revelation 9:20-21). But these escape all spiritual defilement with "the great whore" (Revelation 17:1—18:24). Being called virgins might relate this group to those of Matthew 25:1-13. Such loyalty to Jesus Christ, marked by separation and cleanliness, is enjoined upon believers in this present dispensation (2 Corinthians 11:2).

Verse 4 has a further word about the 144,000.

These were redeemed from among men, being the first-fruits unto God and to the Lamb.

These are kingdom words. Being Jews, they are the "first-fruits" of Israel in the Great Tribulation. The harvest has begun so that there is more to follow. Just as God gives the first-fruits, so He can be depended upon to give the greater harvest which will follow. "And so all Israel shall be saved" (Romans 11:26), "For if the firstfruit be holy, the lump is also holy: and if the root be holy, so are the branches" (Romans 11:16). Now we Christians of this present dispensation are also called "a kind of firstfruits" (James 1:18); however, we are a heavenly people with a heavenly calling and destiny. The 144,000 are a firstfruits of an earthly people, and as such are an earnest of earth's coming blessing and a greater harvest of Jews.

G. *Their Sincerity*

And in their mouth was found no guile: for they are without fault before the throne of God (14:5).

These were truthful. The tribulation period in which they live is peculiarly one when deceit and falsehood reign. The Antichrist will come in the power of Satan with "lying wonders" (2 Thessalonians 2:9), so that the multitudes shall "believe a lie" (2 Thessalonians 2:11). Satan being "a liar, and the father of it" (John 8:44), his man, who is the Antichrist, will appear in the tribulation as "the liar" (1 John 2:22). Zephaniah pictures this remnant in the millennium, "The remnant of Israel shall not do iniquity, nor speak lies; neither shall a deceitful tongue be found in their mouth: for they shall feed and lie down and none shall make them afraid" (Zephaniah 3:13). Over against all the false worship in the tribulation, here is a group which maintains loyalty to God and the Lamb. It is not that they are perfectly sinless, but that they are true when everyone else is conforming to a lie. Well might believers in our own dispensation follow the example of these saints of a far more difficult age.

II. THE SECOND VISION (14:6-7)

And I saw another angel fly in the midst of heaven, having the everlasting gospel to preach unto them that dwell on the

earth, and to every nation, and kindred, and tongue, and
people, Saying with a loud voice, Fear God, and give glory
to Him; for the hour of His judgment is come: and worship
Him that made heaven, and earth, and the sea, and the
fountains of waters (14:6-7).

A. *A Messenger*

The messenger here is *"an angel."* Be certain the Antichrist
will not lay a hand on this servant of God. His pulpit is beyond
the reach of God's enemies. He will herald His message to the
Jewish remnant who in turn will carry it throughout the earth.
God's message must be spoken. If men are silenced, then angels
become vocal. If Satan could slay and silence every human witness of God's truth, then God would see to its proclamation by
some other means. It should be noted that the word "angel"
literally means "messenger," and that it is used at times to
refer to men, as in the seven letters in chapters 2 and 3. The
context must determine whether the angel is a man or a spirit-
being. It appears quite certain that in the present dispensation
of grace angels do not preach the gospel. When Paul wrote,
"But though we, or an angel from heaven, preach any other
gospel unto you than that which we have preached unto you,
let him be accursed" (Galatians 1:8), he was not stating emphatically that angels do preach the gospel in our present age.
An angel told Cornelius to send for Peter in order that Peter
might preach the gospel to him, but the angel made no attempt
to explain the way of salvation (Acts 10). But in the tribulation
the wickedness of man and the power of Satan necessitates a
change in the divine method. God will then resort to a method
He used before Christ came to earth the first time (cf. Hebrews
2:2).

B. *A Message*

The angel's message is *"the everlasting gospel."* There is
nothing in the message about grace, the blood, redemption, or
forgiveness. This is the burden of "the gospel of the grace of

God" (Acts 20:24), which is "the gospel of Christ" (Romans 1:16). The message of the everlasting gospel is essentially that which has been proclaimed since God's earliest dealings with man, namely, God is sovereign, and true happiness comes to those who recognize His sovereign right in the earth. The Creator only, and not the creature, must be worshiped. During the Great Tribulation, when false worship will prevail, God will once again state His claim to the worship of men. The everlasting gospel is a warning of impending judgment against the Antichrist and all who worship him. This is God's last call to a wicked and apostate world, for the hour of judgment has come. The Creator has a claim upon His creature. Presently He attempts to woo men by the Holy Spirit on the ground of Christ's death. Then He summons men by an angel to recognize and reverence Him as the Creator and Sustainer of the universe.

III. THE THIRD VISION (14:8)

And there followed another angel, saying, Babylon is fallen, is fallen, that great city, because she made all nations drink of the wine of the wrath of her fornication (14:8).

A. *A Ruin Is Announced*

Here is a preliminary announcement of the final overthrow of the false and seductive religious system of the end time. It is a mere prophetic glimpse of that which is described fully in chapters 17 and 18. The first Babylon mentioned in the Bible was a city founded by a God-defying rebel named Nimrod (cf. Genesis 10:8-10; 11:1-9). It grew into the first great Gentile world power that oppressed the nations. It was a stronghold of pride and idolatry. But her fall is announced.

Babylon is fallen, is fallen.

Twice the word "fallen" appears, as though she is in for a double portion of divine judgment. Her doom is so certain that she appears here as already "fallen."

B. *A Reason Is Announced*

Because she made all nations drink of the wine of the wrath of her fornication.

Here is a religious system in its most corrupt form. Multitudes are won to it and intoxicated by it. The Prophet Jeremiah described Babylon's condition and coming judgment. "It is the land of graven images, and they are mad upon [or over] their idols" (Jeremiah 50:38). "Babylon hath been a golden cup in the LORD's hand, that made all the earth drunken: the nations have drunken of her wine; therefore the nations are mad. Babylon is suddenly fallen and destroyed" (Jeremiah 51:7-8). Isaiah wrote, "Babylon is fallen, is fallen; and all the graven images of her gods He hath broken unto the ground" (Isaiah 21:9). The reason for her fall is made clear to all. In the last days the harlot church will ally herself with the political powers and thereby seduce the world. Her unholy alliance is her fornication. I see today a strong enthusiasm for a superchurch with Rome taking the lead. But let all be warned that whatever seduces the affections away from the Lord Jesus Christ must needs be the object of God's wrath. Men should think seriously before they affiliate themselves with any church, making certain that it is a true New Testament Church with a genuine interest in the salvation of souls.

IV. THE FOURTH VISION (14:9-11)

And the third angel followed them, saying with a loud voice, If any man worship the beast and his image, and receive his mark in his forehead, or in his hand, The same shall drink of the wine of the wrath of God, which is poured out without mixture into the cup of his indignation; and he shall be tormented with fire and brimstone in the presence of the holy angels, and in the presence of the Lamb: And the smoke of their torment ascendeth up for ever and ever: and they have no rest day nor night, who worship the beast and his image, and whosoever receiveth the mark of his name (14:9-11).

Another angel makes the solemn announcement that the beast worshipers are doomed. They must drink of the wrath of God. Let any and all who entertain light thoughts about the wrath and judgment of God seriously ponder these solemn words. The language is full of awe. Hardly a day passes without our hearing someone mock the idea of hell and coming judgment. Men of God who expound all of God's Word are labeled "hell-fire-and brimstone preachers" and looked upon as a queer lot to be avoided.

But what do the Holy Scriptures say? We read in the book of history, "The sun was risen upon the earth when Lot entered into Zoar. Then the LORD rained upon Sodom and upon Gomorrah brimstone and fire from the LORD out of heaven" (Genesis 19:23-24). Now we know there are unbelievers who refuse to accept this record in spite of the supporting statements of our Lord Jesus Christ, who said, "But the same day that Lot went out of Sodom it rained fire and brimstone from heaven, and destroyed them all" (Luke 17:29). We show these skeptics and scoffers the actual ruins of Sodom and Gomorrah, pointing out the ash heaps uncovered by the spade of the archaeologist, and still they refuse to believe. Well, one day they will know from personal experience that God loves righteousness and hates wickedness (Psalm 45:7 cf. Hebrews 1:9). The "fire and brimstone" in the Revelation passage now under consideration is used in similar passages in this book to describe the torments of hell (Revelation 19:20; 20:10; 21:8). Just as the judgment upon Sodom and Gomorrah was the most terrible that ever fell on this earth, so the doom to come upon the apostates is the fiercest of all dooms.

We may dislike the thought of coming judgment, and fastidiously condemn it, but here it stands. And it does not stand alone! John, writing by inspiration of the Holy Spirit, is echoing that which the prophets wrote by the same Spirit. Isaiah wrote, "For it is the day of the LORD's vengeance, and the year of recompenses for the controversy of Zion. And the streams thereof shall be turned into pitch, and the dust thereof into brimstone, and the land thereof shall become burning pitch. It shall not be quenched night nor day; the smoke thereof shall go up for ever: from generation to generation it shall lie waste; none shall pass through it for ever and ever" (Isaiah 34:8-10). "Awake, awake, stand up, O Jerusalem, which hast drunk at the hand of the LORD the cup of His fury; thou hast drunken the dregs of the cup of trembling, and wrung them out" (Isaiah 51:17). "For thus saith the LORD; Behold, they whose judgment was not to drink of the cup have assuredly drunken; and art thou he that shall altogether go unpunished? thou shalt not go unpunished, but thou shalt surely drink of it" (Jeremiah 49:12). The language is unmistakable. It coincides with the judgment of which John writes. This is God's cup of anger in a day when mercy has been withdrawn forever. "For in the hand of the LORD there is a cup, and the wine is red; it is full of mixture; and He poureth out of the same: but the dregs thereof, all the wicked of the earth shall wring them out, and drink them" (Psalm 75:8).

You may angrily cast off all thoughts of coming doom on the ground that you cannot reconcile such judgment with a God of love, but I can only tell you that which God has written in His Word. The only way man has of knowing what God is like and what He will do is to read what God Himself has said in His Word. God is a holy God and jealous for His character, and because of who He is, He cannot condone sin. Let these verses in the Revelation serve as a warning.

The severity of this judgment cannot be fully imagined. Think of it! *"Torment . . . for ever and ever"* (verse 11), from which there is no relief, *"no rest day nor night."* Robert Govett writes: "After the resurrection, sleep belongs neither to the lost nor to the saved. The saved will not need it; for the body of weakness is shaken off. The lost may not enjoy it. How strange the sinner's infatuation, that after all this solemn warning of the eternity of hell-torments, he will still go on coolly provoking God to cut him down and cast him into the fire!" This divine pronouncement of judgment is in keeping with such Scripture references as Mark 9:43-48 and Luke 12:5, and it is entirely justifiable. They drank of the wine of the harlot's fornication, now they must drink of the wine of God's wrath. Here is a hell-fire-and-brimstone preacher who cannot be silenced.

And yet, with all of the severity of this judgment, I see a fair warning to earth's inhabitants. The judgment does not fall upon men without their being told first that it is coming. It is still future from the moment the angel announces it. If any heed the angel's warning and denounce the Antichrist, they will probably be put to death instantly. But it will be far better to lose one's life on earth and take flight to Heaven in triumph than to suffer the torments of hell forever.

V. THE FIFTH VISION (14:12-13)

> *Here is the patience of the saints: here are they that keep the commandments of God, and the faith of Jesus. And I heard a voice from heaven saying unto me, Write, Blessed are the dead which die in the Lord from henceforth: Yea saith the Spirit, that they may rest from their labours; and their works do follow them* (14:12-13).

Many will not worship the beast, and for their refusal they will be killed. The word *patience* connotes the idea of endurance. These are the saints of the tribulation who refuse to worship the beast. They had no visible means of defence, nor would they have used it if it were offered to them (13:10). Yet they remained loyal to the commandments of God and to Jesus. They were obedient to the law and loyal to the Saviour. God will have His faithful ones, even in the tribulation, who will wait patiently for Him to vindicate them. In their patient endurance they possessed their souls (Luke 21:19). "For what shall it profit a man, if he shall gain the whole world, and lose his own soul?" (Mark 8:36) The threats and torments of the beast for 1,260 days are as nothing when compared with the eternal fire and brimstone judgments of Almighty God. Yet it will take much patient endurance for any person to remain true to God in those tribulation days when Antichrist rules the world.

But what about those who are put to death for refusing to

worship the beast? Do they not lose the special blessing of sharing the earthly rule of Messiah who is to come shortly? John receives a special word from Heaven for them.

> *Blessed are the dead which die in the Lord from hence-forth: Yea, saith the Spirit, that they may rest from their labours; and their works do follow them* (14:13).

The beast may be permitted to put them to death, but God declares them blessed. And what is true of these Jewish saints in the tribulation is true of all saints. All who have ever died in the Lord are blessed. They are blessed because they are absent from the body of suffering in a world where they are despised, and at home with the Lord (2 Corinthians 5:8), and this latter is "far better" (Philippians 1:23). In this sense it is legitimate to use our verse as a funeral text, but in its primary interpretation it is addressed to those Jewish believers who "from hence-forth" (that point of time in the tribulation) are slain for their refusal to worship the beast. It will be better for them to be dead than alive. Their sufferings will have ended forever. More-over, their reward is certain, for He who is about to come said, "And, behold, I come quickly; and My reward is with Me, to give every man according as his work shall be" (Revelation 22:12). What a contrast between the destiny of those who fol-low Christ and them who follow the Antichrist! The efforts of Satan are toward separating men from Christ. But, oh, the blessedness of those who come to the end "in Christ"! And what would those poor dupes of Satan, who end up in hell, give for a bit of this blessing of rest? But the wicked shall have *"no rest"* day or night forever (verse 11).

VI. THE SIXTH VISION (14:14-16)

> *And I looked, and behold a white cloud, and upon the cloud one sat like unto the Son of man, having on His head a golden crown, and in His hand a sharp sickle. And another angel came out of the temple, crying with a loud voice to Him that sat on the cloud, Thrust in Thy sickle, and reap: for the time is come for Thee to reap: for the harvest of the*

earth is ripe. And He that sat on the cloud thrust in His sickle on the earth; and the earth was reaped (14:14-16).

This is a judgment scene. The Judge is about to sweep the earth clean of all evil. He is the Son of Man, the Lord Jesus Christ, in His visible return in glory. All judgment belongs to Him (John 5:27). The harvest here is not the gathering of the good wheat into His garner as in Luke 3:17, but rather the tares which are the children of the wicked one as in Matthew 13:38-42. There is a harvest of evil as well as a harvest of good (cf. Proverbs 13:21; Luke 3:17; Galatians 6:7).

These verses comprising the sixth vision shown to John might well be a preview in brief of Armageddon. Certain prophecies in the Old Testament fit the case. There is the word by Jeremiah, "For thus saith the LORD of hosts, the God of Israel; The daughter of Babylon is like a threshingfloor, it is time to thresh her: yet a little while, and the time of her harvest shall come" (Jeremiah 51:33). Again we read in Joel, "Assemble yourselves, and come, all ye heathen, and gather yourselves together round about: thither cause Thy mighty ones to come down, O LORD. Let the heathen be wakened, and come up to the valley of Jehoshaphat: for there will I sit to judge all the heathen round about. Put ye in the sickle, for the harvest is ripe: come, get you down; for the press is full, the vats overflow; for their wickedness is great. Multitudes, multitudes in the valley of decision: for the day of the LORD is near in the valley of decision. The sun and the moon shall be darkened, and the stars shall withdraw their shining. The LORD also shall roar out of Zion, and utter His voice from Jerusalem; and the heavens and the earth shall shake: but the LORD will be the hope of His people, and the strength of the children of Israel" (Joel 3:11-16). The devil has been sowing his tares during this present age (Matthew 13:25,39), but after the rapture of the Church the reaping will come. It seems that the world is moving toward that reaping. This is not the judgment of the Great White Throne which takes place after the millennium; it is a premillennial judgment upon the wicked nations who have followed evil leaders.

Yes, the Son of Man will come to earth again (Daniel 7:13-

14), in a cloud (Matthew 24:30; Luke 21:27; Acts 1:9-11). This is the last place in the Bible where "Son of Man" occurs. David was the first of the inspired writers to use it, and he looked forward to the coming of the Son of Man as the crowned Sovereign of the earth (Psalm 8:5; 21:3).

John wrote:

> *And the earth was reaped* (14:16).

It is a sad and sorry scene, but it must come. The increasing corruption and rottenness in the earth is objectionable to a holy God. Man cannot continue as he is without the interruption of divine judgment. It is the "earth" that is reaped because this is where men dwell and where they have perpetuated their evil works. The sickle Christ holds in His hand is "sharp." It will not fail to do its work thoroughly. The earth must be reaped of its evil. The cup of iniquity is full, the harvest is ripe, and the time of God's judgment has come.

But while the Church awaits the Rapture, there is a good harvest before us even now. Jesus said, "Lift up your eyes, and look on the fields, for they are white already to harvest" (John 4:35). Our business as Christians is to witness of Christ and His gospel. The world must hear His message of salvation, and we are responsible to tell it to the uttermost part of the earth. "He that goeth forth and weepeth, bearing precious seed, shall doubtless come again with rejoicing, bringing his sheaves with him" (Psalm 126:6).

VII. THE SEVENTH VISION (14:17-20)

> *And another angel came out of the temple which is in heaven, he also having a sharp sickle. And another angel came out from the altar, which had power over fire; and cried with a loud cry to him that had the sharp sickle, saying, Thrust in thy sharp sickle, and gather the clusters of the vine of the earth; for her grapes are fully ripe. And the angel thrust in his sickle into the earth, and gathered the vine of the earth, and cast it into the great winepress of the wrath of God. And the winepress was trodden without the*

city, and blood came out of the winepress, even unto the horse bridles, by the space of a thousand and six hundred furlongs (14:17-20).

This seventh and final vision in this chapter is introduced by two angels. John sees one coming forth from the temple in Heaven *"also having a sharp sickle,"* and another coming out from the altar having *"power over fire."* The angel emerging from the altar is in command, thus he issues the order to the angel which came out of the temple to cut the ripe clusters and cast them into the vat of the righteous wrath of the holy God.

Notice how the peoples of the earth are described as clusters attached to the vine of the earth. Throughout this series of messages we have noted from time to time how Satan, in his attempt to deceive the people, particularly the Jews, produced a clever counterfeit of the blessed Holy Trinity. You will remember how the Lord Jesus said to His disciples, "I am the vine, ye are the branches" (John 15:5). Here in the Revelation we see the false *"vine of the earth,"* the Antichrist, and the clusters of grapes which represent the apostate church which followed him. The Antichrist also has his branches, the wicked nations of the world. As they are ripe for judgment their doom is here graphically described.

In the Old Testament, Israel is symbolized by a vine, but a fruitless, disappointing vine. Moses, in his last song, which was written as a witness against Israel because of her failure, said, "For their vine is of the vine of Sodom, and of the fields of Gomorrah: their grapes are grapes of gall, their clusters are bitter: Their wine is the poison of dragons, and the cruel venom of asps" (Deuteronomy 32:32-33). The Psalmist and the Prophet Isaiah give a summary of the history of this vine in Psalm 80:8-16 and Isaiah 5:1-7. By the time of the end of the Great Tribulation, unbelieving Israel will have degenerated so far as to be allied with the world church headed by the great harlot and the Antichrist. Our Lord confirmed these Old Testament Scriptures, giving Israel's failure His reason for coming into the world as the True Vine and grafting in other branches (Matthew 21:33-43).

When the Great Tribulation concludes with Armageddon, the

luscious-looking clusters of grapes with their false beauty and pride will be destroyed. This is the end of man's glory and Satan's rule in the earth. It will be the worst slaughter of human life in all of history. Ezekiel describes the scene by relating that seven years will be required to rid the earth of the weapons of warfare enmassed by the nations, and seven months to bury the dead (Ezekiel 39:8-16). So great will be the slaughter that in some places the blood will be more than two feet deep. The exact site of this bloody end of the nations is the Valley of Jehoshaphat (Joel 3:10-14; Zechariah 14:1-4). Josephus, in his history of the Roman armies' overthrow of Jerusalem under Titus, said that the dead bodies made the whole city run down with blood. But the blood of Jerusalem and Athens and Stalingrad and Warsaw and Taipan will fade into insignificance when the conflict of the ages is fought, when "the fierceness and wrath of Almighty God" are poured out upon the earth (Revelation 19:15).

Let the unsaved who read these pages turn to Christ at once and thereby escape the unsparing wrath to come. Men ought to praise God that in this day of grace sinners can find refuge in the Lord Jesus Christ. Today God's mercy is extended to all. Oh, yield to the wooing of the Holy Spirit and receive Jesus Christ at once.

THE VIAL JUDGMENTS

Revelation 15:1—16:21

Both the attendance and the attention given to the Word during this series of messages from the Revelation have been most gratifying. However, I do receive an unfavorable response occasionally from someone who is disturbed about my repeated references to coming judgment. Now there are other books in the Bible, the message of which is not one of judgment. But we need to remember that these chapters in the Revelation which we are now studying are prophetic, and that their major message has to do with God's judicial dealings. I bring this to your attention because chapters 15 and 16 show the intensive character of these judgments during the last half of the Great Tribulation. While the time during which these judgments are executed is not a long period, nevertheless the judgments are real. In the last half of Daniel's seventieth week, in the short space of three-and-one-half years, a time period of less duration than World War I, a number of major plagues will fall upon the people of the earth. It is the time of the filling up (or completion) of the wrath of God (Revelation 15:1).

Actually chapter 15 is introductory to chapter 16, the two chapters combining to present one connected vision. There are three judgments presented in sets of seven, each having their introductory vision:

> The Seven Seals—chapters 4 and 5
> The Seven Trumpets—chapter 8:1-6
> The Seven Vials—chapter 15:1-8.

Following is a suggested outline of the vial (or bowl) judgments in chapters 15 and 16:

As we proceed now in our study of the text we will see a detailed recapitulation of the events stated in chapter 14.

I. THE PRELUDE TO THE VIAL JUDGMENTS (15:1-4)

A. *The Sign in Heaven*

And I saw another sign in heaven, great and marvellous, seven angels having the seven last plagues; for in them is filled up the wrath of God (15:1).

In chapter 12 there are two signs, a woman clothed with the sun, who is Israel (12:1), and the great red dragon, who is Satan (12:3). Here in chapter 15 we have another sign, described as "great and marvellous" because terrible things are about to happen. They are described as *"the seven last plagues."* The word "seven" occurs eight times in this brief chapter, and here its use is to announce the last plagues. The Revelation is the book of *"last"* things; thus, with these plagues, judgment upon the earth comes to an end. The cup of God's wrath is full, and the earth dwellers must be made to drink of that wrath. It is about to be poured out. The plagues in Egypt (Exodus 12:29) were but a miniature of these last plagues.

Associated with *"the seven last plagues,"* and included in the sign, are *"seven angels."* These angels are not identified. However, it is not impossible for them to be the seven angels (messengers or pastors) to whom the seven letters were addressed in chapters 2 and 3. The fact that these angels are assigned to the administering of God's judgment, as stated in 15:7 and 16:1, should not surprise the student of Scripture. "Do ye not know that the saints shall judge the world?" (1 Corinthians 6:2)

With this judgment, the purpose of God will be fully accomplished, that is, *"filled up."* What God is about to do through these last plagues is the subject of Old Testament prophecy. The prophet Zephaniah wrote, "Therefore wait ye upon Me, saith the Lord, until the day that I rise up to the prey: for My determination is to gather the nations, that I may assemble the kingdoms, to pour upon them Mine indignation, even all My fierce anger: for all the earth shall be devoured with the fire of My jealousy" (Zephaniah 3:8). God has been longsuffering, and is so even now (2 Peter 3:9), but His wrath is accumulating against all who continue to defy Him and who reject His Son.

B. *The Sea of Glass*

And I saw as it were a sea of glass mingled with fire: and them that had gotten the victory over the beast, and over his image, and over his mark, and over the number of his name, stand on the sea of glass, having the harps of God (15:2).

John does not say that the sea was glass, but *"as it were,"* or *as if it were* a sea of glass. Earlier John saw in a vision "a sea of glass like unto crystal," (4:6), but here it is mingled with fire. Being mingled with fire, judgment is suggested, "for our God is a consuming fire" (Hebrews 12:29). A righteous judgment is about to be precipitated on the whole earth. At the final deliverance of Israel from Egypt, and prior to the judgment plagues upon the Egyptians, the Lord appeared to Moses "in a flame of fire out of the midst of a bush" (Exodus 3:2). By fire the world is at last to be judged (read 2 Thessalonians 1:3-10 and 2 Peter 3:7-13).

John saw a company of people standing on the sea of glass. From the description of them they are that victorious company which has prevailed over the beast, his image, his mark, his number, and his name. These then are tribulation saints. They refused to conform to the beast, and though it cost them their lives to defy the wicked one, they were the real victors. During the Great Tribulation it might have appeared as though they were fools, but their defeat was only apparent. True, each had lost his life, but only to find it again. They obtained the victory, but through no strength of their own. "They overcame him by the blood of the Lamb" (12:11). The martyrs had emerged victorious from their conflict with the Antichrist. It was the very fact that they died that made them conquerors. Had they remained alive by surrendering to the beast and worshiping him, they would have been defeated. But, "to die is gain" (Philippians 1:21).

C. *The Song of Moses*

> *And they sing the song of Moses the servant of God, and the song of the Lamb, saying, Great and marvellous are Thy works, Lord God Almighty; just and true are Thy ways, Thou King of saints. Who shall not fear Thee, O Lord, and glorify Thy name? for Thou only art holy: for all nations shall come and worship before Thee; for Thy judgments are made manifest* (15:3-4).

Like the Israelites who emerged triumphantly from the Egyptians, they sing a song of victory. These are possibly the same blessed dead seen in Heaven in chapter 14:2-5,13. Some expositors believe this song to be the swan song of Moses as recorded in Deuteronomy 31 and 32, because in it Christ and Israel are the two great themes. Here is a song of exultant triumph, ascribing power, glory, and salvation to Jehovah and to the Lamb. It is a witness in the "latter days" (Deuteronomy 31:29). Redeemed people are a singing people, and the songs of redemption which they sing always glorify Christ. There is never a single mention in true gospel songs about man's own goodness or achievements. Those persons who are truly redeemed forget themselves and see only the great purpose and plan of God in redemption. At least, it is that way in Heaven.

In verse 4 the song contains a millennial scene, anticipating the full blessedness of Christ's reign on earth when all nations will worship Him. He is the "King of *nations*" (verse 3), not "King of *saints*" as in the Authorized Version. The time of which these martyred saints are singing will be the fulfillment of Scripture, such as Psalm 2:6-9; 86:8-9; Isaiah 2:2-4; 66:16-17,23; Zechariah 14:16-17; Philippians 2:9-11. The fact that all nations shall worship Christ, rather than the Antichrist, is the reason for the song.

II. THE PREPARATION FOR THE VIAL JUDGMENTS (15:5-8)

A. *The Scene in Heaven*

And after that I looked, and, behold, the temple of the tabernacle of the testimony in heaven was opened (15:5).

The "temple of the tabernacle" is the holy of holies where the ark of the testimony was kept. The ark speaks of the faithfulness of God in keeping His covenants. Under the Law of Moses, the holiest of all was concealed from the eyes of the people. Mystery shrouded that sacred area. But here the mystery of God is "finished" (see 10:7). The way into the holiest is now open to all the redeemed, including the tribulation saints (see 11:19). This is God's dwelling place, where He is approached and worshiped, and from which issue His just judgments.

Notice the sight that meets the gaze of John.

And the seven angels came out of the temple, having the seven plagues, clothed in pure and white linen, and having their breasts girded with golden girdles (15:6).

John does not see the Jewish high priest ministering in the holy of holies, but rather seven angels, or messengers, emerging. And yet they are clothed with the garments of the priest. These angel-priests are about to vindicate the offended holiness and justice of God. A great sacrifice is about to be offered. The servants of God are going to rid the earth of all that has caused creation to groan. God is now going to fulfill His covenant with Israel. Through His servants, who come out from the place where the Law of God rests, God will demonstrate that all men and nations who defy His law must suffer for their sins. The angels, being seven in number, suggest the completeness or perfection of that judgment they are sent to execute. Their solemn task is to carry out the severest of God's judgments upon this earth.

B. *The Seven Vials*

And one of the four beasts gave unto the seven angels seven golden vials full of the wrath of God, who liveth for ever and ever (15:7).

This is the final step of preparation just prior to the actual judgment. The word "vial" (Gr. *phiale*) denotes a bowl, as suggested in the Revised Version. The word contains the idea of a rapid and final emptying of its contents. How significant! We know that these bowls disclose the final series of judgments in which the wrath of God is to be poured out.

In that day there will not be a single scientific or psychological means of pacifying the fears of men. Scientists and psychiatrists themselves will be totally helpless in those days. Men who have refused to drink of the cup of God's salvation must drink from the bowls of His wrath. The Psalmist said, "In the hand of the LORD there is a cup. . . . I will take the cup of salvation, and call upon the name of the LORD" (Psalm 75:8; 116:13). Which cup will you choose? Remember that judgment, just like salvation, comes from the presence of God.

C. *The Smoke in the Temple*

And the temple was filled with smoke from the glory of God, and from His power; and no man was able to enter into the temple, till the seven plagues of the seven angels were fulfilled (15:8).

When the tabernacle in the wilderness was completed, a cloud of glory filled it (Exodus 40:35); likewise when the temple was completed (1 Kings 8:10-11). No smoke was seen in either instance, because the erection of the tabernacle and the temple was not associated with judgment. However, when God gave the law to Moses, the entire Mount Sinai was enveloped in smoke because the law pronounced judgment upon all who failed to obey its demands (Exodus 19:18). When Isaiah saw the temple, "the house was filled with smoke" (Isaiah 6:4), for the prophet was sent by God to Israel with a message of judgment.

In John's vision, judgment is about to descend from God upon the earth. And until the bowls of wrath are emptied, no man can approach God. Until the seven plagues have been completed, no approach to God, by prayer or otherwise, can halt the coming judgment. In this connection the student should read the account of divine judgment upon Korah, Dathan, and Abiram in Numbers 16:1-35.

Presently God is extending His grace to all men. But in the day of His judicial action, none need try to seek Him, for He will not be found. Grace will be withdrawn and prayer will go unanswered. This is the way it will have to be because of the righteous requirements of God's own nature. Heaven will be barricaded so that none can enter until justice is satisfied. Jeremiah prophesied of that day, saying, "Thou hast covered with anger, and persecuted us: Thou hast slain, Thou has not pitied. Thou hast covered Thyself with a cloud, that our prayer should not pass through" (Lamentations 3:43-44).

How great and terrible will be the judgments of God!

III. THE POURING OUT OF THE VIAL JUDGMENTS (16:1-12)

Some portions of the Word of God are preached with great delight. This is not one of them. The mere reading of a Scripture passage such as this causes one to shudder. However, there is a comforting and consoling note for Christians; namely, we do not expect to be on the earth when these judgments are poured out. But why so severe a judgment? There must come a time when judgment can no longer be delayed.

The first commandment God gave to Moses for the people contained a clear word, "Thou shalt have no other gods before Me" (Exodus 20:3).

The second commandment is a detailed warning against the fashioning of any image and the bowing down to an image, upon pain of a divine visitation in judgment. Here are God's own words, "Thou shalt not make unto thee any graven image, or any likeness of any thing that is in heaven above, or that is in the earth beneath, or that is in the water under the earth: Thou shalt not bow down thyself to them, nor serve them: for I the LORD thy God am a jealous God, visiting the iniquity of the fathers upon the children unto the third and fourth generation of them that hate Me; And shewing mercy unto thousands of them that love Me, and keep My commandments" (Exodus 20:4-6). The vision which John saw is that visitation of judgment. Satan's desire for worship has been satisfied in men worshiping the image of the beast (cf. Isaiah 14:12-14; Matthew 4:8-10). But God will never allow His glory to be given to another. When men turn from God completely, giving themselves to the worship of the devil, then God steps in to vindicate His sovereignty, righteousness, and holiness. The pouring out of the seven vials is that vindication.

> *And I heard a great voice out of the temple saying to the seven angels, Go your ways, and pour out the vials of the wrath of God upon the earth* (16:1).

The hour for judgment can no longer be delayed. From the smoke-filled temple there comes a *great* voice commanding the seven angels to proceed with the execution of judgment. The adjective *great* appears not less than eleven times in this one chapter. With the passing of time the world employs the extravagant use of adjectives to peddle its wares. Cigarettes, beer, cosmetics, sporting events, and motion picture and television productions are billed as fabulous, amazing, colossal, unbelievable, stupendous, sensational, incredible, gigantic, super, spectacular, and great. But man will have produced nothing to compare with the greatness of the coming judgments upon the earth.

Let us keep in mind the fact that these judgments are future and literal. The bowl judgments were not fulfilled in the French Revolution, the oppression of Napoleon, the pressures of popery, or the machinations of Hitler and his slaughter of six million Jews. These events in history, and others like them, were mere rehearsals for the great and final drama of the last judgment on earth.

A. *The First Vial*

And the first went, and poured out his vial upon the earth; and there fell a noisome and grievous sore upon the men which had the mark of the beast, and upon them which worshipped his image (16:2).

This first judgment is directed at the worshipers of the beast. It is aimed particularly at idolatry. Here is a physical malady, possibly in the form of bodily sores or boils. God had warned Israel that such a plague would be forthcoming if they violated His law (Deuteronomy 28:27,35). The people knew that God meant exactly what He said. He plagued them when they worshiped the golden calf that Aaron made (Exodus 32:35). This same type of judgment came upon Egypt in the sixth plague (Exodus 9:8-12). A similar plague fell upon Miriam (Numbers 12:10). It was an affliction resembling this that God permitted Satan to bring upon Job (Job 2:7-8). In the last days many will be seduced into apostasy, but they must pay for their idolatry. This first plague is described as *"noisome,"* that is, painfully bad. It will fall upon all who have on them the mark of the beast. By the true Messiah diseases were healed. Under the false messiah such afflictions can neither be prevented nor cured.

B. *The Second Vial*

And the second angel poured out his vial upon the sea; and it became as the blood of a dead man: and every living soul died in the sea (16:3).

You will recall that at the breaking of the second seal, there was much human blood shed upon the earth (6:3-4), and at the sounding of the second trumpet, a third part of the sea became blood (8:8). But here it seems that all the water is affected. The awful stench, which is as the blood of a dead man, will be world wide. As all the great bodies of water in the earth congeal, shipping will be affected and all fish will die. This will be a death blow to the fishing and shipping industries. The plague on Egyptian waters, when God turned that water into blood, was literal (Exodus 7:18 cf. Psalm 105:29) even as the plague will be in the latter days preceding the return of Christ to the earth. I am not saying that the water becomes literal blood, for the text says, "It became *as* the blood of a dead man." What I am saying is that I believe there will be a literal plague which will affect the seas.

C. *The Third Vial*

And the third angel poured out his vial upon the rivers and fountains of waters; and they became blood. And I heard the angel of the waters say, Thou art righteous, O Lord, which art, and wast, and shalt be, because Thou hast judged thus. For they have shed the blood of saints and prophets, and Thou hast given them blood to drink; for they are worthy. And I heard another out of the altar say, Even so, Lord God Almighty, true and righteous are Thy judgments (16:4-7).

It would seem here that the third angel extends the blood-like judgment to the fresh-water rivers and lakes as well as the springs which feed them. The angel vindicates God's judgment as just. To the testimony of the angel is added another voice which is heard coming out of the altar.

There might be some reading this message who feel that God is unjust in meting out such punishment. That is because we do not have perfect knowledge, nor are we perfect in righteousness. But God is both omniscient and righteous. As the Judge of all the earth He will do right (Genesis 18:25). The deadliness and destruction upon the earth will not meet with objection in eternity. Both in Heaven and hell men will acknowledge the righteousness of the eternal God who had so judged. The justice of this judgment lies in the fact that the wicked are being judged on the basis of their judgment upon innocent victims (see Matthew 7:1-2). They shed the blood of saints and prophets; now they must reap that which they have sown. Read the prophecy in Deuteronomy 32:40-43. The angel's voice and the voice from the temple are both right. In eternity, that is, in the life to come, the righteous judgments of God will never be brought into question.

D. *The Fourth Vial*

And the fourth angel poured out his vial upon the sun; and power was given unto him to scorch men with fire. And men were scorched with great heat, and blasphemed the name of God, which hath power over these plagues: and they repented not to give Him glory (16:8-9).

For many millenniums, how long we have no way of knowing, God had made the sun to rise on the evil as well as the good (Matthew 5:45). But in the Great Tribulation it shines only upon the evil, and then with such intensity that many will die. This greater of lights was given by God to rule the day for the blessing of man (Genesis 1:16). Yet most of us have known something of a heat wave when people were stricken with sunstroke and some died, and when cattle died in the fields. But the world has never known a heat wave comparable to this one that is to come. Those who do not die because of it will be made to suffer the more because of their bodily sores and the awful stench arising from the polluted rivers and lakes. This is one of our Lord's predicted signs of the times (Luke 21:25), as well as the message of Old Testament prophets (Isaiah 24:6; 42:25; Malachi 4:1). The effects of this judgment will not change men's hearts. They only blasphemed God the more and refused to repent. Nor should the attitude of men's hearts then surprise us. If a man rejects the kindness and love of God, judgment will hardly change his heart. If the mercy and grace of God do not change his heart, all the heat of a "purgatory," *even if there were such a place,* would not cause him to repent. They made their decision. Their will was fixed. I have seen a sample of this bitterness in men and women in some of our nation's penitentiaries. One comforting prospect is the fact that the tribulation saints will not be affected by this heat (Revelation 7:16).

E. *The Fifth Vial*

And the fifth angel poured out his vial upon the seat of the beast; and his kingdom was full of darkness; and they gnawed their tongues for pain. And blasphemed the God of heaven because of their pains and their sores, and repented not of their deeds (16:10-11).

The concentration of God's wrath is now directed at the very source of the wickedness in the world, namely, the "seat" (or throne) of the beast (cf. 2:13). He is the one whom the people on earth will be worshiping at that time. They will see that their leader is helpless in the face of the judgments of Almighty God. The "darkness" which describes his kingdom is that moral and spiritual darkness which results, not from ignorance, but from willfully rejecting the truth. (See Matthew 6:22; John 3:19-21; Colossians 1:12-13). It is to the very heart of this darkness that God turns His attention. By this time the judgments have become so severe that people bite their tongues from pain. They continue to blaspheme the God of Heaven, but they are made to punish their own tongues which they use to offend God. This could be the fulfillment of Zechariah 14:12. We are not surprised that Satan sees to it, for the most part, that the book of the Revelation remains closed.

F. *The Sixth Vial*

And the sixth angel poured out his vial upon the great river Euphrates; and the water thereof was dried up, that the way of the kings of the east might be prepared (16:12).

The outpouring of the sixth bowl of wrath resembles closely the sixth trumpet judgment. Both have to do with the Euphrates River (see Revelation 9:13-21). I understand the drying up of this river to be literal. God dried up a path through the Red Sea for Israel, and then duplicated the miracle forty years later at the Jordan River. John's vision in the Revelation might well be a fulfillment of Isaiah's prophecy (Isaiah 11:15-16). If the Euphrates River is to be the eastern boundary of the revived Roman Empire, it will be a simple matter for God to remove that boundary. At this point we need to be reminded that this bowl, like the five preceding it, is connected with judgment, not with mercy. This fact should be made more clear as we proceed in our study.

IV. THE PURPOSE OF THE VIAL JUDGMENTS (16:13-14)

And I saw three unclean spirits like frogs come out of the mouth of the dragon, and out of the mouth of the beast, and out of the mouth of the false prophet. For they are the spirits of devils, working miracles, which go forth unto the kings of the earth and of the whole world, to gather them to the battle of that great day of God Almighty (16:13-14).

Most commentaries I have examined on these verses include them as a part of the sixth bowl judgment. However, it seems to me that we have here the action of the evil trinity—the dragon, the beast, and the false prophet—which action discloses, in part at least, the purpose of the bowl judgments. The evil trinity will persuade the kings of the earth to join forces in battle against the people of God in Jerusalem. A part of their activity will be the revival of spiritism. Men will be possessed by demons with the power to do great signs and miracles to deceive the nations of the earth. They will draw the nations toward Palestine for the purpose of an all-out global war, a war to include *"the kings of the earth and of the whole world."* This will be the great and final conflict, called *Armageddon*. When the nations have assembled to fight against God and Jesus Christ, divine judgment will be perfected. These verses (13-14), then, disclose the purpose of the judgments, namely, to settle once and for all among every nation on earth the absolute authority of Christ over the whole earth. When all the nations converge on Jerusalem, the seventh bowl will be poured out, followed by the personal return of Christ.

V. THE PARENTHETICAL WARNING BEFORE THE LAST VIAL (16:15)

Behold, I come as a thief. Blessed is he that watcheth, and keepeth his garments, lest he walk naked, and they see his shame (16:15).

Before the last bowl judgment is poured out upon the nations, there is a solemn pause, and the Lord Himself speaks. He reminds them of His soon, sudden coming, and the subsequent battle of that great day. He says that He will come *"as a thief,"* showing that the Church will not be on earth at that time, for the Thessalonian Christians were assured that that day could not overtake them as a thief (1 Thessalonians 5:4; cf. 2 Peter 3:10). Here is a final warning to those tribulation saints to watch for His coming and to keep themselves unspotted from defilement and from the Satan-inspired activities of those last days. The *garments* here are not literal, but they speak of character, as in other Scripture references. The nakedness is their exposure of any defilement at Christ's coming to the earth. Concerning the *garments,* Philip Mauro says, "When about to go to sleep one lays aside his garments; but when awake he keeps them. Now if something suddenly happens, such as the arrival of the Lord, one who is asleep does not readily get himself clothed; but he who is in a wakeful attitude is safe also in respect to his clothing." How gracious of God to warn believers of what lies ahead!

VI. THE PERFECTING OF THE VIAL JUDGMENTS (16:17-21)

A. *The Seventh Vial*

And He gathered them together into a place called in the Hebrew tongue Armageddon. And the seventh angel poured out his vial into the air; and there came a great voice out of the temple of heaven, from the throne, saying, It is done. And there were voices, and thunders, and lightnings; and

there was a great earthquake, such as was not since men
were upon the earth, so mighty an earthquake, and so great.
And the great city was divided into three parts, and the cities
of the nations fell: and great Babylon came in remembrance
before God, to give unto her the cup of the wine of the fierce-
ness of His wrath. And every island fled away, and the moun-
tains were not found. And there fell upon men a great hail
. . . for the plague thereof was exceeding great (16:16-21).

"It is done!" Here is the perfecting of the judgments, the consummation of God's wrath, the final overthrow of all opposition. Once before our Lord uttered similar words from the cross when He cried, "It is finished" (John 19:30), and at that time there was an earthquake (Matthew 27:51). But then He was bearing the judgment for man's sin. However, the next time He speaks of a finished work, it will be the consummation of judgment upon all who have rejected Him. It is the comprehensive finality of judgment upon the earth and its inhabitants.

The judgments in these verses I take to be literal. What is described here is both possible and probable. With the exception of the hail and lightning, man could produce the same effects with the multimegaton bombs now in his possession. Mountains will disappear and islands will be submerged.

The seventh angel tips the seventh bowl of judgment in "the air," the present headquarters of Satan (Ephesians 2:2), followed by thunders, lightnings, and hailstones weighing upwards to one hundred pounds. This is the final destruction of every religious, political, and educational institution that man has built apart from God. It is the collapse of all man's hopes and dreams. But with all of this, men still refuse to submit to God's rule. Men boast of their scientific progress, but it will all come to nought. All that men consider stable, they must watch crumble. Many people marvel at such descriptions of the severity of God. I marvel at the unconcern and wickedness of men's hearts. William Barclay has said, "The most terrible situation in life is when Almighty God is powerless to gain an entry into the citadel of the human heart, for God has given men the terrible responsibility of being able to lock their hearts against Him."

THE JUDGMENT OF THE GREAT WHORE

Revelation 17:1-18

The chapter before us is devoted to a solemn subject. It is the doom of a vast international system of error, religious in character, and so close in resemblance to Christianity that millions are deceived by it. The system is called "the great whore" (or harlot) (17:1). It is a combination of apostate protestantism, Romanism, and atheism. It is the huge ecumenical church of the last days. This religious monstrosity is taking shape before our eyes even now, and it is being heralded as a step forward toward unity and world peace. But because it is apostate, it is doomed and must come under the judgment of God. This chapter in the Revelation spells out that doom.

In the minds of millions of people, such a prediction of doom upon so large an ecclesiastical body is fantastically unbelievable. But when one examines the description of her, as given by the Holy Spirit, there is no longer surprise at the prediction of the coming judgment of God upon her. Professor Moorehead said, "The harlot is Christendom estranged from God and become thoroughly secularized and degenerated."

A wife who is unfaithful to her husband is an adulterous woman. A church which calls itself Christian, and which courts an alliance with the godless world-system, commits spiritual adultery (James 4:4). God calls her a harlot. And in the key verse of chapter 17, which is verse 1, her judgment is pronounced.

In the book of the Revelation, the figure of a woman is used symbolically of religion. Jezebel represents the pagan idolatry of the past (2:20); the woman clothed with the sun represents

Israel (12:1); the Bride of Christ represents His true Church (19:7-8; 21:9; cf. Ephesians 5:25-26), and the great whore represents the apostate church (19:2). This judgment upon the great whore, then, is a divine judgment upon apostate religion.

Three times the apostle is bidden to "come hither":

"Come hither" (4:1)—The vision in Heaven
"Come hither" (17:1)—The judgment of the great whore
"Come hither" (21:9)—The Bride, the Lamb's wife.

Before we see the Lamb's wife in her perfection, we see the harlot, the illegitimate leader of apostate religion, judged. The woman and the beast must be judged before the Bride and the Lamb are presented. Final judgment precedes the final blessing. The object of this vision, then, is to show to John the judgment of the great harlot. She professes to be Christ's great witness and His true church, but she has stooped to ally herself with the corrupt political system of the last days. She is Satan's counterfeit religion, an imitation of the true Church, the Bride of Christ.

The judgment before us in chapters 17 and 18 is prophecy yet to be fulfilled, and not history which has already been fulfilled. The judgment will take place at the close of the Great Tribulation, after the true Church, the Body of Christ, has been taken from the earth to Heaven. At the close of the previous chapter we read that "great Babylon came in remembrance before God, to give unto her the cup of the wine of the fierceness of His wrath" (16:19). (See also 14:8.) But now the specific details of her judgment are described.

It is not easy to preach from this chapter in the Bible. During the Kennedy-Nixon campaign for the office of president of the United States, the word "bigot" was taken out of mothballs and leveled at all persons who dared to speak about Mr. Kennedy's Roman Catholic religion. Since that time little has been said against any religion because of the fear of inviting accusations of being narrow-minded or conceited.

Since the late Pope John ascended the papal throne, there has been a growing movement toward the merging of all religions into a world church. And now, at the risk of being charged with bigotry, I invite you to examine those Scriptures which reveal the culmination of the ecumenical church under the curse and wrath of God.

Anyone reading the New Testament can see clearly that the Holy Spirit pictures the church of the last days in a state of corruption and degeneracy. There will be progressive unbelief and apostasy. The Apostle Paul wrote, "Now the Spirit speaketh expressly, that in the latter times some shall depart from the faith, giving heed to seducing spirits, and doctrines of devils" (1 Timothy 4:1). "This know also, that in the last days perilous times shall come" (2 Timothy 3:1). Men are described as "Having a form of godliness, but denying the power thereof: from such turn away" (2 Timothy 3:5). The Apostle Peter wrote, "But there were false prophets also among the people, even as there shall be false teachers among you, who privily shall bring in damnable heresies, even denying the Lord that bought them, and bring upon themselves swift destruction. And many shall follow their pernicious ways; by reason of whom the way of truth shall be evil spoken of" (2 Peter 2:1-2).

When the Lord Jesus Christ appears in the air, He will catch away, to be with Himself, every true believer who by virtue of being born again is in His Church, which is His Body. All who have not been born again, though they be in some church or religious system, will be left on earth to pass through the Great Tribulation to experience the wrath of God. I understand the great harlot in Revelation 17 to be that religious system, ecumenical, or world-wide, in scope. Now many persons within Christendom have professed to know Christ and have rendered lip service to Him, but in personal experience they are strangers to His saving grace. This great harlot may claim to be the Bride of Christ, but she proves to be an adulteress who is unfaithful to Him.

Now is the great harlot the Roman Catholic Church? Not merely! The great harlot is called, *"the mother of harlots"* (17:5). If she is the mother of harlots, her origin must be traced back beyond Romanism, for there was no pope before the fourth century. The insidious principles of Babylonianism might be found within the Roman Catholic Church; however, they were practised long before the Roman Catholic Church came into existence. The Roman Catholic Church is an old church, but certainly she is not the oldest church.

In order to identify Babylon, we are led back to an early period in the history of the human race. In Genesis 10 we are introduced to a man named Nimrod, a fourth-generation descendant from the time that God judged the earth by means of the flood. Nimrod's grandfather was Ham, meaning "the swarthy one," and his father was Cush, meaning "the blackened one." Ham was the evil son of Noah who uncovered his father's nakedness, so Nimrod did not have too good a start. A significant statement about Nimrod is that "the beginning of his kingdom was Babel" (Genesis 10:10). Dr. Ironside calls Nimrod "the arch-apostate of the patriarchal age. . . . With all the effrontery of modern apostates, they called their city and tower Bab-El, 'the gate of God'; but it was soon changed by divine judgment into Babel, 'confusion.' It bore the stamp of unreality from the first, for we are told, 'They had brick for stone, and slime had they for mortar.' An imitation of that which is real and true has ever since characterized Babylon, in all ages" (cf. Genesis 11:1-9). The spirit of Babylon was a manmade way of salvation through works as opposed to God's way of grace. In Nimrod's day men sought a federation of power that would make them secure, but God scattered them in judgment.

The spirit of Babylon is seen later under the rule of Nebuchadnezzar. That first mighty Gentile world ruler made a huge image of himself and attempted to bring all people by force to worship his image (Daniel 3). But God was not in his religion nor in his kingdom (Daniel 4:28-30). This dream of a superstate with its federation of nations and one universal religion, which began with Nimrod, is with us still. What Nimrod and Nebuchadnezar and the Caesars and Constantine failed to do, will be attempted once more in an all-out effort under the head of the restored Roman Empire. Even today there is a revival of the spirit of Babylonianism. The Roman Catholic Church, under the reign of the late Pope John, has taken the lead in this. Councils have been called for the purpose of exploring the prospects of an ecumenical church which will embrace all religious faiths. This action has brought visits to the pope from such men as the Archbishop of the Church of England and the son-in-law of Russia's Premier Khrushchev. The idolatrous system of the same ilk as Babylon of old is rising before our very eyes. The Babylon of the Revelation is an apostate religious system clearly identifiable with all of Christendom, with papal Rome taking the lead in its formation. It is the same old evil of idolatry which came forth from Nimrod and ancient Babylon, and which had its headquarters in Pergamos in the days of the early Church (Revelation 2:12-13).

When Pope John XXIII was elected on October 28, 1958, some looked upon his election as a delaying action. People thought that because of his advanced age, he would merely hold the office, do little, and leave the big decisions for another pope who would follow him. But by now Pope John is looked upon as one of the most popular popes in the Roman Church's history. And why? Simply because this ingenious innovator has expressed in his papal encyclical the desire for a one-world government and a one-world church. He called two councils for the express purpose of setting the wheels in motion toward the forming of the ecumenical church. Even communistic Russia was represented at the council. On March 18, 1963 *U.S. News and World Report* said, "There had been other signs of easier relations between the Vatican and the Kremlin. Russian Orthodox priests were permitted by the Kremlin to attend the Ecumenical Council in Rome last autumn."

The world might applaud such a union, but we may be certain that God is not in it. It is all man's doing. The adamant stand against communism which was taken by Pope Pius XII was abandoned by John XXIII. This attitude eased tensions between the Kremlin and the Vatican and it gave rise to further negotiations between these two world powers. This is the final stage of Babylon in the making.

Let us now view the text under three headings:

> The System Is Exposed—17:1-6
> The Secret Is Explained—17:7-15
> The System Is Extinguished—17:16-18.

I. THE SYSTEM IS EXPOSED (17:1-6)

> *And there came one of the seven angels which had the
> seven vials, and talked with me, saying unto me, Come
> hither; I will shew unto thee the judgment of the great whore
> that sitteth upon many waters: With whom the kings of the
> earth have committed fornication, and the inhabitants of
> the earth have been made drunk with the wine of her forni-
> cation. So he carried me away in the spirit into the wilder-
> ness: and I saw a woman sit upon a scarlet coloured beast,
> full of names of blasphemy, having seven heads and ten
> horns. And the woman was arrayed in purple and scarlet
> colour, and decked with gold and precious stones and pearls,
> having a golden cup in her hand full of abominations and
> filthiness of her fornication: And upon her forehead was a
> name written, MYSTERY, BABYLON THE GREAT, THE
> MOTHER OF HARLOTS AND ABOMINATIONS OF
> THE EARTH. And I saw the woman drunken with the
> blood of the saints, and with the blood of the martyrs of
> Jesus: and when I saw her, I wondered with great admira-
> tion* (17:1-6).

This false church which dominates the world scene in these
climactic hours immediately preceding the second coming of
Christ to earth, is shown first as a woman, a filthy and dissolute
harlot. She is seen *"sitting upon many waters"* (17:1). The
symbolic phrase "many waters" is interpreted in the chapter,
and it means *"peoples, and multitudes, and nations, and
tongues"* (17:15). This shows the scope of the seducing harlot's
influence. She sways the surging masses of humanity throughout the whole earth in an ecclesiastical rule.

Keep in mind the fact that this superchurch, made up of all
religious faiths, is now in the making. On April 12, 1963, the
New York Times published a report of J. Irwin Miller, president
of the National Council of Churches, in which he said: "We
are gratified at the growing area of agreement among leaders
and peoples of the Judeo-Christian heritage, and of other religious faiths on basic matters affecting the peace of the world
and the well-being of God's whole family." We are not sur-

prised, then, when we see men and women of various religious faiths making pilgrimages to Rome to see a man who has been exalted as "the holy father," "the voice of God," and then bowing down to him as though he were a god. The Roman Catholic Church is playing her most strategic role in world affairs. Never before has she wooed and won so many devotees of other religions. Indeed we are moving toward the end of the age.

The character of this religious system, under the symbol of a harlot woman, is described in verse 2. Why call this world church a harlot? Because she has committed fornication with the kings and inhabitants of the earth. Her illicit intercourse with the world-system is contrary to the behavior of Christ's true Church. His Church (Gr. *ekklesia*) is a called-out assembly to be separated from the world (Acts 15:14; Romans 12:2; 1 John 2:15; James 4:4). While the true Church dare not be isolated, she must be separated. However, the "great harlot," the apostate religious system of the last days, forms an unholy intrigue with the political leaders of the earth. Christians are to obey rulers in civil matters (Romans 13; 1 Peter 2:13-17), and pray for them (1 Timothy 2:2), but never surrender Christian principles for money, honor, or position in this world. The union of the church and the state is a union of the church with the world. Christ's true Church will never compromise with the world. The great harlot professes to be Christ's Church, but Christ has never received her. She is a center of influence over the earth, and her doctrines and views have an intoxicating influence over the minds of the people. Under the sanction of her assumed authority she is able to keep the nations in her power.

In verse 3 John sees the woman sitting *"upon a scarlet coloured beast."* The beast is the Antichrist, the same beast who appeared in chapter 13. Here he is seen supporting the harlot woman. Of course he does so for the sake of the advantage he hopes to derive from her in his bid for power during the last part of the tribulation. The *"ten horns"* represent the ten confederated kingdoms, the revived Roman Empire, which will be under his jurisdiction. Here the woman, the great religious system of the end times, is controlling and directing the beast. This superchurch will actually be ruling the nations, an ambition the Roman Catholic Church has had for centuries. But the world she rules is a spiritual "wilderness," the true Church having been taken from the earth by her Lord.

The seven heads are the seven mountains, on which the woman sitteth (17:9).

Every high school graduate knows that Rome is known as *the seven-hilled city*. Propertius spoke of it as "the lofty city on seven peaks, which rules the whole world." Here then is a prophecy referring to papal Rome, not history referring to pagan Rome. I know of no more direct explanation than that Rome is the city intended. All religions will unite with Romanism. The headquarters will be in Rome, and under this religious system with world-wide influence, all political and educational systems will submit.

In verse 4 the woman's wealth is described. The huge amount of wealth accumulated in religious traffic is hardly believable to the average person. The wealth of the Roman Catholic Church and the Protestant denominations combined adds up to many billions of dollars. The major religious denominations are not poor, but possess rich holdings in real estate, stocks, cash, and many different kinds of investments. In 1952, J. J. Van Gorder stated that a survey showed that the Roman Catholic Church maintained in the United States "337 seminaries, 228 colleges, 1,596 high schools, 7,777 elementary schools, 348 orphan asylums, 731 general hospitals, 110 special hospitals, 244 homes for the aged." Add to this the wealth of Jews and Protestants held in the name of religion, and you have a possible contributing factor to the alliance between the Antichrist and the great world church, called here the *"great whore."* In verse 4 we see a symbol of the wealth and luxury of the ecumenical church under the leadership of Rome. But in reality she is the rich poor church of this Laodicean period, to whom our Lord addressed His solemn warning in Revelation 3:14-22.

The system is exposed further in verse 6. It will stop at nothing to achieve world dominion, not even the death of those who refuse to join its ranks. Nebuchadnezzar had his fiery furnace for those who would not bow down to his image, and Rome has had hers. Her hatred is against the *"saints."* Rome makes her own saints, but those whom she has put to death are God's saints. Sir Robert Anderson, of Scotland Yard fame, estimated that Rome was guilty of the death of 50,000,000 Christians. The Inquisition, the stake, and the torture chambers are all history. Recent persecutions against Christians in Spain, Colombia, and elsewhere confirm this. While Rome has put to death her millions, we must keep in mind the fact that Babylonianism did likewise before Rome came into existence. But here John is permitted to see the bloody martyrdoms to take place at the hands of the harlot at the close of the tribulation. These persecutions might well be those spoken of by the Psalmist (see Psalm 44:22; 79:1-3).

Babylon has not changed. She continues to the end as she began in Genesis. This we should expect for if she loves the world, she will hate the saints who "love not the world" (1 John 2:15) and will rejoice in their death. Robert Govett has pointed out that when the massacre of St. Bartholomew took place, and Protestants throughout France were butchered, Rome appointed religious services of thanksgiving, and struck medals in commemoration of the joyful event. It is strange, yet true, that while claiming to be Christ's church, she persecutes to death Christ's true followers.

II. THE SECRET IS EXPLAINED (17:7-15)

And the angel said unto me, Wherefore didst thou marvel? I will tell thee the mystery of the woman, and of the beast that carrieth her, which hath the seven heads and ten horns. The beast that thou sawest was, and is not; and shall ascend out of the bottomless pit, and go into perdition: and they that dwell on the earth shall wonder, whose names were not written in the book of life from the foundation of the world, when they behold the beast that was, and is not, and yet is. And here is the mind which hath wisdom. The seven heads are seven mountains, on which the woman sitteth. And there are seven kings: five are fallen, and one is, and the other is not yet come; and when he cometh, he must continue a short space. And the beast that was, and is not, even he is the eighth, and is of the seven, and goeth into perdition. And the ten horns which thou sawest are ten kings, which have received no kingdom as yet; but receive power as kings one hour with the beast. These have one mind, and shall give their power and strength unto the beast. These shall make war with the Lamb, and the Lamb shall overcome them: for He is Lord of lords, and King of kings: and they that are with Him are called, and chosen, and faithful. And he saith unto me, The waters which thou sawest, where the whore sitteth, are peoples, and multitudes, and nations, and tongues (17:7-15).

The name of the harlot, written on her forehead, is *"MYS-TERY"* (17:5). The vision to this point caused John to marvel, so he writes:

And the angel said unto me, Wherefore didst thou marvel? I will tell thee the mystery of the woman, and of the beast that carrieth her, which hath the seven heads, and ten horns (17:7).

The angel will now explain the literal meaning of the symbols. The word "mystery" does not mean "mysterious," but rather *secret,* that which has hitherto been hid but which is now revealed. The mask is now to be stripped from the mother of harlots, that which has been shrouded in secrecy is now to be explained.

The woman is associated with the beast having *"ten horns."* The ten horns upon the beast are quite likely to be identified with the ten toes in the image of Nebuchadnezzar's dream in Daniel 2:40-44 and the ten horns on the fourth beast of Daniel 7:7. Long centuries before John's vision on Patmos, six to be exact, it was revealed by God to Daniel and to Nebuchadnezzar that the power of world government should pass through the hands of four empires: the Babylonian, the Medo-Persian, the Grecian, and the Roman. The last of these, the Roman Empire, came into being in the middle of the eighth century B.C., and was overthrown in A.D. 476. However, the influence of pagan Rome was not completely wiped out. While it has not risen as a political force, as was *pagan* Rome, a smoldering flame has been kept alive during the past fifteen centuries through the influence of *papal* Rome. As a political force she will rise again. *"The ten horns which thou sawest are ten kings"* (17:12). Here, then, is the revived Roman Empire, the ten toes of Nebuchadnezzar's dream image, to arise just prior to the establishment of Christ's kingdom on earth (Daniel 2:41-44).

Babylon is clearly identified. *"The seven heads are seven mountains, on which the woman sitteth"* (17:9). History knows of only one city which is so designated. It is Rome, called "the lofty city of seven peaks." The first signification of the *"seven heads"* then is geographical, or territorial. They are identified with the woman, pointing her out clearly to be Rome. The names of the seven hills are Aventine, Caelian, Capitoline, Esquiline, Palatine, Quirinal, and Viminal. Students of ancient coins remind us that the coin of Vespasian represents Rome seated on seven hills. The Roman Catholic Church itself, in the Confraternity Edition of the New Testament (new edition, New York, 1963, page 337), claims that Rome is Babylon.

The second signification of the *"seven heads"* is personal. John adds, *"And there are seven kings"* (17:10). Double types are not uncommon in Scripture. For example, Satan is likened to a lion (1 Peter 5:8), as also is Christ (Revelation 5:5). The woman Hagar is a symbol of both a mountain and a covenant (Galatians 4:24-25). The heads of the Roman Empire, then, are indicated here. When John received his vision, five had fallen. They were Julius Caesar, Tiberius, Caligula, Claudius, and Nero. The angel then said to John, *"and one is,"* meaning, I take it, Domitian, the last of the Caesars who was alive when John wrote.

> *And the other is not yet come; and when he cometh, he must continue a short space* (17:10).

The identity is clear. Pagan Rome is but the forerunner of papal Rome. Another head of the revived Roman Empire is to arise. He is the Antichrist who was alive, is now dead, but who comes to life again (17:8,11; cf. 13:3). The extent of their rule, under the influence of the harlot woman, will be the whole inhabited earth (17:15). But that rule will not be for long, only *"a short space"* (17:10). Three-and-one-half years will be a short time.

Now the true character of this whole apostate system is shown for what it is.

> *These shall make war with the Lamb, and the Lamb shall overcome them: for He is Lord of lords, and King of kings: and they that are with Him are called, and chosen, and faithful* (17:14).

The opposition all along has been against Christ. This verse (14) introduces the final conflict described in chapter 19. With self-confidence and daring the Antichrist leads his empire against the Son of God. The anti-God system reaches its zenith before it is finally overthrown in the last great conflict to take place on the earth. At once we can see that Satan has been the power behind every operation of this combined religious and political ecumenical system. How blind can intelligent men become? Already we can see the power of Satan deceiving the minds of world leaders, both Romanists and Protestants. If only men would study the Bible and accept it literally for what the Holy Spirit says in it.

III. THE SYSTEM IS EXTINGUISHED (17:16-18)

> *And the ten horns which thou sawest upon the beast, these shall hate the whore, and shall make her desolate and naked, and shall eat her flesh, and burn her with fire. For God hath put in their hearts to fulfil His will, and to agree, and give their kingdom unto the beast, until the words of God shall be fulfilled. And the woman which thou sawest is that great city, which reigneth over the kings of the earth* (17:16-18).

The ten horns, the federated states of Europe, that great political power, turn against the harlot with hatred. Realizing that they are nothing but puppets under the ecumenical church led by Rome, this coalition of nations rises up and completely wipes out this system. The description of the destruction of all religion, with headquarters at the Vatican, is set forth in detail in chapter 18. God permits the ecumenical church to develop until it has seduced the whole world, and then He puts it in the hearts of the political antireligious leaders to overthrow her. Then the church will have ceased forever to dictate the policies of the state. Religious Babylon must come to nought.

Why is Babylon called a "city" in verse 18? For the same reason that Old Jerusalem is called Sodom and Egypt (11:8). Jerusalem has become so corrupt and blinded by sin, that when Christ came, she nailed Him to the cross. The superchurch of the last days will duplicate the spirit of Babylon. And because of her apostasy she is loathed and looked upon with disgust by the leaders of the confederated nations. She is stripped of her purple and scarlet robes and her wealth. But keep in mind that all of this carnage is the execution of the sovereign will of God. Babylon from the beginning has been the fountainhead of all idolatry. Rome and the ecumenical church had their source in this fountainhead, therefore the whole system must be judged. She has been pampered and extolled for centuries by the nations of the world, but this must all come to an end. First they were all for her, but now they are united in a bold stand against her. They want both her power and her wealth. The beast, weary of the domination of the harlot, turns against her with hatred. But he is fulfilling the will of God. Once more God will make the wrath of man to praise Him (Psalm 76:10), even as He used Nebuchadnezzar to punish Judah (Jeremiah 25:9-12). What a change! At last the religious forces of the world meet their doom, and the secular powers confiscate their wealth.

The Word of God spoken to His people centuries ago is most fitting in view of what we have been studying. "Flee out of the midst of Babylon, and deliver every man his soul: be not cut off in her iniquity; for this is the time of the LORD's vengeance; He will render unto her a recompence. Babylon hath been a golden cup in the LORD's hand, that made all the earth drunken: the nations have drunken of her wine; therefore the nations are mad. Babylon is suddenly fallen and destroyed: howl for her; take balm for her pain, if so be she may be healed. We would have healed Babylon, but she is not healed: forsake her, and let us go every one into his own country: for her judgment reacheth unto heaven, and is lifted up even to the skies" (Jeremiah 51:6-9).

THE COLLAPSE OF THE WORLD MARKET

Revelation 18:1-24

In this chapter the subject is still the fall of Babylon. We saw something of the collapse of her ecclesiastical power in chapter 17. However, we must remember that her influence rises to be felt quite strongly both politically and commercially as well. But the system must come to nought in its entirety. When this superchurch loses its hold religiously, it follows that she must come to nought in every other way. God's judgment upon her is complete.

Our day has revealed the unusual way in which the principles and practices of this vast system have permeated the entire life of our civilization. But those principles and practices of the great harlot do not have God's sanction upon them. Therefore, before the ideal society can be ushered in at the Lord's return, the way must be prepared through the destruction of Babylon.

I. THE ANNOUNCEMENT OF JUDGMENT (18:1-3)

And after these things I saw another angel come down from heaven, having great power; and the earth was lightened with his glory. And he cried mightily with a strong voice, saying, Babylon the great is fallen, is fallen, and is become the habitation of devils, and the hold of every foul spirit, and a cage of every unclean and hateful bird. For all nations have drunk of the wine of the wrath of her fornication, and the kings of the earth have committed fornication with her, and the merchants of the earth are waxed rich through the abundance of her delicacies (18:1-3).

305

Another mighty angel is seen coming down from Heaven with great power. His glory is so brilliant that the entire earth is lightened by it. Some teachers identify this angel with the Lord Jesus Christ as in 8:3 and 10:1. The fact that he has "great power" does not necessitate his being Christ. Some angels are more distinguished and have greater authority than do others of the angelic hosts. This angel could be Christ, but we do not know for certain, nor does it really matter.

The announcement he makes is the important factor here. He proclaims publicly Babylon's downfall. She has come to the day of her accounting. Having been full of everything that God hates, the time of her destruction has arrived. She *"is become the habitation of devils* [demons]*"* (18:2).

Here is an amazing revelation. A religious system which claims to be Christ's true church houses demons whose abode is the abyss in the underground world. The true Church is the habitation of God through the Holy Spirit (Ephesians 2:22), but Babylon has become *"the hold of every foul spirit";* the "spirit of the world" (1 Corinthians 2:12); "the spirit that now worketh in the children of disobedience" (Ephesians 2:2); "the spirit of error" (1 John 4:6); "the spirit of bondage" (Romans 8:15); and "the spirit of man" (1 Corinthians 2:11). There are many foul spirits contending for the mastery of man's mind. We need to heed the admonition, "Beloved, believe not every spirit, but try the spirits whether they are of God: because many false prophets are gone out into the world" (1 John 4:1).

"And a cage of every unclean and hateful bird" (18:2). In our Lord's parable of the mustard seed Christendom is depicted as an abnormal mustard "tree" in whose branches the birds of the air have come to lodge (Matthew 13:31-32). Throughout that series of parables recorded in Matthew 13, Mark 4, and Luke 8, the birds are used symbolically of Satan (Matthew 13:4,19; Mark 4:15; Luke 8:12). Here is Christendom at the end of the age, a monstrosity, a freak. The church had a humble beginning, but gradually it was infiltrated by unregenerated men. Today the huge organization which calls itself the church of Jesus Christ is taken over by men who do not

subscribe to the essential doctrines of historic Christianity as
set forth in the Bible. Satan's emissaries are occupying the
top branches in Babylon's great religious system. They are
being taken in by it, so that after the true Church has been
caught up from the earth to be with her Lord, the residue of
religious leaders, by far in the majority, will be literally caged
(or imprisoned) within the Babylonian system. There are
some today who are caught in it and feel they cannot get out.
Yes, Babylon is the habitation, not of saints and angels, but of
demons and every foul spirit.

The extent of Babylon's influence is stated once more in
verse 3. She has wooed and won the nations by her flirtations.
She becomes the pride of the world as she makes the nations
rich through the abundance of her delicacies. The peoples of
the earth have drunk so eagerly from her intoxicating cup,
they no longer have power to resist her. I watched the na-
tionally-televised funeral of Pope John XXIII and saw the
masses of men, women, and children, Protestant and Roman
Catholic, drinking from Rome's cup. They sip slowly at first,
perhaps a bit doubtful and apprehensive, but after a while
they gulp it freely, too intoxicated to know its contents.

II. THE APPEAL TO GOD'S PEOPLE (18:4-8)

*And I heard another voice from heaven, saying, Come out
of her, My people, that ye be not partakers of her sins, and
that ye receive not of her plagues. For her sins have reached
unto heaven, and God hath remembered her iniquities. Reward her even as she rewarded you, and double unto her
double according to her works: in the cup which she hath
filled fill to her double. How much she hath glorified herself,
and lived deliciously, so much torment and sorrow give her;
for she saith in her heart, I sit a queen, and am no widow,
and shall see no sorrow. Therefore shall her plagues come in
one day, death, and mourning, and famine; and she shall be
utterly burned with fire: for strong is the Lord God who
judgeth her* (18:4-8).

Here is a clear call to separation. In its primary interpretation it is prophetic, addressed to the tribulation saints of that

day. However, it is a warning to believers in our own day who even now can discern the true character of this rising religious system. There are always those well-meaning people who feel that they can remain within an apostate religious system and reform it. But the command from Heaven is unmistakably clear, *"Come out of her, My people, that ye be not partakers of her guilt"* (18:4). To just what degree they would have been requited, we have no way of knowing. Achan paid with his life for hiding the Babylonish garment in his tent (Joshua 7:16-26). Dr. Ironside has said, "And there is many a Babylonish garment today hidden in Protestant tents, or even displayed upon Protestant shoulders."

The call to separation has come to the people of God in every age. It came to Abraham (Genesis 12:1); to Lot (Genesis 19:12-14); to Moses (Numbers 16:23-26). "Go ye forth of Babylon" (Isaiah 48:20), said God to His people Israel. "Remove out of the midst of Babylon" (Jeremiah 50:8). "Flee out of the midst of Babylon" (Jeremiah 51:6). "My people, go ye out of the midst of her, and deliver ye every man his soul from the fierce anger of the LORD" (Jeremiah 51:45). And in the New Testament we read, "Be ye not unequally yoked together with unbelievers. . . . Wherefore come out from among them, and be ye separate, saith the Lord" (2 Corinthians 6:14,17). "Neither be partakers of other men's sins: keep thyself pure" (1 Timothy 5:22).

God's people are not of this world system (John 17:14,16). When professing Christians ally themselves with Babylon, or with any other worldly society, on the pretence that they are going to give a testimony and attempt to change those who are in it, they violate the plain teaching of God's Word. The reason why is plain. *"For her sins have reached unto heaven, and God hath remembered her iniquities"* (18:5). Babel's tower of stones did not reach to Heaven, but her sins did. God says of His own people, "For I will forgive their iniquity, and I will remember their sin no more" (Jeremiah 31:34), but the sins of unchanging, unrepentant Babylon He will remember and punish. Therefore, *come out of her!* (The student should examine Isaiah 47:1-15 and Jeremiah 51:24).

> *Reward her even as she rewarded you, and double unto her double according to her works: in the cup which she hath filled fill to her double* (18:6).

The character of her retribution described here, and in verses 7 and 8, is further reason why the Lord's own must separate from her. In chapter 17 her religious system is destroyed, and now her political and economic power must suffer a like fate. Her economic collapse will come in *"one day"* (18:8), even within the space of *"one hour"* of that day (18:10,17,19). Let not any person belittle the possibility of so sudden an economic downfall. The economic depression in America in the thirties followed the sudden collapse of the stock market. And even in these inflationary times it is not beyond sound reasoning to suggest the possibility of another similar downfall. I believe that Americans could arise on any one morning to learn that the American dollar is not worth the paper on which it is printed. The suddenness and intensity of Babylon's coming judgment, as described in this chapter, is certain, because *"strong is the Lord God who judgeth her"* (18:8). Therefore, *come out of her!*

III. THE AGONY OF THE WORLD'S MERCHANTS (18:9-19)

> *And the kings of the earth, who have committed fornication and lived deliciously with her, shall bewail her, and lament for her, when they shall see the smoke of her burning. Standing afar off for the fear of her torment, saying, Alas, alas that great city Babylon, that mighty city! for in one hour is thy judgment come. And the merchants of the earth shall weep and mourn over her; for no man buyeth their merchandise any more: The merchandise of gold, and silver, and precious stones, and of pearls, and fine linen, and purple, and silk, and scarlet, and all thyine wood, and all manner vessels of ivory, and all manner vessels of most precious wood, and of brass, and iron, and marble. And cinnamon, and odours, and ointments, and frankincense, and wine, and oil, and fine flour, and wheat, and beasts, and sheep, and*

horses, and chariots, and slaves, and souls of men. And the fruits that thy soul lusted after are departed from thee, and all things which were dainty and goodly are departed from thee, and thou shalt find them no more at all. The merchants of these things, which were made rich by her, shall stand afar off for the fear of her torment, weeping and wailing, And saying, Alas, alas that great city, that was clothed in fine linen, and purple, and scarlet, and decked with gold, and precious stones, and pearls! For in one hour so great riches is come to nought. And every shipmaster, and all the company in ships, and sailors, and as many as trade by sea, stood afar off. And cried when they saw the smoke of her burning, saying, What city is like unto this great city! And they cast dust on their heads, and cried, weeping and wailing, saying, Alas, alas that great city, wherein were made rich all that had ships in the sea by reason of her costliness! for in one hour is she made desolate (18:9-19).

We shall not attempt a detailed study of these verses, but merely point out the world's lamentation over Babylon's judgment, and why. The entire population of the earth will be affected by her judgment. It must be remembered that *"the merchants of the earth are waxed rich through the abundance of her delicacies"* (18:3). The power and influence of this superchurch will extend to all nations, and when the fornication and luxury afforded by her is cut off, their source of gain will be gone.

The first to bemoan her fate will be the kings and rulers of the earth (18:3). The next to lament her collapse will be the merchants of the world (18:11-16). Twenty-eight categories of merchandise, including the *"souls of men,"* are listed. The last commodity, the souls of men, reveals how low Babylon has stooped in order to fill her coffers with the wealth of this world. The unscriptural doctrines of purgatory, the last rites, and masses for the dead have brought untold wealth into the treasury of their iniquitous system. Little wonder that the *"merchants of the earth shall weep and mourn over her; for no man buyeth their merchandise any more"* (18:11).

The last to bemoan the fall of Babylon are the vast shipping companies (18:17-19). All the transporters of merchandise must shut down their operations because the world's commercial center has been destroyed. The transport companies will have made their money and expanded their operations by means of Babylon's influence and needs. But now all business comes to a standstill. The teamsters' unions are powerless. They cease operations, not by their own choice as they have done so often in the past when strikes were called to achieve some goal of their own, but because the world's center of commerce has collapsed. There is no one to buy or sell. The false bottom of Babylon's economic pail has dropped out.

In each of these three groups the expression, "Alas, alas," is used (18:10,16,19). It is a term denoting disappointment, consternation, and at times an expected disaster, an exclamation of sorrow or regret. In the day of Babylon's final collapse, which will spell the utter disintegration of the world market, the peoples of the world in every walk of life will be saying, "Alas, alas." Their source of gain, which included everything from gold to the souls of men, will be taken from them.

The agony of the world's merchants can be understood when the suddenness with which the world market collapses is seen. It all takes place on *"one day"* (18:8), within *"one hour"* (18:10,17,19). The end of this great system comes with suddenness. She had boasted, *"I sit [as] a queen . . . and shall see no sorrow"* (18:7), but her sorrow is to come upon her suddenly. She must fall to rise no more. Imagine the horror and dismay to grip those who are linked with her and who have depended upon her for their support. They will learn, but too late, that it is better to trust in the Lord than to put confidence in man or in a religious system.

But the lament of the merchants is purely selfish. Their agony grows from the fact that the market from which they derived their wealth has collapsed. This only increases their hatred for Babylon. They never were bound to her by love or loyalty, but only by the trade she made possible to them. They are bewailing their lost money and the defunct markets.

IV. THE ATTITUDE OF HEAVEN (18:20-24)

Rejoice over her, thou heaven, and ye holy apostles and prophets; for God hath avenged you on her (18:20).

While the rulers, merchants, and shippers of the world are bewailing their losses, all of Heaven rejoices. The day of God's vengeance has come. "For it is written, Vengeance is mine; I will repay, saith the Lord" (Romans 12:19 cf. Deuteronomy 32:35). The judgment upon her is a sore one indeed. God says: *"Reward her even as she rewarded you, and double unto her double according to her works: in the cup which she hath filled fill to her double. How much she hath glorified herself, and lived deliciously, so much torment and sorrow give her: for she saith in her heart, I sit a queen, and am no widow, and shall see no sorrow"* (18:6-7). God cannot be silent forever and allow Babylon's abominations to continue. Iniquity and violence cannot be tolerated forever without divine intervention.

Someone might object to the attitude of rejoicing over the judgment of Babylon. True, such an attitude is a far cry from forgiving our enemies and from praying for those who despitefully use us and persecute us. However, there are several things we should remember. First, the actions and attitudes are ordered by God and not man, and this we have no right to question. Secondly, the day of grace will have come to its end. Today every Christian is keenly aware of the fact that his salvation is all of grace, that he does not deserve to be saved, and knowing the terror of the Lord he shrinks from the thought that any man must come under the anathema of Almighty God. Thirdly, the rejoicing is in the triumph of God over evil. There is no personal bitterness or malice here, but only a deep and sincere devotion to the holiness of God. There is always a note of rejoicing when one sees God triumphing ultimately over evil.

The attitude of rejoicing grew out of the final overthrow and obliteration of Babylon, a system which had defied God and debauched the nations. Notice in the six "no more's" how complete is her overthrow.

> *And a mighty angel took up a stone like a great millstone,*
> *and cast it into the sea, saying, Thus with violence shall*
> *that great city Babylon be thrown down, and shall be found*
> *no more at all* (18:21).

There has been much speculation as to the meaning of the great millstone. Robert Govett sees the stone representing the great city, a picture taken from Jeremiah 51:63-64. We are reminded of the words of our Lord in reference to those who neglect the spiritual care of children (Matthew 18:6). Herman Hoyt says that the stone is the Lord Jesus Himself (Daniel 2:34-35, 44-45), and when He falls upon the city He produces catastrophic results. I will not venture to identify the stone; suffice it to say that the city and the system are utterly destroyed and shall be "no more." The language depicts the swiftness and completeness of Babylon's destruction.

> *And the voice of harpers, and musicians, and of pipers,*
> *and trumpeters, shall be heard no more at all in thee* (18:22).

No more mirth and no more music. How sad! All entertainers and entertainment disappear forever. But it was not the kind of music that honored God. Earth's music had its origin with Jubal, a descendant of Cain and son of Lamech, the first polygamist (Genesis 4:16-21). Dr. Ironside said, "Music charmed the weary sons of Cain as they sought to make themselves happy in this world apart from God." The world today attempts to escape the realities of life by listening to modern jive and jazz from morning till night, but all to no avail. One day the Lord will blot it all out. "And I will cause the noise of thy songs to cease; and the sound of thy harps shall be no more heard" (Ezekiel 26:13).

> *And no craftsman, of whatsoever craft he be, shall be found*
> *any more in thee* (18:22).

No mechanic will ply his trade again. The tools of the craftsmen will be forever silent. This means that the wheels of industry will cease and all trade unions collapse. There shall not be one single building program in operation.

And the sound of a millstone shall be heard no more at all in thee (18:22).

The ancient handmills, like the modern milling centers, are essential to grind grain for human consumption. But the day will come when they shall grind no more.

And the light of a candle shall shine no more at all in thee (18:23).

The lamp and light of hearth and home shall be no more. The streets will be turned into caverns of darkness.

And the voice of the bridegroom and of the bride shall be heard no more at all in thee (18:23).

Many a marriage and many bridal tours took place in Babylon, but never again shall the marriage vows be taken. Never again will there be the sounds of rejoicing as heard at the wedding feasts, for even love will die. The desolation is complete. These "no more's" were prophesied by Jeremiah (see Jeremiah 25:9-11). The headquarters of the world's superchurch shall become a barren and an abandoned place.

Three reasons are given for this divine sentence of judgment upon Babylon.

For thy merchants were the great men of the earth; for by thy sorceries were all nations deceived. And in her was found the blood of prophets, and of saints, and of all that were slain upon the earth (18:23,24).

She will be judged because she worshiped wealth and luxury, playing harlot to the great merchants of the world. She will be judged because she led many astray with her witchcraft and doctrines of demons, her spiritism and necromancy, her bewitching attractiveness by which she lured the world to her feet. She will be judged because of the untold number of victims whom she slaughtered in the Inquisition and in St. Bartholomew's Massacre. She must pay for those shocking murders and for the many bloody persecutions which followed.

The day of reckoning is coming. This is the fate of Babylon. *"Come out of her, My people, that ye be not partakers of her sins."*

THE MARRIAGE SUPPER OF THE LAMB

Revelation 19:1-21

The title I have given to this chapter does not do justice to it because it contains more than that one event called "the marriage supper of the Lamb." Actually there are two scenes, one in Heaven, and one on the earth. The scene in Heaven is one of joy; the scene on earth is one of judgment.

I. THE JOY SCENE IN HEAVEN (19:1-10)

A. *The Manifestations of Praise*

The chapter opens" with four "alleluias" (19:1,3,4,6). From this point on we shall use the word "hallelujah," because "alleluia," without the initial "h," is a misspelling, having been robbed of its initial aspirate. The word means "praise the LORD." It occurs as a short doxology in the translated form, "Praise ye the LORD," both at the beginning and end of some of the psalms (see Psalms 146-150). In the New Testament it is found only here in the Revelation. It is the happy expression of the people of God. None save the redeemed can sing it or speak it, for it is Heaven's language.

First, there is the Hallelujah of *redemption*.

> *And after these things I heard a great voice of much people in heaven, saying, Alleluia; Salvation, and glory, and honour, and power, unto the Lord our God* (19:1).

I have called this the hallelujah of *redemption* because the first note of praise is *salvation*. Christ is about to appear with

His Church to complete the redemption He began at Calvary. One final conflict remains and then, after Armageddon, the swords of men shall be beaten into plowshares, the earth will be redeemed, and the lamb and the lion shall lie down together. While Satan is the prince of this world now, Christ holds the title deed to the earth, and the day is coming when He shall possess that which is His own by creative right and redemptive right. There has been much speculation in the many attempts to identify the *"much people in heaven"* who utter the first hallelujah. But what does it matter? Let us all join in the chorus. The great day of deliverance for all creation will surely come. Hallelujah!

Secondly, there is the hallelujah of righteous *retribution*.

> *For true and righteous are His judgments: for He hath judged the great whore, which did corrupt the earth with her fornication, and hath avenged the blood of His servants at her hand. And again they said, Alleluia. And her smoke rose up for ever and ever* (19:2-3).

All of God's judgments, upon the good and the evil, are true and righteous. The great harlot has received a just retribution for her evil, and her doom is an everlasting witness to the righteous judgment of God. He has avenged the blood of His servants who died at her hand. The hallelujah here is expressed because God has gotten the victory over His foes. One mention of the word hallelujah, translated in the Old Testament, "Praise ye the LORD," is uttered in connection with the righteous judgments of God against the wicked. The Psalmist wrote, "Let the sinners be consumed out of the earth, and let the wicked be no more. Bless thou the LORD, O my soul. Praise ye the LORD" (Psalm 104:35). The permanence and finality of God's judgment upon all evil is cause for the rejoicing of God's people. Hallelujah!

Thirdly, there is the hallelujah of *realization*.

> *And the four and twenty elders and the four beasts fell down and worshipped God that sat on the throne, saying, Amen; Alleluia. And a voice came out of the throne, saying,*

Praise our God, all ye His servants, and ye that fear Him, both small and great (19:4-5).

This is the last mention of the elders in the Revelation. They join in a hallelujah as the volume of praise gains momentum. I see in this third hallelujah a realization of the greatness of God. It corresponds to some degree to the usage of the term in its first mention when the ark was installed in David's tent and a feast was held in connection with it (1 Chronicles 16:4). The ark was to Israel a reminder of the realization of God's greatness and majesty. Blessed is that Christian who gets quiet each day to read God's Word and pray in order that he might contemplate his Lord's greatness. To contemplate the greatness and grace of God is to awaken gratitude and praise in every believer. Hallelujah!

Fourthly, there is the hallelujah for Christ's *reign*.

And I heard as it were the voice of a great multitude, and as the voice of many waters, and as the voice of mighty thunderings, saying, Alleluia: for the Lord God omnipotent reigneth (19:6).

This final shout of praise comes from the whole host of the redeemed. The Psalmist wrote, "The LORD reigneth; let the earth rejoice; let the multitude of isles be glad thereof" (Psalm 97:1). And why not? For centuries men have been praying, "Thy kingdom come," and now that prayer is to be answered. The time for the reign of the King of kings has come. The hallelujah time for Heaven and earth is at hand. It is the hour for the King to be set upon His holy hill in Zion and to receive the uttermost parts of the earth for His possession (Psalm 2:6,8). It is the moment when every knee shall bow and every tongue confess that Jesus Christ is Lord to the glory of God the Father (Philippians 2:11). This is the moment anticipated by all the redeemed. When Jesus came the first time, He was rejected and nailed to the cross. When He comes again, all men, rich and poor, high and low, will bow in homage at His feet. Hallelujah!

B. *The Marriage of the Lamb*

Let us be glad and rejoice, and give honour to Him: for the marriage of the Lamb is come, and His wife hath made herself ready. And to her was granted that she should be arrayed in fine linen, clean and white: for the fine linen is the righteousness of saints (19:7,8).

The great event, to which the Triune God and the Church have looked forward, has at last arrived. This marriage of the Lamb has been the long-looked-for event of the ages. The central figure of attraction is the Bridegroom, the Lamb, who is none other than the Lord Jesus Christ. In our marriage ceremonies, at which a man and a woman are united in wedlock, it is the bride who gets most of the attention. The guests watch for her appearing. The organ plays, "Here comes the bride." But here the multitude is heard in one united voice, saying, *"Let us be glad and rejoice, and give honour to Him"* (19:7). Here comes the Bridegroom!

It was said of Babylon that "the voice of the bridegroom and of the bride shall be heard no more at all in thee" (18:23), but now that the harlot has been exposed and expelled, the true Church, which is the Bride of Christ, is brought into view. There has been no mention of the Church since chapter 4, where she is caught up to Heaven. During the tribulation, the saints were in Heaven preparing for this important event. The marriage of the Lamb is a heavenly scene; therefore the Bride, the Lamb's wife, could hardly be Israel. It is difficult to conceive that Abraham, or any other Old Testament saint, will make up the Body of Christ, the Lamb's Bride. I believe that the Church for whom Christ gave Himself, and which will be presented to Him "holy and without blemish," is made up of those saints from Pentecost to the Rapture (Ephesians 5:25-27). This is the full and final union between Christ and His Church.

Now I am aware of the marriage symbolism in the Old Testament used to express the relationship between God and His people. This is clear in such passages as Isaiah 54:6; Jeremiah 3:14; Ezekiel 16; Hosea 2:19-20. But Israel is divorced

(Jeremiah 3:8), and as a widow (Lamentations 1:1). The prophesied union between God and Israel is an event to take place on the earth, and must not be confused with the marriage of the Lamb to His Bride, which takes place in Heaven. Now I will not deny the possibility of two marriages, one at which the Church and Christ will be united, and one at which Israel and Jehovah will be united. Nor is it impossible that each might attend the marriage feast of the other. But to fail to distinguish between the two of these actions only tends to confuse the whole issue. In the Revelation passage the Lamb's wife is the Church, not Israel. In Revelation 21:9-10, the Lamb's wife is seen descending out of Heaven as the heavenly Jerusalem, a city being used symbolically for the Bride just as the city Babylon is used symbolically of the harlot. Further comments will be made on this subject when we take up the study of chapter 21.

Now notice a statement concerning the Lamb's wife.

> *And His wife hath made herself ready. And to her was granted that she should be arrayed in fine linen, clean and white: for the fine linen is the righteousness of saints* (19:7-8).

Why is it stated that she has made herself ready? Is not salvation entirely of grace apart from works? The answer to these and related questions is found, in part, in the American Standard Version as well as in some other versions, where we read, "the fine linen is the righteous acts of the saints." The original Greek text shows that the word "righteousness" is literally *righteousnesses,* or *righteous deeds.* Here the righteous deeds of the saints are not to be confused with the righteousness of God, which is imputed to each believing sinner at the time of conversion (Romans 3:21-22). No sinner can work for this righteousness, as it is received only by faith. It is true of all unsaved persons that "all our righteousnesses are as filthy rags" (Isaiah 64:6). But when we receive Jesus Christ as Saviour and Lord, we can say,

> "Dressed in His righteousness alone,
> Faultless to stand before the throne."

However, what are in view here in Revelation 19:8 are the righteous acts of the saints, right doing while we are here on earth as saints. It is sad, but true, that all saints will not be ready to meet Christ when He comes for His Church. Some will be ashamed before Him at His coming. Many saints are guilty of committing unrighteous acts. These are unfit garments to be wearing on their wedding day. So while God has been preparing the earth for the reign of the saints, He must also prepare the saints to be presented to a prepared earth. The fact that the Lamb's wife has made herself ready suggests that she was not ready before. Too many Christians have assumed the attitude that just because they are saved they can live careless lives but nevertheless go to Heaven. Now it is true that when Christ appears at the Rapture, all saints of the Church Age, both living and dead, will be caught up to be with Him. But before they can reign with Him there must be a reckoning and a readiness.

Has it ever occurred to you, my Christian friend, that at the marriage of the Bride to the Lamb, each of us will be wearing the wedding garment of our own making? We must confess to our shame that the Bride is not now ready for the wedding. There are many carnal, selfish Christians who live worldly lives, and all such must pass through the fires of the Judgment Seat of Christ before they qualify to reign with Christ. The Judgment Seat, which follows the Rapture, will not be a happy experience for every Christian. I know that for some of us there will be loss and shame (Romans 14:10; 1 Corinthians 3:11-16; 2 Corinthians 5:10). But we *must* all appear before Christ for the final inspection and necessary readiness for the marriage.

Dr. DeHaan says, "In Ephesians 5:26 we are told that Christ will sanctify and cleanse His Church by the washing of water by the Word. The two words used, 'sanctify' and 'cleanse,' are not the same in the Greek. The word translated 'cleanse' in this verse is *katharizō*, from which our English word 'cathartic' is derived. God uses two methods of making us clean. One is by 'sanctifying,' by washing by the Word. If we refuse this method, He will give us a 'cathartic,' but He will have us clean. How much better to take the gentle course now than to wait until the Judgment Seat of Christ and be purged by fire!"

The wedding gown, then, will be made up of the good works that remain after the testing of the Judgment Seat of Christ. Now you can see how the wife makes herself ready. It used to be customary for the bride to make her own wedding dress. When a girl would meet a young man and he began to court her, she would acquire a hope chest and commence to lay away lovely, clean pieces of apparel in anticipation of her wedding day. She would work diligently to prepare her own bridal gown. Christian, what are we putting in the bridal chest for that day? Of what will your wedding garment and mine be made? The fruit of a good and godly life will make a lovely garment for that glorious occasion. The white linen of the holy and useful life of Christ's dedicated followers stands out in bold contrast to the purple and scarlet, the gold, precious stones, and pearls of the harlot (cf. 17:4).

C. *The Marriage Supper*

And he saith unto me, Write, Blessed are they which are called unto the marriage supper of the Lamb, And he saith unto me, These are the true sayings of God. And I fell at his feet to worship him. And he said unto me, See thou do it not: I am thy fellowservant, and of thy brethren that have the testimony of Jesus: worship God: for the testimony of Jesus is the spirit of prophecy (19:9-10).

The marriage supper is an event separate from the marriage. Those "which are called unto the marriage supper of the Lamb" are invited guests. Every wedding has its guests. Now the guests are not the bride. Certainly the bride is not invited to her own wedding supper, for she has a place of honor next to the bridegroom. It is quite possible that the guests here are the Old Testament saints and those saints who were saved in the tribulation. John the Baptist, who died before the death of our Lord, will be there as one of the guests. You will remember that he called himself "the friend of the bridegroom" (John 3:29).

The marriage takes place in Heaven, but it would seem that the marriage supper occurs on the earth, the latter when the Bridegroom returns with His Bride. This I believe explains the parable of the ten virgins in Matthew 25:1-13. William L. Pettingill has drawn to our attention the fact that the Latin Vulgate adds the words "and bride" to the first verse of Matthew 25, so that it reads, "Then shall the kingdom of heaven be likened unto ten virgins, who took their lamps, and went forth to meet the bridegroom and bride." The Vulgate also reads "marriage feast" instead of "marriage" in verse 10. The Revised Version has made this latter change. It certainly seems that the parable of the ten virgins fits into the marriage supper of the Lamb.

Another parable of a wedding supper spoken by our Lord is recorded in Matthew 22:1-14. This one also might well fit into the marriage supper of the Lamb. Psalm 45, called "a song of loves," probably has as a historical basis the marriage of Solomon to the daughter of the King of Egypt (1 Kings 3:1). But in its broader application and prophetic anticipation it is Messianic, and points to the heavenly Bridegroom and His Bride. It is the marriage of the King of kings to His elect spouse.

II. THE JUDGMENT SCENE ON EARTH (19:11-21)

These verses introduce that great event anticipated for centuries and about which the Old Testament prophets wrote. It is the golden age on earth when all creation shall be subject to its Creator and Redeemer. But before He reigns He must subdue every enemy and opposing force. Daniel's seventieth week has just about run its course. The conflict of Armageddon is about to occur. Up to this point Christ has been directing earth's judgments from His throne in Heaven, but now He leaves Heaven and descends to earth for the purpose of completing the work of judgment before He establishes His millennial Kingdom.

A. *The Advent of Christ*

> *And I saw heaven opened, and behold a white horse; and He that sat upon him was called Faithful and True, and in righteousness He doth judge and make war. His eyes were as a flame of fire, and on His head were many crowns; and He had a name written, that no man knew, but He Himself. And He was clothed with a vesture dipped in blood: and His name is called The Word of God* (19:11-13).

Here we see the commencement of the apocalypse of Jesus Christ, His real and actual appearing on the earth. For centuries the scoffers have tauntingly asked, "Where is the promise of His coming?" (2 Peter 3:4) Now they are about to be silenced. He is seen here as the Rider on a white horse. The white horse rider in 6:1-2, who appears at the opening of the first seal, is not Christ.

John sees *"heaven opened"* for His descent. In chapter 4, verse 1, a door was opened in Heaven. Here Heaven is opened. These two openings (4:1 and 19:11) present the pivotal points of the book. They mark the clear distinction between Christ's coming *for* His saints and His coming *with* His saints. The first discloses the *Rapture;* the second unfolds the *Revelation.* All who enter Heaven through the door in 4:1 will come again with Christ when Heaven is opened in 19:11.

He is called *"Faithful and True."* The rider on the white horse in chapter 6 was faithless and untrue. Christ was presented as "the faithful and true witness" in the letter to the Laodiceans (3:14). He is seen coming to execute righteous judgment on the earth, as He said. His promises and warnings have been rejected by many, but in that day all will know that He is faithful and true to His word. When He appears on earth again it will be to *"judge and make war,"* but His judgment and His war will be those of the perfect man, the Faithful and True One.

"And His name is called the Word of God." This is the name whereby His majesty will be manifested, for when He comes to earth again it will be with all authority. Christ was always

the eternal Word (John 1:1), but when the Word became flesh (John 1:14), His own people would not receive Him (John 1:11). And yet it was this very Word who spoke the worlds into being (Psalm 33:6). As the eternal Word He was always the expression of God, but at His next appearing on the earth He will exercise full authority in expressing the Father's judicial attitude. Of the eight writers who penned the New Testament, John only uses this title of Christ (John 1:1,14; 1 John 1:1; 5:7). As words are a vehicle of expression to the mind and heart of some personality, so Christ, the Word of God, is the only perfect expression of God. Spoken words are not merely a sound; they are wonderfully alive, and this is more true of the Divine Word (Hebrews 4:12). Here Christ is both the Warrior and the Word.

B. *The Armies of Christ*

And the armies which were in heaven followed Him upon white horses, clothed in fine linen, white and clean (19:14).

Here we see the mighty Captain leading His armies from Heaven to earth. These are the soldier-saints whom He took to Heaven. The plural "armies" suggests more than one company. It is quite possible that they include the Old Testament saints, the Church, and the saints of the tribulation. Their clothing indicates that they are all saved people. What a magnificent army this is! The Lamb's Bride will be with Him; however, she is viewed here not ready for the wedding but for the war. Here the redeemed are a militant force. Doubtless there will be a host of angels in that army because our Lord did tell His disciples that the holy angels would be with Him when He returned in glory (Matthew 25:31). This mighty event was divinely revealed to Enoch, the seventh generation from Adam, for Jude writes, "And Enoch also, the seventh from Adam, prophesied of these, saying, Behold, the Lord cometh with ten thousands of His saints, To execute judgment upon all, and to convince all that are ungodly among them of all their ungodly deeds which they have ungodly committed, and of all their hard speeches which ungodly sinners have spoken against Him" (Jude 14-15).

Paul prophesied of this same event when he wrote, "And to you who are troubled rest with us, when the Lord Jesus shall be revealed from heaven with His mighty angels, In flaming fire taking vengeance on them that know not God, and that obey not the gospel of our Lord Jesus Christ: Who shall be punished with everlasting destruction from the presence of the Lord, and from the glory of His power; When He shall come to be glorified in His saints, and to be admitted in all them that believe (because our testimony among you was believed) in that day" (2 Thessalonians 1:7-10).

These armies are not mere symbols; they are real! Christ is the Lord of Hosts, Jehovah-Sabaoth, and the armies of Heaven are as real as the Lord Himself.

C. *The Authority of Christ*

And out of His mouth goeth a sharp sword, that with it He should smite the nations: and He shall rule them with a rod of iron: and He treadeth the winepress of the fierceness and wrath of Almighty God. And He hath on His vesture and on His thigh a name written, KING OF KINGS, AND LORD OF LORDS (19:15-16).

This description of Christ, namely, a sword issuing out of His mouth, was given in 1:16. Here we see the fulfillment of the great Messianic prophecy which reads, "And He shall smite the earth with the rod of His mouth, and with the breath of His lips shall He slay the wicked" (Isaiah 11:4). The "sharp sword," I take it, is the Word of God (Hebrews 4:12). He will need only to speak and His enemies will fall in utter defeat. He demonstrated such authority when He was here on the earth. John writes, "As soon then as He had said unto them, I am He, they went backward, and fell to the ground" (John 18:6). This would be a strange campaign equipment to the average warrior, but our Commander-in-Chief has never resorted to carnal weapons. And please notice that He is the only One who engages in the conflict. It is He who smites the nations. The armies merely view the battle. Most battles are fought by the armies while the general directs from a vantage point. But this General is unique, and He has never lost a battle. Having been given full authority in Heaven and on earth, He is seen here coming to exercise that authority.

As Christ led His armies forth, John perceived that upon His garments, in the region of the thigh, He had His name written: "KING OF KINGS, AND LORD OF LORDS." As the absolute Sovereign and sole Ruler of the earth, He now presents Himself as such. This is His official title and it belongs to Him. As the Nobleman who went into a far country, He now returns to establish His kingdom (Luke 19:12-27). At last "the government shall be upon His shoulder. . . . Of the increase of His government and peace there shall be no end, upon the throne of David, and upon His kingdom, to order it, and to establish it with judgment and with justice from henceforth even for ever. The zeal of the LORD of hosts will perform this" (Isaiah 9:6-7). It is the complete fulfillment of Psalms 2 and 24.

D. *The Avenging of Christ*

And I saw an angel standing in the sun; and he cried with a loud voice, saying to all the fowls that fly in the midst of heaven, Come and gather yourselves together unto the supper of the great God; That ye may eat of the flesh of kings, and the flesh of captains, and the flesh of mighty men, and the flesh of horses, and of them that sit on them, and the flesh of all men, both free and bond, both small and great. And I saw the beast, and the kings of the earth, and their armies, gathered together to make war against Him that sat on the horse and against His army. And the beast was taken, and with him the false prophet that wrought miracles before him, with which he deceived them that had received the mark of the beast, and them that worshipped his image. These both were cast alive into a lake of fire burning with brimstone. And the remnant were slain with the sword of Him that sat upon the horse, which sword proceeded out of His mouth: and all the fowls were filled with their flesh (19:17-21).

These verses depict the final vanquishing of all of Christ's enemies on earth. It is the long-looked-for conflict of Armageddon (16:16). All of the demon-inspired nations are completely overthrown.

First, we observe the *vulturous fowls* (19:17-18). This scene is a true and literal one. God, through an angel, summons the vultures and other birds of prey to eat the flesh of the slain. As the rulers of the earth converge on the city of Jerusalem in their last strenuous effort to destroy the Jews, their end will come suddenly with the descent of the King of kings. It is a grim and terrible picture, I admit, but one that we must expect to come to pass. Ezekiel prophesied concerning it (Ezekiel 39:17-20), and our Lord warned that "wheresoever the carcass is, there will the eagles be gathered together" (Matthew 24:28). The vultures devouring the flesh of the hundreds of thousands of fighting men from Europe and Asia is called here a "supper." In this one chapter there are two suppers, one of joy which follows the wedding, and one of judgment which follows the war. Take your choice!

Secondly, we observe the *vanquished foes* (19:19-21). Here is the confederacy of evil forces under the leadership of the beast and the false prophet arrayed against Christ. They are seen *"gathered together to make war against Him"* (19:19). The revived Roman Empire, including the monarchs of the ten kingdoms, will assemble together in a futile attempt to withstand the King of kings. What daring audacity! Owning the Antichrist as its only leader, all earth defies the Lord Jesus Christ. The wickedness of man has come to its full, so the wrath of God now reaches its peak. Because this vast confederacy has subdued the earth, it now boldly attacks Heaven. But to no avail. The creature is a fool who fights against his Creator. Already in our day God has been ordered off parts of His creation. Our own Supreme Court has banned Him from the public schools, and we can expect the revolt against the Almighty to rise higher until all the earth's hostile forces assemble themselves to defeat Him.

Judgment fell first upon the beast and the false prophet. *"Both were cast alive into a lake of fire burning with brimstone"*

(19:20). No natural weapon was used against them, but the doom of these supermen is certain. The great drama of earth's hostilities is drawing to a close. The Seed of the woman will bruise the serpent's head. Satan's two emissaries are still found alive in the lake of fire at the close of the thousand years (20:10).

The followers of these wicked men once said, "Who is like unto the beast? Who is able to make war with him?" (13:4). Now they have the answer as their leaders are cast alive into the lake of fire. Two Old Testament saints, Enoch and Elijah, were taken up alive to Heaven, but these two enemies of Christ are cast alive into hell. Daniel saw their end in a vision (Daniel 7:11).

Let the doom of these two men and their followers serve as a solemn warning to all who are still rejecting Christ. I sound this alarm because I feel I must. God has done everything to save you. You must come to Christ at once and receive Him. Rebellion against Him means doom, for no weapon formed against Him can prosper. If you decide to take issue with these things, you must deal with Him who is the Author of them.

THE THOUSAND YEARS AND
THE GREAT WHITE THRONE

Revelation 20:1-15

Every student of the Revelation is aware of the fact that this chapter is a highly controversial one. The disagreement among students revolves around the phrase "a thousand years," appearing six times in this chapter (verses 2,3,4,5,6,7). Three schools of eschatology have taken their positions in this battleground.

Amillennialism. This is the newest of the three schools, having become popular only in recent years. It holds to the literal coming of Christ, but its chief weakness is that it spiritualizes the 1,000 years, as it does most of the book of Revelation. The amillennialist is actually a nonmillennialist.

Postmillennialism. This school does not deny that there will be a literal return of Christ, nor that there will be a literal millennium on the earth, but it does assume falsely that Christ does not come back until the conclusion of the 1,000 years. This theory was an optimistic view at the beginning of the twentieth century, but it could not survive the first half of the century which produced two world wars and a disastrous depression. It held that man would bring in the kingdom through his own efforts, and then Christ would return. Many of those who once held this view no longer respect the prophetic Scriptures.

Premillennialism. This school takes the position that Revelation 20 must be interpreted literally. The 1,000 years are treated as 1,000 years. Christ comes back to earth at the close of Daniel's seventieth week before the millennium. There can be no kingdom on earth until Christ the King returns and Satan is removed from the earth. This I believe to be the true Biblical position.

There are some who refuse to accept the literalness of the thousand-year period, but they will accept the literalness of the angel, Heaven, the bottomless pit, Satan, the nations, and the resurrections mentioned in the context of Revelation 20. I know of no principle of Biblical interpretation that would allow for the literalness of those things while denying the literalness of the time element which is said to be *"a thousand years."* The amillennialist who attempts to spiritualize the *"thousand years"* will defend his position by quoting the following verses: "For a thousand years in Thy sight are but as yesterday when it is past, and as a watch in the night" (Psalm 90:4). "But, beloved, be not ignorant of this one thing, that one day is with the Lord as a thousand years, and a thousand years as one day" (2 Peter 3:8). But please notice the words "in Thy [God's] sight" and "with the Lord." True, a thousand years is as a "watch" and as "one day," but only in God's sight, only with Him. But it is not so with us, and the Bible was written for us to whom a thousand years means a thousand years.

The time of the millennium is given by our Lord in His words, *"Immediately after the tribulation* of those days shall the sun be darkened, and the moon shall not give her light, and the stars shall fall from heaven, and the powers of the heavens shall be shaken: And then shall appear the sign of the Son of man in heaven: and then shall all the tribes of the earth mourn, and they shall see the Son of man coming in the clouds of heaven with power and great glory" (Matthew 24:29-30). Here Christ places the theocratic kingdom immediately after the seventieth week of Daniel as mentioned in Daniel 9:27).

The form of government during the millennium will be a theocracy. In both the Old and New Testaments it is stated that God will rule in the Person of Jesus Christ (Psalm 2:6-9; Jeremiah 23:5; Luke 1:30-33).

The seat of God's rule in the earth will be Jerusalem (Isaiah 2:2-4; Matthew 19:28). God's people Israel will be restored to their own land a united people. The breach caused by Rehoboam will be healed (Isaiah 11:11-16; Jeremiah 16:14-16;

Ezekiel 34:11-16), and Israel will once more be the chief of the nations (Deuteronomy 28:13).

The conditions on the earth during the millennium will be ideal. There shall be peace in the animal kingdom (Isaiah 11:7-9) as well as earthwide peace among men (Isaiah 2:4; 54:13-14). There will be one language with the curse of Babel removed (Zechariah 3:9). All of the physical creation will be delivered from the curse resulting from the fall (Romans 8:19-21; Isaiah 11:6-9; 35:1-2).

All of the events so far in the book of Revelation have been premillennial, that is, they all occur before Christ returns to earth to reign. In this chapter the events are millennial. During the millennium God will bring to pass certain of His plans and purposes, and then after the 1,000 years have run their course, the millennium will merge into the eternal state.

This chapter contains five major emphases. They divide the chapter and should be considered one at a time.

I. THE REMOVAL OF SATAN (20:1-3)

And I saw an angel come down from heaven, having the key of the bottomless pit and a great chain in his hand. And he laid hold on the dragon, that old serpent, which is the Devil, and Satan, and bound him a thousand years. And cast him into the bottomless pit, and shut him up, and set a seal upon him, that he should deceive the nations no more, till the thousand years should be fulfilled: and after that he must be loosed a little season (20:1-3).

In these verses we have God's final answer to the puny excuses of men as to the cause of evil in the world. One sociologist insists that environment is the cause of man's moral ills. Another blames evil on our educational system. For these and other reasons men have concentrated their efforts on improving these areas of life. But changing a man's environment does not change the man. In fact, while environmental change has characterized recent generations, the world has been growing increasingly worse just as the Word of God predicts (2 Timothy 3:1-7; 13).

From the very beginning of man's history the existence of a personal enemy of God and man is in evidence. That enemy is referred to first as "the serpent" (Genesis 3:1), and finally as "the great dragon . . . called the Devil, and Satan, which deceiveth the whole world" (Revelation 12:9). Between Genesis and Revelation there are repeated references to his nature and nefarious practices. Jesus said that he is a "murderer" and a "liar" (John 8:44). The name "devil" means a slanderer, a malignant liar. This foe of God and man is the great power behind the whole antichristian system. He it is who controls the beast, the false prophet, and the harlot, and by whose instigation wars are undertaken.

In order that righteousness and peace might rule on earth, this evil one must be removed. But what man has been unable to do, and never can do, God does. At the close of the Great Tribulation, and just before Christ appears on the earth to bring in His kingdom, which is characterized by spiritual, moral, and physical perfection, God sends an angel from Heaven to bind Satan.

Who this angel is we are not told. Some teachers believe He is Christ Himself. Others are satisfied that he is a created angel. He could be the Lord Jesus Christ, for He has appeared at other times in the character of the Angel of Jehovah, and He does have "the keys of hell and of death" (1:18). But the point is of no importance either way. Whether the angel is Michael (see 12:7), or another created being, or Christ, the fact is that he does his job well.

He comes with a *"great chain in his hand"* with which he binds Satan for one thousand years. This may or may not be a literal chain, as we know a chain, but whatever its nature, it is a literal chain of God's making, capable of binding a spirit. It is called "a *great* chain" since it is to bind "the *great* dragon" (12:9). With similar chains evil angels are kept bound even now awaiting the day of judgment (Jude 6). Satan and his demons can break the chains and fetters that men may fashion (Mark 5:1-5), but the "great chain" of God's making not even Satan himself can resist or shake off. It is adequate for the purpose of binding him a helpless prisoner.

The place where Satan is incarcerated during the millennium is called in the Authorized Version *"the bottomless pit."* It is a noun denoting the abyss, the immeasurable depth of the underworld, the lower regions, the intermediate abode of evil demons which are doomed forever. This word appears seven times in the Revelation (9:1,2,11; 11:7; 17:8; 20:1,3). The bottomless pit, or abyss, is not the lake of fire which is the final hell. It is a sort of prison-house in which evil spirits are confined, awaiting final judgment. These have no share in Christ's redemption.

That old serpent, the devil, who has been responsible for the evil in the world, will be imprisoned then during the millennium. The object of his imprisonment is not to render his due punishment, but rather to remove him from the earth and thereby restrain his evil machinations. So long as he is at liberty to act he will not rest from deluding men with lies, and seeking their destruction. And let each one of us be reminded that Satan is not bound now. He would have us believe that he is, but the Word of God says, "Be sober, be vigilant; because your adversary the devil, as a roaring lion, walketh about, seeking whom he may devour" (1 Peter 5:8).

The duration of Satan's imprisonment in the abyss is said to be *"a thousand years"* (20:2). This covers the entire period of the millennium. This period when Satan is cast into the abyss, and the abyss closed, locked, and sealed, is prophesied in the Old Testament. Isaiah wrote, "And it shall come to pass in that day, that the Lord shall punish the host of the high ones that are on high, and the kings of the earth upon the earth. And they shall be gathered together, as prisoners are gathered in the pit, and shall be shut up in the prison, and after many days shall they be visited" (Isaiah 24:21-22). We may be certain that this prophecy is yet future by reading verse 23, for that verse describes the golden age that follows immediately after the shutting up in prison of the hosts of the high ones on high. These hosts are none other than the devil and his demons.

II. THE REIGN OF SAINTS (20:4-6)

And I saw thrones, and they sat upon them, and judgment was given unto them: and I saw the souls of them that were beheaded for the witness of Jesus, and for the word of God, and which had not worshipped the beast, neither his image, neither had received his mark upon their foreheads, or in their hands; and they lived and reigned with Christ a thousand years. But the rest of the dead lived not again until the thousand years were finished. This is the first resurrection. Blessed and holy is he that hath part in the first resurrection: on such the second death hath no power, but they shall be priests of God and of Christ, and shall reign with Him a thousand years (20:4-6).

Here is a group of whom it is written, *"they lived and reigned with Christ a thousand years."* They occupy thrones, and the authority to judge is given to them. Who are they? They are all those who belong to the "first resurrection." They are Old Testament saints, Church saints, and tribulation saints. The occupants of these thrones are the same as those in chapters 4 and 5, including those saints who suffered martyrdom during the tribulation and those to whom our Lord spoke in Luke 22:29-30. The thrones that John saw are judicial seats of regal authority. They are not displayed for mere empty show. The sitters upon them are described in the passage under consideration as *"priests of God and of Christ, and shall reign with Him a thousand years."* They constitute Christ's "royal priesthood" (1 Peter 2:9), those whom He has made "kings and priests" (Revelation 1:5-6; 5:9-10). John says expressly that *"judgment was given unto them."* Once God's saints were judged and persecuted by the world, and are so treated even now, but the day will come when "the saints shall judge the world" (1 Corinthians 6:2). Victory belongs to the King of kings and Lord of lords, and He will share it with His redeemed ones on the earth for one thousand years. The longest human life on earth fell short of one thousand years (Genesis 5:27), but that same length of time, during which the devil is bound, the saints will live gloriously.

But the rest of the dead lived not again until the thousand years were finished. This is the first resurrection (20:5).

All of these mentioned in verse 4 will be raised from the dead at different stages. Notice that both verses 5 and 6 speak of *"the first resurrection,"* which is set in contrast to a second resurrection. The first resurrection is a resurrection to everlasting life (Daniel 12:2), which includes saints only. It is called "the resurrection of the just" (Luke 14:13-14), "the resurrection of life" (John 5:29), "a better resurrection" (Hebrews 11:35). The first resurrection takes place at different stages, but it includes all who are God's own, raised to everlasting life. All such are said to be "blessed and holy" (20:6).

Many have erred in assuming that there is but one general resurrection and one general judgment for all mankind, saved and lost alike. When our Lord was here on the earth He did teach that all men, saved and unsaved alike, will be raised again at some future time. His words are clear when He says, "All that are in the graves . . . shall come forth" (John 5:28-29). Paul said, "There shall be a resurrection of the dead, both of the just and unjust" (Acts 24:15), but there is not the slightest implication that both classes would be raised at the same time. Revelation 20:5 makes it clear that between the two resurrections there will be the space of one thousand years.

Paul wrote further by inspiration, "But now is Christ risen from the dead, and become the firstfruits of them that slept . . . But every man in his own order [or rank]: Christ the firstfruits; afterward they that are Christ's at His coming" (1 Corinthians 15:20,23). There are at least three, and possibly four different ranks connected with the "first resurrection." First, there is Christ's resurrection. Secondly, there is the resurrection of the saints of the Church Age (1 Thessalonians 4:16). Thirdly, there is the resurrection of the tribulation saints. Not all teachers of the Bible are agreed as to the time of the resurrection of Old Testament saints. Some believe they are raised when the Church saints are raised at Christ's appearing in the air to raise and rapture the Church; others hold to the view that they are raised at the close of the tribulation. To me this is not a point of major significance. The Old Testament saints will be raised and will be in one of the ranks even though we cannot be certain as to exactly which rank.

In connection with this subject some have asked in which rank do we place those who were raised from the dead at the time of Christ's resurrection, and of whom it is written, "And the graves were opened; and many bodies of the saints which slept arose" (Matthew 27:52). Actually theirs was not a resurrection to immortality, but rather a resuscitation like the resurrection of Lazarus, the daughter of Jairus, the son of the widow of Nain, and others. These all must have died again, else they would be living somewhere today. Because they are saints, they will be raised to immortality either with the Church saints or else with the tribulation saints.

Those who spiritualize the Revelation passage stumble at the word *"souls"* in verse 4. Others who criticize the Bible use this word to obscure a plain doctrine of God's Word which they do not like. Any honest reader of the Bible knows that the word "soul" is not used merely to denote the spirit of a man out of his body. When speaking of Noah and his wife, their three sons and their wives, the Bible calls them "eight souls" (1 Peter 3:20). Jacob and his family who went down into Egypt are spoken of as "threescore and six souls" (Genesis 46:26). The converts on the Day of Pentecost are referred to as "about three thousand souls" (Acts 2:41). In all of these passages disembodied spirits are out of the question. The word "souls," as used in John's vision of the martyrs, indicates persons who were slain on account of their faith. Since they lived again and reigned with Christ a thousand years, they had to be in their bodies. The soul never dies, that is, never lapses into a state of sleep or unconsciousness. When the Bible speaks of resurrection, it always means the resurrection of the body. The only resurrection of which the dead are capable is the resurrection of the body.

Of these saints God says, *"On such the second death hath no power"* (20:6). The phrase *"second death"* actually means a second *kind* of death. There are two kinds of death, namely, physical and spiritual. We all are acquainted with the general idea of physical death, that moment when the body dies and is vacated by the spiritual part of man.

But spiritual death is quite different. As we have already stated, the spiritual part of man never sleeps nor becomes unconscious. Spiritual death means alienation from the life of God (Ephesians 4:18), the state of every unbeliever (Ephesians 2:1). When the unbeliever receives Christ by faith, he is born again and thereby receives the life of God (John 3:16; 5:24; 1 John 5:12). As long as man is physically alive and conscious, there is hope and the possibility of his escaping from spiritual death. However, if he dies physically in unbelief, or if he is alive and continues to reject Christ until the Rapture, or if during the tribulation he follows the Antichrist instead of Christ, then there is no escape from the "second death." All such will be banished from God forever. The phrase "second death" appears not less than three times in the Revelation (20:6,14; 21:8). "The lake of fire" (20:14), "which burneth with fire and brimstone . . . is the second death" (21:8). The saints, who are the blessed and holy ones, and who will be in the first resurrection, will escape the *"second death."*

III. THE RETURN OF SATAN (20:7)

And when the thousand years are expired, Satan shall be loosed out of his prison (20:7).

During the millennium, the earth will experience the answer to millions of prayers, "Thy kingdom come. Thy will be done, as in heaven, so in earth" (Luke 11:2). The chant of victory will contain the words, "The kingdoms of this world are become the kingdoms of our Lord, and of His Christ; and He shall reign for ever and ever" (Revelation 11:15). There shall be peace and righteousness at last among all nations, a peace and righteousness that man could not effect, but which Christ Himself has perfected. Revelation 20 contains merely a statement of the dispensation of the kingdom, the 1,000 years of Christ's rule on earth. Other Scripture references give to us a more detailed description of those days.

But now there is added a most amazing prophecy that will be fulfilled at the end of the millennium. Satan is to be released from the prison that will hold him and he will return to the earth. In verse 3 it was stated *"that he should deceive the nations no more, till the thousand years should be fulfilled: and after that he must be loosed a little season."* Here in verse 7 we have this fact reiterated.

But why *"must"* Satan be released and permitted to return to the earth? Indeed there must be a reason, else the necessity of it would not be stated so emphatically. It must be known by all, men and angels, that time does not change the nature and character of Satan or man. Both Satan and human nature are incurably evil and impossible of self-improvement. From Satan's first rebellion (Isaiah 14:12-23) to his final rebellion, pride rules his heart (1 Timothy 3:6-7), and the destruction of all men who refuse to worship him is his goal. In every dispensation both the devil and unregenerated man remain unchanged. This is proved conclusively at the end of the millennium.

It has been argued by some that good parentage and good environment produce good children, and that poor parentage and poor environment produce bad children, the conclusion being that a good society will produce a generation free of strife, immorality, and poverty. But this argument is disproved at the close of the millennium. The one-thousand-years reign of Christ will begin with all redeemed people. No unsaved person will enter the millennium (Isaiah 60:21; Joel 2:28). But during the millennium children will be born of saved people, and then after having been born and reared in a perfect moral and spiritual society, they will be easily deceived by the devil, choosing to follow him while they turn their backs on Christ. Evil nature, whether confined in a prison or subject to righteous rule, does not change. The leopard cannot change its spots. "The carnal mind is enmity against God: for it is not subject to the law of God, neither indeed can be. So then they that are in the flesh cannot please God" (Romans 8:7-8).

IV. THE REVOLT OF SOCIETY (20:8-10)

And shall go out to deceive the nations which are in the four quarters of the earth, Gog and Magog, to gather them together to battle: the number of whom is as the sand of the

sea. And they went up on the breadth of the earth, and com-
passed the camp of the saints about, and the beloved city:
and fire came down from God out of heaven, and devoured
them. And the devil that deceived them was cast into the
lake of fire and brimstone, where the beast and the false
prophet are, and shall be tormented day and night for ever
and ever (20:8-10).

Even after 1,000 years of a righteous and peaceful reign, Satan by his deception is able to discredit God's dealings and thereby lead the nations astray in a revolt against God. Those born during the millennium will not be willing subjects of the King of kings, but will render mere lip service. Their subjection to Him will be by restraint, much like the underworld characters are restrained by law. For just as soon as Satan is released, they yield a ready allegiance to his deceptions. The masses come from the four corners of the earth in so large an assemblage, their number is *"as the sand of the sea."* If one wonders where these masses of people come from, he need only be reminded that the millennium will be the time of earth's greatest population explosion, because the curse will be removed from the physical earth, thereby yielding its greatest food production. Likewise disease will be eliminated. Only the human heart will remain unchanged, this being the reason for the revolt.

The "Gog and Magog" here are not necessarily the Gog and Magog of Ezekiel 38 and 39. While the names are the same, the conflicts differ as to time, location, and participants. The battles, however, are the same in nature, that is, Satan inspires men to war against God.

The attack is against Jerusalem, called *"the beloved city"* (20:9). God's enemies are bent on destroying the place of Christ's throne on the earth. But the attack is quickly ended when God sends fire from Heaven to devour them. These might well be natural forces, an explosion of atoms. "For our God is a consuming fire" (Hebrews 12:29). By this same means Gog and Magog are destroyed in the first great conflict (Ezekiel 38:22).

Without further delay Satan is cast into the lake of fire.

> *And the devil that deceived them was cast into the lake of fire and brimstone, where the beast and the false prophet are, and shall be tormented day and night for ever and ever (20:10).*

There, together with his accomplices, he is tormented day and night forever and ever. Satan's judgment was assured at the cross (John 12:31-33; 16:11), but the actual execution of the sentence awaits the end of the millennium and his last rebellion. Hell is the place prepared for him (Matthew 25:41), and the place in which fallen angels have been cast (2 Peter 2:4). The one who has brought untold sorrow and suffering to all mankind must now suffer for all eternity without relief. Little wonder Satan hates the book of Revelation and prevents so many from preaching its message!

V. THE RESURRECTION OF SINNERS (20:11-15)

> *And I saw a great white throne, and Him that sat on it, from whose face the earth and the heaven fled away; and there was found no place for them. And I saw the dead, small and great, stand before God; and the books were opened: and another book was opened, which is the book of life: and the dead were judged out of those things which were written in the books, according to their works. And the sea gave up the dead which were in it; and death and hell delivered up the dead which were in them: and they were judged every man according to their works. And death and hell were cast into the lake of fire. This is the second death. And whosoever was not found written in the book of life was cast into the lake of fire (20:11-15).*

These verses are among the most solemn in the Bible. They tell us of that dread and final assize called the *"great white throne"* judgment. The judicial benches of this world pale into insignificance when placed alongside the staggering scene of this throne and the judgment which issues from it. In our chapter on Revelation 4, we noted that the book commences with a throne (1:4), and concludes with a throne (22:3). Thrones often speak of judgment, and this is precisely the purpose of the throne in the verses we are now to study.

It is called a *"great"* throne. The sinners who stand before it have rejected a *"great* salvation" (Hebrews 2:3), and now they must stand before a great Judge to listen to their final sentence. How different from the rainbow-encircled throne in Revelation 4! Great is the occasion on which this throne appears.

It is called a *"white"* throne. Everything connected with this throne will be right. The judgment will be in righteousness (Psalm 9:7-8; Romans 2:5). The treatment the unsaved receive will be just and fair, unlike the treatment our Lord received in Pilate's court. The greatness and the whiteness, then, are suggestive of power and purity.

"Him that sat on it" is the eternal God and only perfect Judge. Is He the Father, the Son, or the Holy Spirit? It would seem from John 5:22; Acts 17:31; and Romans 2:16 that Christ Himself will be the Judge. It is He who opens the seals (Revelation 6:1) and who "treadeth the winepress of the fierceness and wrath of Almighty God" (19:15). No one is better qualified than He for this task. Having done all that could be done to save man, He is the One whom those who rejected Him must now face as their Judge.

"From whose face the earth and the heaven fled away; and there was found no place for them." The awesomeness of this throne and the One who is seated upon it are so great that even the earth and the heaven flee. This might well be the day described in 2 Peter 3:10-12. This does not imply the annihilation of the very elements which make up the earth and the heaven. We have a similar expression in Isaiah 34:4; 51:6; and Daniel 2:35. In Revelation 6:12-17 we have a reiteration of our Lord's statement in Matthew 24:29. The removal of a person or thing does not imply extinction. To pass away does not mean to cease to be. Our Lord spoke about heaven and earth passing away in Matthew 5:18; 24:34-35; but He did not necessarily mean their annihilation. In the last two chapters of Revelation nations are seen inhabiting the earth (21:24; 22:2), so the earth does not cease to be. I do not know all that is involved in the phrase *"the earth and the heaven fled away."* But in that day all mystery will have cleared away and we shall know.

And I saw the dead, small and great, stand before God. . . . And the sea gave up the dead which were in it; and death and hell delivered up the dead which were in them (20:12).

These are the judged, "the rest of the dead" mentioned in verse 5. There are no saved among them. They are the wicked dead raised to appear at the last judgment. They are classified as the "small" and the "great," but they are all lost, having never turned to God for salvation. Their bodies are brought forth from every depository that holds their dust. Whether the remains of the wicked dead are in the sea or in the earth, God will see to it that they are raised. Big sinners and little sinners, criminals known and unknown, rich and poor, rulers and subjects, the learned and the ignorant, the employers and the employees, all stand before the "great white throne." All ranks and degrees of unsaved sinners will be there.

"Death," that is, the graves of earth which hold the bodies, and "hell" (hades), that is, the abode of the soul and spirit, yield their victims. The resurrection of the wicked dead will be a literal bodily resurrection which necessitates the spirit and soul returning to the body. It is clear that "death" and "hades" are distinct places, each having custody of some part of man between death and resurrection. They are the enemies of man for which Satan must bear full responsibility. And now, just before the eternal state, John sees in the vision that *"death and hell were cast into the lake of fire"* (20:14). "Then shall be brought to pass the saying that is written, Death is swallowed up in victory" (1 Corinthians 15:54; cf. Isaiah 25:8; Hebrews 2:14). "The last enemy that shall be destroyed is death" (1 Corinthians 15:26).

And the books were opened: and another book was opened, which is the book of life: and the dead were judged out of those things which were written in the books, according to their works (20:12).

This verse speaks of "books" (plural) and "the book of life." The "books" contain the record of the unbeliever's works. "The book of life" has in it the names of all who will be saved. But these who come forth in the second resurrection at the close of the millennium will have had their names blotted out from "the book of life." Nothing is said here as to the exact content of the "books," nor need we speculate as to what is written in these books beyond what is here stated in God's Word. The words, *"according to their works"* (verses 12-13) suggest the possibility of the "books" having in them God's record of the sinner's deeds. These "books" will contain the evidence to show just cause why those who come forth in the second resurrection are not written in the book of life. Precise and indisputable records will be available as evidence to prove the sinner worthy of hell. God keeps books, and His books are accurate, so that no one at His bar of justice will be able to find fault with the final decision He makes.

These "books" are not for the purpose of determining who is to go to hell. That matter was settled and sealed by each sinner for himself, and finalized at his death. The purpose of the "books" and the sentence pronounced upon the wicked is to determine the various degrees of punishment in the lake of fire. All unsaved must go to the lake of fire and suffer the second death, but not all will suffer the same degree of punishment. Some will be beaten with many stripes; others, with few (Luke 12:47-48). It will be more tolerable for some than for others (Matthew 11:22-24). If man can invent machines and electronic computers to detect whether a person is lying or telling the truth, and to record an accurate account of men's actions and whereabouts, surely God will have no problem in doing the same. Whoever you are, your biography is written in God's books.

It is but wishful thinking on the part of the unbeliever who says there is no resurrection. Recently I read about a remarkable discovery. A vase, closely sealed, was found in a mummy pit in Egypt. In it were a few peas, old, wrinkled, and hard as stone. The peas were removed from the vase and planted carefully under a glass. At the end of thirty days they sprang into life after having lain dormant in the dust of the tomb for almost 3,000 years. Here is a faint illustration of the mortal body which shall put on immortality, the redeemed to eternal life, and the unsaved to eternal conscious torment.

And whosover was not found written in the book of life was cast into the lake of fire (20:15).

There are those who argue that the language here is merely figurative and that a place is not even suggested in these words. I believe that such reasoning is the devil's lie. The lake of fire must be a locality, for when human beings are raised from the dead, they cannot be nowhere, neither everywhere, but they must be somewhere. Thus the lake of fire is local, circumscribed. Exactly where it is, I have never found distinctly stated in Scripture. We know it is a place of punishment and of divine origin, with God Himself inflicting the punishment (Luke 12:5; Hebrews 10:27,30,31; 12:29). It is eternal in duration, for there the fire is not quenched (Matthew 25:46; Mark 9:44). The punishment is painful in character, for their worm dieth not (Mark 9:44,48). All of this is supported by the fact that the beast and the false prophet are cast into the lake of fire at the beginning of the thousand years reign of Christ (19:20), and they are still there when Satan is cast in after his final rebellion (20:10). There is much about the lake of fire I do not know, and I am trusting God's Word and Christ's finished work that I shall never find out.

As I write these words, I am encouraged only by the fact that there are millions of redeemed persons who will spend eternity in Heaven. I would like to believe that there is no such place as the "lake of fire," but the Bible depicts it clearly and Christ spoke of it often. I can only plead with you to call upon the Saviour now and receive Him, for He has said, "Him that cometh to Me I will in no wise cast out" (John 6:37).

THE ETERNAL STATE

Revelation 21 and 22

The book of the Revelation has traced the history of the Church, Israel, and the Gentile nations through our present age and right on to the end of the millennium. The scenes before us in these last two chapters are postmillennial. Satan and the wicked angels have been judged, and they, along with all the wicked of the human race, have been cast into the lake of fire. The bitter conflict between good and evil is past. John is now given a vision of the eternal state. From here on all is new.

I. THE PASSING OF THE OLD ORDER (21:1)

> *And I saw a new heaven and a new earth: for the first heaven and the first earth were passed away; and there was no more sea* (21:1).

John states merely that the first heaven and the first earth are passed away. He gives no details as to how or to what extent this takes place. For details we must examine other Scriptures.

First, the apostle was given to see *"a new heaven . . . for the first heaven . . . passed away."* Both the Bible and science agree that there are three heavens: the atmospheric heaven immediately surrounding our earth where the birds fly; the planetary or stellar heavens where the sun, moon, and stars are; the third heaven, or the Heaven of heavens, the abode of God. The latter of these, designated "the third heaven," is the place where the spirits of the saints go at death (2 Corinthians 12:2). The Bible says nothing of a "seventh heaven." Now the heaven that is purged, or "passed away" is the heaven that became defiled because of Satan and his wickedness. This is the atmospheric heaven surrounding our earth, the domain of Satan (Ephesians 2:1-2; 6:12). We know that nothing that defiles has entered God's dwelling place.

The writer continues, *"the first earth . . . passed away."* Now keep in mind that the purpose for the passing of this present order is that it should be replaced with a new order, *"a new heaven and a new earth."* A big question that is raised is how heaven and earth will be replaced. The two possibilities are by annihilation or renovation. I accept the latter view. A new heaven and a new earth do not necessarily indicate another heaven and another earth. It is not likely that the present heaven and earth will become extinct.

We know that since the fall of Lucifer and the subsequent fall of our first parents, the earth has been under a curse (Genesis 3:17), and "the heavens are not clean in His [God's] sight" (Job 15:15). After Satan and wicked angels and wicked men, who by their persistent evil have corrupted this earth, have been cast into the lake of fire, then God will thoroughly purge away all that has become defiled by them. While matter in itself is not inherently evil, we do know that just as Canaan was defiled by the abominations of its inhabitants (Leviticus 18:25-27), even so "the earth is polluted under the inhabitants thereof" (Isaiah 24:5).

We know that this future purging of the heaven and earth will be by fire. A former renovation of the earth was performed by God with water, after which God made a covenant with Noah that He would not again judge the earth with water (Genesis 9:11-17). However, there is abundant evidence in the Bible that it will be purged by fire. The Apostle Peter wrote, "Whereby the world that then was, being overflowed with water, perished" (2 Peter 3:6). The word "perished" here does not suggest annihilation. We know that the world of Noah's day did not become extinct; it did not cease to exist. It did not lose its being, but rather its well-being. This latter thought, namely, the loss of well-being, is the whole idea in the word "perish" when it is used in relation to man in John 3:16 and in 2 Peter 3:9. The unsaved man who is said to "perish" does not cease to be, but he does lose his well-being. In much the same way the present heaven and earth will be judged with fire.

Peter continues, "But the heavens and the earth, which are now, by the same word are kept in store, reserved unto fire against the day of judgment and perdition of ungodly men. . . . But the day of the Lord will come as a thief in the night; in the which the heavens shall pass away with a great noise, and the elements shall melt with fervent heat, the earth also and the works that are therein shall be burned up" (2 Peter 3:7,10). There is an analogy between verses 6 and 7. The earth will not be annihilated, but renewed, regenerated. When the believing sinner is regenerated (Titus 3:5), he becomes a "new creation" (2 Corinthians 5:17). While old things are said to have "passed away," the old nature is not eradicated, that is, the "old man" does not cease to exist. Jesus told His disciples that the earth would be regenerated (Matthew 19:28), and John sees the old things "passed away." The Psalmist wrote, "Of old hast Thou laid the foundation of the earth: and the heavens are the work of Thy hands. They shall perish, but Thou shalt endure: yea, all of them shall wax old like a garment; as a vesture shalt Thou change them, and they shall be changed" (Psalm 102:25-26 cf. Hebrews 1:10-12).

There was a time, not long ago, when men scoffed at such an idea, and ministers and theologians spiritualized those Scripture passages which spoke of a coming judgment of fire to the earth. But fewer intelligent people would scoff at this teaching today. The discovery and development of the atom bomb have frightened most critics into silence. Then, too, the very structure of our earth has a tremendous potential in this area. We humans live on the outer crust of a planet, 25,000 miles in circumference and 8,000 miles in diameter, whose heart is molten heat. Inside there is a seething, boiling liquid lake of fire. When these elements get too near the surface, and pressure builds up, a piece of crust blows off. This we call a volcanic eruption. Our earth is a giant bomb.

Our Lord taught a coming fiery judgment upon the earth. He reminded His hearers of judgment by fire which fell upon Sodom and Gomorrah (Genesis 19:23-24), saying, "But the same day that Lot went out of Sodom it rained fire and brimstone from heaven, and destroyed them all. Even thus shall it be in the day when the Son of man is revealed" (Luke 17:29-30). And if anyone is wondering why God does not send the sparks now that will ignite the earth, let me remind you that it is His long-suffering, for He is "not willing that any should perish, but that all should come to repentance" (2 Peter 3:9).

This idea of a new heaven and a new earth is not confined to the New Testament. God foretold these things to Israel, saying, "For, behold, I create new heavens and a new earth: and the former shall not be remembered, nor come into mind" (Isaiah 65:17). "For as the new heavens and the new earth, which I will make, shall remain before Me, saith the Lord, so shall your seed and your name remain" (Isaiah 66:22). Now I am not insisting that these passages in Isaiah have exactly the same significance and that they must be interpreted precisely the same as Revelation 21:1. Isaiah might be speaking of a moral newness to prevail during the millennium when heaven and earth will be rid of Satan and his evil influence, a period when righteousness will *reign* in contrast to the eternal state wherein righteousness will *dwell* (2 Peter 3:13). We do know that the eternal state follows immediately after the millennium, and that it is not impossible that the one grows out of the other. The idea is one of transition, not extinction.

II. THE PRESENTATION OF THE NEW ORDER (21:2)

And I John saw the holy city, new Jerusalem, coming down from God out of heaven, prepared as a bride adorned for her husband (21:2).

There are two Jerusalems, one earthly and the other heavenly (Galatians 4:25-26; Hebrews 12:22). It is in the earthly Jerusalem that Christ establishes His throne during His one thousand years reign. The Jerusalem in the eternal state is not the city of Jerusalem we know today. It is possibly that place which our Lord has gone to prepare for His own (John 14:3).

It is called the *"holy city"* and is described *"as a bride adorned for her husband."* In verses 9 and 10, where the angel tells John that we will show him *"the bride, the Lamb's wife"* (verse 9), that promise is fulfilled by the angel showing him *"that great city, the holy Jerusalem, descending out of heaven from God"* (verse 10). There are those who teach that the New Jerusalem is not an actual city, but that it is merely a symbol teaching us something about the eternal relationship of the Church. I believe that this is a real city in which the Bridegroom shall dwell with His perfected Bride. Both the measurements (verses 15-17) and the materials (verses 18-21) indicate a literal city. Men build cities out of concrete and steel and wood. But Christ is the Builder of this city, and He has everything at His command to build a mansion. While I am not going to attempt a detailed explanation of each item of which the New Jerusalem is made, I will mention the fact that everything in this "holy city" expresses the many-sided glories of God. It is His glory that gives light to it; thus John speaks twice of *"the glory of God"* (verses 11,23).

From the viewpoint of the people in it, the New Jerusalem is *"the Lamb's wife."* From the standpoint of the place, it is an actual city. But the people cannot be disassociated from the place. The size of a city is not determined by square miles only, but by its population. A city is usually described and designated by the character of its people. If the inhabitants are wicked, the place is known as a wicked city.

"No more sea." I take this to be literal. Three-quarters of our globe at present is occupied by seas. A feature of the new earth is the complete absence of the seas. It seems to us now that the seas are necessary to our existence and essential to animal and vegetable life. But they will not be needed in the eternal state. It is difficult for us to conceive the conditions of life in an immensely expanded land surface without sea, so we must wait until the time comes when we shall see and know even as we are known. John was given a vision of it and told to write what he saw. One day we too shall see the new heaven and the new earth, but we shall never see an ocean again. God created the sea (Exodus 20:11; Revelation 10:6), and so He will dispense with it when He is pleased to do so. Presently the seas serve as a boundary and a barrier, limiting communication among na-

tions. But in the final restoration, the sea disappears forever. There will be no need for the process of evaporation, distillation, and condensation. We may learn from all of this that the climate and living conditions will be changed in the eternal state.

III. THE PRESENCE OF GOD IN THE NEW ORDER (21:3-7)

And I heard a great voice out of heaven saying, Behold, the tabernacle of God is with men, and He will dwell with them, and they shall be His people, and God Himself shall be with them, and be their God. And God shall wipe away all tears from their eyes; and there shall be no more death, neither sorrow, nor crying, neither shall there be any more pain: for the former things are passed away. And He that sat upon the throne said, Behold, I make all things new. And He said unto me, Write: for these words are true and faithful. And He said unto me, It is done. I am Alpha and Omega, the beginning and the end. I will give unto him that is athirst of the fountain of the water of life freely. He that overcometh shall inherit all things; and I will be his God, and he shall be My son (21:3-7).

The provision in the eternal state rests with the Lord Jesus Christ. The Bride's sufficiency will be in the Bridegroom. We are assured that in Him we shall be well provided for. We see Him in several descriptive phrases in these verses.

"The tabernacle of God is with men." The ancient tabernacle in the wilderness represented God's presence and glory in the midst of Israel (Leviticus 26:11-12; Ezekiel 37:17). All of the rich meaning symbolized in the tabernacle of Israel was fulfilled in Jesus Christ. The word translated "tabernacle" is *skene,* which literally means "the place where God dwells." This means that God will make His tabernacle with His saints forever and ever; He will give His presence to them forever and ever. "Behold the tabernacle [*skene*] of God is with men, and He will tabernacle [*skenosei*] with them." At once it becomes clear why He did not say that the *temple* of God is with men. In the eternal state we will not be engaged with a temple made with men's hands (see Acts 17:24), but with God Himself. Not even

the gorgeous and elaborate temple which Solomon built could contain Him (2 Chronicles 6:18).

God chose to tabernacle among men on one other occasion, but it was merely for the brief span of thirty-three years (John 1:1,14). John sees Him, in the Patmos vision, dwelling in a body with His Church throughout eternity. Jesus Christ, the second Person of the Holy Trinity, is the only member of the Trinity who dwelled in His own body prepared especially for Him (Hebrews 10:5). Christ is the unique Man of the ages, the only man who is God. He is the God-Man. For this reason, I believe He will be the only Person in the Trinity whom we shall see with our eyes in that day. God is in His children now in the Person of the Holy Spirit (John 14:17; 1 Corinthians 3:16; 6:19-20), but He is not visible. We cannot see Him with our eyes. He walked with Adam in the garden as He walks with us today. He appeared to the patriarchs of Israel as He appears to us today. But in the eternal state we shall behold Him in His glorified body in the Person of Jesus Christ. Peter, James, and John caught a glimpse of His deity when He was transfigured before them on the holy mount, but we shall behold Him in the full display of His glory throughout eternity. This is no mere figure of speech, but a coming glorious reality.

We see further evidence in these closing chapters that Christ will be the central figure in the eternal state. He said to John, *"I am Alpha and Omega, the beginning and the end"* (21:6). At the commencement of our study we came upon this claim made by Christ (1:8; see also 22:13). This is the same claim of deity made to ancient Israel when He said, "Thus saith the LORD the King of Israel, and his redeemer the LORD of hosts; I am the first, and I am the last; and beside Me there is no God" (Isaiah 44:6).

What did Jesus mean when He said, "I am Alpha and Omega"? *Alpha* is the first letter of the Greek alphabet and *Omega* is the last letter. Christ is the beginning and the end. He is the beginning, not merely first in point of time, but the source and origin of all things. All things have their beginning through Him (John 1:1-3; Colossians 1:16; Hebrews 1:1-2). He is the end, not merely in point of time, but the goal, the consummation, the One through whom all things reach their grand climax. "For of Him, and through Him, and to Him, are all things: to whom be glory for ever. Amen" (Romans 11:36). Christ is the A to Z in wisdom, power, and glory. He only can say, *"It is done"* (16:17; 21:6). Nothing that He has anything to do with can end in failure.

That He is the Divine Presence in the new order is further attested by other identifying terms. It is He who offers the *"water of life"* (21:6 cf. John 4:13-14; 7:37). He is the "Lamb" (21:9,23,27; 22:1,3,4). It is Christ who is coming again (22:7,12,20). And finally, He says *"I Jesus have sent mine angel to testify unto you these things in the churches. I am the root and the offspring of David, and the bright and morning star"* (22:16).

IV. THE PERFECTION OF THE NEW ORDER
   (21:1,4,22-27; 22:5)

The eternal state will be a perfect order. Its perfection is due to the fact that all which is imperfect is banished.

> *And there shall in no wise enter into it any thing that defileth, neither whatsoever worketh abomination, or maketh a lie: but they which are written in the Lamb's book of life* (21:27).

No wicked person or evil thing will be permitted to enter the portals of the New Jerusalem. The gates to the city will remain open at all times (21:25), so it is obvious that they are not for protection. The Lord Himself will see to its protection. And right here I must remind the sinner who has rejected Christ that, unless he repents and receives the Lord Jesus Christ, he will be barred from the city of God.

The perfection of our eternal home is depicted in a list of those things which are missing. I have called these the "no mores." Leon Zucker used to say that the book of Romans is the book of the "much mores" (see Romans 5:9,10,15,17,20; 9:22; 11:12,24), and that the book of the Revelation is the book of the "no mores." There are not less than ten "no mores" in this book.

No more sea (21:1). While there is no inherent evil in the sea, these huge bodies of water have proved to be man's enemy. They have created a barrier between nations and have claimed the lives of untold thousands, all of whom will be raised (20:13). (See paragraph above on *"no more sea."*)

No more death (21:4). Death was caused by sin (Genesis 2:16-17; Romans 5:12; James 1:15), and it is man's worst enemy, his last enemy to be destroyed (1 Corinthians 15:26). We cannot face a day in which we hope to escape seeing the undertaker's place of business, the hearse, the funeral procession, the cemetery, the obituary column. On every hand we see death. And if our Lord Jesus does not come in our lifetime, we ourselves are waiting, not knowing what year, or month, or day, or hour we shall leave this life by means of death. But in the eternal state death shall be no more. Then the desire of the prophets and the promise of God to them will be fulfilled, for Isaiah wrote, "He will swallow [hath swallowed] up death in victory [for ever]; and the Lord GOD will wipe away tears from off all faces; and the rebuke of His people shall He take away from off all the earth: for the LORD hath spoken it" (Isaiah 25:8). Thank God, in "that city foursquare" there will be no more sad farewells caused by death.

No more sorrow (21:4). In the more than thirty passages in the New Testament where the words "sorrow" and "sorrowful" are found, there is the idea of grief, pain, distress and travail. No matter what path of life we choose, we cannot escape sorrow. Like a shadow, it follows rich and poor alike. The word translated "sorrow" in 21:4 is the same word translated "wailing" (mourning) in 18:15). Many souls are in mourning, in heaviness of heart, but, thank God, there is a boundary where sorrow cannot cross, for in the eternal state it is forever banished.

No more crying (21:4). *"God shall wipe away all tears from their eyes."* The Bible speaks often of those who cry. Jesus told His disciples that they would weep. We read of weeping saints

(John 16:20-22); weeping soul-winners (Psalm 126:5-6; Acts 20:31); weeping sinners (Matthew 22:11-14); weeping sorrowers (Luke 7:12-15; John 20:11-15); weeping servants (Acts 20:19), and the weeping Saviour (John 11:35; Luke 19:41). Not all tears are justified. I don't believe that God has any respect for the tears of self-pity which are shed merely to draw attention to ourselves. But the tears of many a saint have flowed for a worthy cause. Jeremiah felt the burden of a good cause when he said, "Oh that my head were waters, and mine eyes a fountain of tears, that I might weep day and night for the slain of the daughter of my people!" (Jeremiah 9:1) It is good for us when we weep over our own sins and the sins of others. But soon our crying will be over. "Weeping may endure for a night, but joy cometh in the morning" (Psalm 30:5).

No more pain. Until this writing I have known little pain, for which I am thankful. And I shall be deeply grateful if God spares me from pain in the years ahead. But in my twenty-five years as a pastor I have witnessed hundreds of persons suffering with the racking torments to which these mortal bodies are subjected. Thank God the saints can look ahead to a time and place when those things which cause human anguish and misery will be no more.

> *And I saw no temple therein: for the Lord God Almighty and the Lamb are the temple of it* (21:22).

No temple. The tabernacle in the wilderness and the temple in Jerusalem served a purpose in their day. And the temples men build in our day are not all without value. But no temple will be needed in this city. Earthly temples are supposed to symbolize the presence of God, but in God's Holy City, the Lord Jesus Christ, who is the image of the invisible God, is the Temple. In Christ dwells all the fulness of the Godhead (Colossians 1:19; 2:9), therefore there will be no need for signs, symbols, sacraments, and systems. Buildings and liturgy do not make a church, nor do they prove that God is there. But in God's city His presence will be continually there.

> *And the city had no need of the sun, neither of the moon, to shine in it: for the glory of God did lighten it, and the*

> *Lamb is the light thereof. . . . And there shall be no night
> there; and they need no candle, neither light of the sun; for
> the Lord God giveth them light: and they shall reign for ever
> and ever* (21:23; 22:5).

No sun . . . no moon . . . no night. In that city which
Christ has prepared for His own there will be no created light,
simply because Christ Himself, who is the uncreated Light
(John 8:12), will be there. Then shall be fulfilled the ancient
prophecy which says, "The sun shall be no more thy light by
day; neither for brightness shall the moon give light unto thee:
but the LORD shall be unto thee an everlasting light, and thy God
thy glory" (Isaiah 60:19). The created lights of God and of
men are as darkness when compared with our blessed Lord. The
light He diffuses throughout eternity is the unclouded, un-
dimmed glory of His own holy Presence. In consequence of the
fulness of that Light, there shall be no night. Think of it! No
darkness forever!

> *And the nations of them which are saved shall walk in the
> light of it: and the kings of the earth do bring their glory
> and honour into it* (21:24).

As the New Jerusalem is suspended over the earth, the nations on the earth will receive the benefit and blessing of the
divine effulgence. By this holy Light the nations shall walk. It
is the Light of life, truth, holiness, and righteousness. The world
today is not seeing that Light as it should (Matthew 5:16), but
in that day all nations shall walk in it.

> *And there shall be no more curse* (22:3).

No more curse. This is another consequence flowing out of a
perfect state, for there shall be nothing in the holy city to re-
quire the curse of God. The first Paradise was perfect until sin
entered it. But after man had yielded to Satan, God said,
"Cursed is the ground for thy sake; in sorrow shalt thou eat of
it all the days of thy life" (Genesis 3:17). The idea of God's
cursing a thing always grows out of man's obstinacy in refusing
to obey the divine will. This is why the earth on which we live
bears the scars of sin. But in the New Jerusalem every restraint

will be placed upon evil so that sin and its subsequent curse cannot enter. In the first Paradise the wicked Cain was cursed (Genesis 4:11) as were all who subsequently broke God's Law (Galatians 3:10). In the heavenly city the curse will be done away because no accursed thing will be there.

V. THE PORTION OF THE UNSAVED (21:8)

The perfection of the eternal state of the saved is further assured by one final reminder that the wicked of this earth will not be there. The unsaved will be conscious in an eternal state, but in an entirely different location and condition from that of the saved. The saved will live eternally in the place "prepared" for them by Christ (John 14:3), while the unsaved will live eternally in a placed "prepared" for the devil and his angels (Matthew 25:41).

The Apostle John continues:

> *But the fearful, and unbelieving, and the abominable, and murderers, and whoremongers, and sorcerers, and idolaters, and all liars, shall have their part in the lake which burneth with fire and brimstone: which is the second death* (21:8).

The first feature of this passage is that the creation of new heavens and a new earth does not affect or alter the condition of the lake of fire and those who will be in it. The doom of sinful man is fixed for eternity. They are here described as:

"The fearful." These are the cowards who would not confess Christ for fear of the reproach of men. William Barclay says that the Authorized Version gives a wrong impression when it translates the word *deilos* by the word "fearful." It is not fear that is condemned. The highest courage is to be desperately afraid and in spite of that fear to do the right thing, and to hold fast to loyalty. What is condemned is the cowardice which denies Christ for safety's sake. Because they refused to own and confess Christ, they must at that day be denied by Christ (Matthew 10:32-33; Romans 10:9). How true is the proverb, "The fear of man bringeth a snare" (Proverbs 29:25). It is better to

fear God and the consequences of sin and ally one's self with Christ and His cause.

"And unbelieving." Behold the awful fate of them who will not trust God and His Word, who declare that His Truth is not worthy of their confidence. To resent those who do not trust us is a normal reaction. How much more is God justified in punishing them who reject in unbelief the merits of His crucified Son. "He that believeth on Him is not condemned: but he that believeth not is condemned already, because he hath not believed in the name of the only begotten Son of God" (John 3:18). Jesus said that the Holy Spirit would reprove the world "of sin, because they believe not on Me" (John 16:8-9).

"And the abominable." These are the *polluted,* those who have allowed themselves to become stained and contaminated with the filthy evils of this world. If only men would realize that when they debase themselves with the uncleanness and abominations of this present evil world, they are heaping upon themselves a fiery judgment for eternity. Let each reader pause here and examine carefully Romans 1:14-32 and Genesis 19.

"And murderers." Ever since Cain murdered Abel (Genesis 4:8), there has been a growing disregard for human life. Men kill without the faintest flicker of fear or conscience. The taking of human life is a growing menace throughout the world. Even though the murderer be caught and tried and made to pay with his life, let him be reminded that unless he repents and turns to Christ, there is another sentence beyond the death of the body.

"And whoremongers." These are *fornicators* who regarded lightly the ruin of virtue. Sexual promiscuity is sanctioned widely in our day. But God's law still stands which says, "Thou shalt not commit adultery" (Exodus 20:14). "Marriage is honourable in all, and the bed undefiled: but whoremongers and adulterers God will judge" (Hebrews 13:4). Our modern society sanctions fornication, but all fornicators God will judge.

"And sorcerers." Witchcraft, spiritism, magic, and demon worship were the stock in trade of the ancient world. The Christians in the early Church were confronted with this evil constantly. It thrived in cities like Ephesus (Acts 19:19-24). Under the Mosaic law such practices were punishable by death

(Deuteronomy 18:10-12). In our modern twentieth century the number of adherents to spiritism in its various forms is increasing rapidly. But the lake of fire is the divinely appointed doom for all who traffic in this evil. Idolatry and witchcraft are listed among "the works of the flesh," and of all persons who practice such it is written that "they shall not inherit the kingdom of God" (Galatians 5:20-21).

"And idolaters." There are those who worship idols and false gods, an evil practice prohibited by God (Exodus 20:1-5). But in the broadest and strictest sense of the word, idolatry is the giving of the heart to covetousness and selfishness, equally forbidden by God (Exodus 20:17; Proverbs 28:16; Ephesians 5:3,5; Colossians 3:5).

"And all liars." Satan was the first liar, therefore he is the father of lies (John 8:44). The *liars* are those who are guilty of falsehood, either in speech or in silence. God condemns all who make a lie, speak a lie, or act out a lie.

All these classes are to spend eternity *"in the lake which burneth with fire and brimstone: which is the second death"* (21:8). The devil, the beast, and the false prophet have already experienced their doom in this place, where they "shall be tormented day and night for ever and ever" (20:10). And now men learn that they too must suffer the same judgment. They cannot enter the new order of the redeemed lest they sow the seeds of wickedness that would defile the new heavens and the new earth. How solemn is this statement of finality! Let it settle all doubt in the mind of every unbeliever as to the eternal doom of all who reject Jesus Christ.

Their doom is called *"the second death."* This means literally *the second kind of death.* The Bible speaks of two kinds of death, physical and spiritual. Death in either instance means separation. Physical death is the separation of the spiritual part of man from his body. This is the first (or first kind of) death. Spiritual death is the separation of the whole man from God. This is the second (or second kind of) death. Paul wrote about the first death (2 Corinthians 5:8; Philippians 1:23), and also the second kind of death (Ephesians 2:1; 4:18). The second death is the final banishment from God of all who refused to be reconciled to Him through faith in the death of His Son. They shall suffer in the fire which shall never be exhausted and where there is consciousness and activity of spirit (Luke 16:19-31; Revelation 6:9-11).

While we cannot identify the exact location of the lake of fire, we know that it is local and circumscribed. It is some-place. And we know that it is eternal separation from God.

VI. THE PROVISION OF THE NEW ORDER (22:1-2)

First, there is the:

Water of life, clear as crystal, proceeding out of the throne of God and of the Lamb (22:1).

Ezekiel saw healing waters proceed from the altar in the temple, the place of *sacrifice* (Ezekiel 47:1), but in the new order it issues forth from the throne, the place of *sovereignty,* for in that day there will be no need for a sacrifice.

In the first Eden there was a river which divided into four branch rivers (Genesis 2:10). In the new Jerusalem God's throne is the spring and source of the water of life. It is not uncommon to hear of a shortage of water in large cities, but in the eternal city there shall be no lack of this commodity. A city without water would be a most disconsolate place.

It is interesting, and even amusing at times, to read what some interpreters say about this "water of life." The water has been interpreted to mean nations (based on 17:15), the Holy Spirit, baptism, the cleansing influence by which the nations are to be kept pure. But why cannot we simply accept it for what the Word itself says? This river is part of a literal city, a heavenly city to be occupied by a heavenly people. Therefore its waters are literal waters, of a nature corresponding to that of the city of which it is a part. This could well be the city of the Psalmist's song (Psalm 46:4). The life which this water symbolizes and sustains is divine life, and it is for the people of God. Someone has asked whether or not we will need water in eternity. I don't know! But we will have access to it. Did Jesus need food after His resurrection? I don't know!

But He ate it. I find no occasion to spiritualize and symbolize this river.

Then, John saw:

> *The tree of life, which bare twelve manner of fruits, and yielded her fruit every month: and the leaves of the trees were for the healing of the nations* (22:2).

The tree of life, once in the garden of Eden, now flourishes in the streets of the New Jerusalem. This tree provided eternal life for the body. If you ask whether or not glorified saints will have need of food, I can only answer now that it will be available to us if we want it. Access to the tree of life was promised to the overcomers (2:7). We are not told whether the fruit will be a necessity or a luxury, but it will be there nevertheless. And there will be variety, a different fruit for each month of the year.

> *And the leaves of the tree were for the healing of the nations.*

No further details are given to explain this statement. Some take it to mean that the leaves have in them some medicinal value which, when applied, serves as a preventive from sicknesses and ailments. Others believe that the bodies of the earth dwellers will need renewing from time to time. This is a difficult passage, and I prefer to leave it for the present.

VII. THE PROMISE OF CHRIST'S COMING (22:7,12,20)

As this book comes to a close, our Lord assures His Church that He is coming again. *"Behold, I come quickly"* (22:7,12). *"Surely I come quickly. Amen"* (22:20). The book opened with the words, "Behold, He cometh" (1:7), and it concludes with Christ's promise that He will surely come. "The Spirit and the bride say, Come" (22:17), that is, the Church indwelt by the Holy Spirit is longing for His return. When His Church is dwelling in Him, "A glorious church, not having spot, or wrinkle . . . but . . . holy and without blemish" (Ephesians

5:27), then He shall be satisfied. And not until He appears will the Church be fully satisfied.

The word "quickly" means speedily, rapidly. When our Lord comes for His own it will be with lightning-like speed, "In a moment, in the twinkling of an eye" (1 Corinthians 15:52). His appearing will be with such suddenness that it will catch unawares all who are unprepared. In this connection observe verse 11, "He that is unjust, let him be unjust still: and he which is filthy, let him be filthy still: and he that is righteous, let him be righteous still: and he that is holy, let him be holy still." Here we are confronted with the awful fact that a man's character becomes fixed and unchanging at death. The unjust and filthy will always be unjust and filthy, and the righteous and holy will always be righteous and holy. Here is a challenge to be ready for His Coming.

These last three promises of Christ's return are connected with our responsibility to obey the Word (22:7), with our stewardship and reward (22:12), and with our comfort and consolation (22:20). What a difference there would be in our individual lives, in our homes, and in our churches if we held these facts before us daily!

VIII. THE PERMANENCE OF THIS BOOK (22:18-19)

> *For I testify unto every man that heareth the words of the prophecy of this book, If any man shall add unto these things, God shall add unto him the plagues that are written in this book: And if any man shall take away from the words of the book of this prophecy, God shall take away his part out of the book of life, and out of the holy city, and from the things which are written in this book* (22:18-19).

Here we see the inviolability of the things recorded in this book. As there is a special blessing promised to all who read and heed the message of this book, so there is a pronouncement of woe upon all who detract from, or add to, those things which God has written in this book. So important is the message in the Revelation that God solemnly warns every man not to tamper with its contents. He will not tolerate any attempt on man's part at forgery. The warning is stern and the penalty severe. Let the corrupters of these prophecies beware.

There are similar warnings in other parts of the Bible. God had said, "Ye shall not add unto the word which I command you, neither shall ye diminish ought from it, that ye may keep the commandments of the LORD your God which I command you" (Deuteronomy 4:2). "Every word of God is pure: He is a shield unto them that put their trust in Him. Add thou not unto His words, lest He reprove thee, and thou be found a liar" (Proverbs 30:5-6). "But though we, or an angel from heaven, preach any other gospel unto you than that which we have preached unto you, let him be accursed. As we said before, so say I now again, If any man preach any other gospel unto you, than that ye have received, let him be accursed" (Galatians 1:8-9). In the days of Moses, Solomon, Paul, and John, such warnings from God were quite apropos inasmuch as all books were hand-copied by scribes. This would be particularly the case with the Septuagint, the Greek version of the Hebrew Bible copied by seventy Jewish scholars. It would be very easy for a scribe to make an omission or an addition or to alter a phrase or even a word.

But this warning must apply to men of our day as well. Modern scholars who reject the plenary inspiration of the Holy Scriptures, and who abridge and add, suppress and stultify the Word of God to satisfy their own minds, will do well to heed Christ's warning. Men like R. H. Charles brush aside this warning by saying that it is perfectly possible that this warning is not a part of the original book at all. But by what right or authority do men cast such wicked aspersions? As I read our Lord's warning, I feel somewhat like Dr. Seiss must have felt when he wrote: "If I have read into this book anything which Christ has not put there, or read out of it anything which He has put there, with the profoundest sorrow would I recant, and willingly burn up the books in which such mischievous wickedness is contained. If I err, God forgive me! If I am right, God bless my feeble testimony! In either case, God speed His everlasting truth!"

IX. THE POSTLUDE (22:20-21)

John's last words, written by divine inspiration, are a fitting climax to the Revelation.

Even so, come, Lord Jesus (22:20).

That for which the suffering servant of Christ looked and hoped and expected was never realized before he died. But he did know the blessed reality of Christ's promise to another suffering servant of His, namely, our Lord's words to Paul, "My grace is sufficient for thee" (2 Corinthians 12:9). And so John closes the masterpiece of prophecy with the words:

The grace of our Lord Jesus Christ be with you all. Amen (22:21).

The final message to the Church is that our Lord will come back again. And until He appears for His own, His infinite and inexhaustible grace reaches out to sustain us. But while we wait, let us watch and work, "That, when He shall appear, we may have confidence, and not be ashamed before Him at His coming" (1 John 2:28).

BIBLIOGRAPHY

AINSLIE, EDGAR. *The Dawn of the Scarlet Age*

BARCLAY, WILLIAM. *Letters to the Seven Churches*

BARCLAY, WILLIAM. *The Revelation of John* (*2 vols.*)

BARNES, ALBERT. *Barnes Notes on the New Testament* (*Revelation*)

BLACKSTONE, W. E. *Jesus Is Coming*

BLOOMFIELD, ARTHUR E. *All Things New*

BOWMAN, JOHN WICK. *The Drama of the Book of Revelation*

BOYD, ROBERT. *The Book of Revelation*

DAVIDSON, FRANCIS. *The New Bible Commentary*

DEAN, JOHN T. *The Book of Revelation*

DEHAAN, M. R. *Revelation*

ELLICOTT, CHARLES JOHN. *Revelation*

ENGLISH, E. SCHUYLER. *Re-Thinking the Rapture*

ERDMAN, CHARLES R. *The Revelation of John*

GAEBELEIN, ARNO C. *The Revelation*

HOYT, HERMAN. Unpublished notes on Revelation

HUMBERD, R. I. *The Book of Revelation*

IRONSIDE, H. A. *Revelation*

KIDDLE, MARTIN. *The Revelation of St. John*

KUYPER, ABRAHAM. *The Revelation of St. John*

LANG, G. H. *The Revelation of Jesus Christ*

LANGE, J. P. *The Revelation of John*

LARKIN, CLARENCE. *The Book of Revelation*

MAURO, PHILIP. *Of Things Which Soon Must Come To Pass*

MILLIGAN, WILLIAM. *The Book of Revelation*

MOOREHEAD, WILLIAM C. *Studies in the Book of Revelation*

NEWELL, WILLIAM R. *The Book of the Revelation*

NILES, D. T. *As Seeing The Invisible*

OTTMAN, FORD C. *The Unfolding of the Ages*

PEAKE, A. S. *The Revelation of St. John*

PFEIFFER and HARRISON. *The Wycliffe Bible Commentary*

PIETERS, ALBERTUS. *Studies in the Revelation of St. John*

RAMSAY, SIR W. M. *The Letters to the Seven Churches of Asia*

SCOTT, WALTER. *Exposition of the Revelation of Jesus Christ*

SCROGGIE, W. GRAHAM. *The Great Unveiling*

SEISS, J. A. *The Apocalypse*

SMITH, J. B. *A Revelation of Jesus Christ*

STANTON, GERALD. *Kept From The Hour.*

STOTT, JOHN R. W. *What Christ Thinks of the Church*

SWETE, HENRY BARCLAY. *The Apocalypse of John*

TALBOT, LOUIS T. *An Exposition on the Book of Revelation*

TENNEY, MERRILL C. *Interpreting Revelation*

TENNEY, MERRILL C. *Proclaiming the New Testament (Revelation)*

TONIOU, G. A. HADJIAN. *The Postman of Patmos*

TRAPP, JOHN. *Trapp's Commentary on the New Testament*

VAN RYN, AUGUST. *Notes on the New Testament (Revelation)*

INDEX

OF

SCRIPTURE TEXTS

INDEX OF SCRIPTURE TEXTS